PRAISE

MAKING THE ROUNDS

"*Making the Rounds* is a wonderful book that flows from page to page keeping its readers engaged in Patricia's story and wanting to know where it will go next. Inspiring, heartfelt, and brutally honest at times, this is a book that will give women and those who care about them the strength and motivation to persevere through the trials and tribulations in life."

—*Seattle Book Review*

"*Making the Rounds* is an important piece of history served up in a crisp writing style, entwined with beautiful sensory details. Grayhall's point of view is candid, self-deprecating, and genuine. She is obviously accomplished, but what comes through is her openness and honesty—qualities rarely seen in similar works. This is a book you do not want to miss."

—MORGAN ELLIOT, author of *Stroke of the Brush* and *The Crying Chair*

"Well-written, fast-paced, and inspiring—Patricia Grayhall's memoir is an authentic, accurate, and brave portrayal of her lived experience in times that were exciting and expansive, but often confusing, challenging, and uncharted."

—MARGARET DOZARK, MD,
emergency and internal medicine specialist

"Patricia Grayhall has much to teach us in this well-paced and deeply humanizing memoir of what it means to seek both belonging and love—and to find both, always in the most surprising of ways."

—SUSAN MEYERS, professor of creative writing, Seattle University

"Patricia Grayhall's writing style is seamless in the way it flows gently across the pages. She is a very talented storyteller, weaving a narrative filled with fortitude, courage, and passion as she faces the uphill battle to be her authentic self in an environment of patriarchal supremacy and homophobia. I thoroughly recommend this wonderfully written book to anyone."

—ALEXIS HUNTER, author of *Joy Lansing: A Body to Die For*

"*Making the Rounds* is a fast-paced, inspiring, and accessible true story of a young lesbian's struggle to enter the male-dominated profession of medicine in the '70s while concurrently learning, through a series of heartbreaking and endearing encounters, to be her authentic self in a loving relationship with another woman. I highly recommend this book—a great read exploring issues that are as relevant today as ever."

—ROBIN TYLER, producer, activist, and comic

"Grayhall skillfully depicts the problems confronting any ambitious person in search of stable romantic relationships . . . those professional challenges resonate throughout this fast-paced, immersive, and weighty memoir that will resonate with anyone who has experienced the hardships of being true to yourself."

—BookLife Reviews

"Entertaining, informative, and important, especially to those in the process of coming out, *Making the Rounds* is a superbly written memoir that will find a permanent niche in LGBTQ+ literature."

—GRADY HARP, poet and author of *War Songs*

"In *Making the Rounds*, Patricia Grayhall has granted us access into her world, and into the life of a complex woman we will not soon forget."

—SHARON DUKETT, author of *No Rules: A Memoir*

"Female professionals—gay or straight, doctor or other—owe a debt of gratitude for the tribulations women like Grayhall endured to hew the path we now traverse. Reverberating with personal angst and professional certitude, *Making the Rounds* is about life. I highly recommend it to anyone who's ever lived one."

—ADELE HOLMES, MD, author of *Winter's Reckoning*

MAKING

the

ROUNDS

MAKING
the
ROUNDS

Defying Norms in
Love and Medicine

PATRICIA GRAYHALL

SHE WRITES PRESS

Published 2022
Printed in the United States of America
Print ISBN: 978-1-64742-273-8
E-ISBN: 978-1-64742-274-5
Library of Congress Control Number: 2022906480

For information, address:
She Writes Press
1569 Solano Ave #546
Berkeley, CA 94707

She Writes Press is a division of SparkPoint Studio, LLC.

Book design by Stacey Aaronson

To David, and to all the women I've loved before.

AUTHOR'S NOTE

There are no composite characters in this memoir. To protect my
privacy and that of some of my characters, I am writing under a
pen name. I have also changed the names of some characters to
further protect their privacy—Cass, Anna, Sara, Rebecca, Gillian,
Gabrielle, Dani, Dr. Nelson, and all patients.

Memory is never perfect, and others may remember events
differently. This is what *I* remember.

PREFACE

*N*o *Signposts in the Sea*, the title of one of Vita Sackville-West's books, sums up my experience studying and training to be a doctor in the early 1970s before Title IX, which prohibited discrimination in education based on sex. As only one of five women in a class of one hundred in Salt Lake City, and the only woman in my internship in Boston, I encountered few, if any, female role models that could affirm my ambition or provide encouragement.

Tossed around in the rough seas of medical training, chronically exhausted, and emotionally drained, I yearned to have a stable love relationship that would offer the same care and support my male colleagues seemed to find in their wives and girlfriends. Though I loved women, the only model of relationship I knew was heteronormative. My exposure to the women's movement in Boston in the '70s taught me female eroticism was cause for celebration, but it provided few models for how to sustain a relationship with a woman beyond desire. Being open with such love also threatened my ambition to become a doctor.

This book is the story of how I navigated those seas without signposts, tossed by the tempest—battered, but never broken.

PART I

THE ONLY LESBIAN
IN ARIZONA

"The privilege of a lifetime is to become who you truly are."
—CARL GUSTAV JUNG

CHAPTER ONE

Being a lesbian in the 1960s was considered a mental illness and, for some, a death sentence. On March 13, 1964, a man stabbed Kitty Genovese to death, a lesbian living with her girlfriend in Queens, New York, while she walked to her apartment complex. Decades later, society would label this a hate crime—but not then.

I was in elementary school when I discovered my attraction to girls—first Georgina and Becky in my classes, then Elizabeth Taylor in the movies, and my teacher, Miss Chiono.

Playing Red Rover with the neighborhood kids one summer day, I stood—taller than most of the boys, wearing jeans and a red T-shirt—in the middle of the line. We called Becky over to our side, yelling, "Red Rover! Red Rover! Send Becky over!"

With her long brown hair, summer tan, and blue eyes, Becky ran headlong into me. I let go of the others, put my arms around her, and held on. We both fell to the grass, my flat chest on hers, her heart pounding against mine. I looked into her blue eyes, her lips only inches from mine, and a thrill ran through me as heat rushed to my face.

Growing up, I played with the boys in my neighborhood: exploring abandoned houses, building forts, and climbing trees. I ran around shirtless in the hot Phoenix summers—just like the boys—until a friend's mom shamed me into wearing a top. When watching Hollywood romances, I often identified with the man, and I was in love with Katharine Hepburn as Jo in *Little Women*.

Mom, however, strove to fashion me into the beautiful girl she'd declared me to be. I had big brown eyes with long lashes, unruly auburn curls, and very fair skin like my handsome father, and she cried when the school determined I needed glasses. It must've been obvious to Mom early on that I wasn't like other girls. I didn't plaster my bedroom walls with posters of the Beatles or the Rolling Stones and preferred jeans to dresses. Still, she forced me, crying and protesting, into those dresses I hated, and inspected my attire before I could leave the house.

Mom was a stately five-ten and sensitive about her height, but she always dressed in the latest fashions. She impressed upon me that the ideal woman should be beautiful, well-dressed, and above all, thin. When I sprouted up taller than all my peers at age eleven, she took me to a physician in San Francisco who gave me high-dose estrogen to stop my growth. It made me puke for days. In defiance, my body shot up to my full six feet. My sister Terri, five years younger, better fit Mom's expectations: more compliant, happy in a dress or a hula skirt, and content to play dolls with her girlfriends in her bedroom.

In the fall of 1965, my best friend, Aileen, who had just gotten her driver's license, drove over to my house. We'd gone to the same elementary school, but she'd ended up going to a different high school and had since become a popular party girl. We didn't hang out together much anymore. At fifteen, I was taller than most boys, though now with breasts and hips. I had fewer friends than I'd once had and was uncoordinated, bespectacled, and studious.

Aileen and I sat together on my bed with the door closed. The late-afternoon sun glinted off her blonde hair, and we were close enough for me to smell her shampoo. Her blue-gray eyes danced with excitement. "I met this new boy in my history class who just transferred from another high school. I think he might be a bit of a rebel," she confided with a nervous smile.

"Do you like him?" I asked, eager to hear about sexual escapades in any context. But it disappointed me she was so interested in boys.

I'd been attracted to Aileen when we hung out together in grade school. We'd been co-leaders of our little gang who broke rules, measured the teacher's broad behind when she bent over, and left crawdads in the drawer of her desk. I'd listened to other girls gushing about the boys they had crushes on. Even at that age, I'd known better than to mention my crushes on girls.

That day, Aileen told me about the stolen kisses she and her boyfriend shared in the stairwell between classes. The thought of stealing kisses with her flashed through my mind.

Just then, Mom burst through the door and screamed at Aileen, "Did you give my daughter this filthy trash on lesbians?" Her face contorted in anger as she held up the offending magazine in her right hand.

I recognized the March 1965 issue of *The Ladder*; I had hidden it in my underwear drawer. My heart threatened to explode with rage and embarrassment.

Aileen stared at her, wide-eyed, her face reddening. My breath caught in my chest, a rushing sound in my head. I stood paralyzed—mouth open, unable to speak.

Aileen jumped up with a look of stunned horror. "No . . . uh . . . I don't know what you mean," she stammered, then turned and bolted past Mom, down the hall, and out the door. Seconds later, I heard the screech of her tires as she drove off.

7

"Well?" Mom demanded, fixing me with a hard stare.

I was shaking, knees weak, but when I regained my ability to speak, I didn't confess the literature was mine. *If she is so disgusted by a mere magazine, how will she feel about her daughter being gay?* Instead, I yelled, "What were you doing in my underwear drawer?"

Her lips pressed into a thin, disapproving line. She didn't answer or question me further; she whirled around and took the magazine out to the trash at the curb.

After seeing the expressions on Aileen's and Mom's faces, I concluded the worst thing I could be was a lesbian.

I never saw Aileen again.

A few weeks before Mom found *The Ladder* in my drawer, I'd been lying on my bed in my room, studying biology. Down the hall, I'd heard Mom explaining to my father what the word lesbian meant.

"Lesbians are women who love women." Her voice dripped with disdain.

My head shot up, and my chest tightened. *Is she talking about me? Is that what I am? Is that why I have crushes on some girls in my class?* It sounded like a bad thing to be.

Mom lowered her voice, and I couldn't hear the rest.

The following weekend, I'd taken the bus to the Phoenix Public Library. On my own, I searched for books on homosexuality. Secluded in a private corner, I read everything I could find.

The books said homosexuality was a mental illness caused by difficulties in childhood that prevented normal psychological development. Treatment was often unsuccessful, and homosexuals lived unhappy lives. They could not sustain relationships or hold down jobs.

Loving other girls is a disease? And I'm doomed to be unhappy?
My shoulders slumped, and I was too despondent to read further.

Still, I was reluctant to accept my feelings for other girls
meant I was mentally ill. Mom worried I might be susceptible to
mental illness because of my father's chronic depression and
always told me I was too sensitive when she found me crying over
some hurt. I'd had an obsessive-compulsive germ phobia and
washing habit when I was younger. I'd grown out of that, but I
still struggled with the fear I might become like my father and
suffer from depression.

One book I found mentioned the Daughters of Bilitis, a lesbian organization, started in the 1950s as a social and then a political group. It was headquartered in San Francisco. As soon as I
arrived home, I called directory assistance in San Francisco and
got their number, hoping to meet other girls who felt like I did. I
carried the number in my pocket for a few days, trying to gather
the nerve to call from the landline in the hallway. *What will it
mean if I do? How will I know if I'm a lesbian if I don't?*

My stomach was in a knot, imagining I was the only girl who
might be a lesbian in Arizona. I wanted desperately to talk to
somebody about the feelings surging in me for girls like Becky.

I called collect, not wanting Mom to see the call on her
phone bill. I kept an ear out for Mom's car swinging into the
drive or my father padding down the hall as the phone rang.

"Hello," a gruff woman's voice answered.

The operator asked if she would accept long-distance charges
for a collect call.

"Yup," she said in her gravelly voice.

My palms sweated, my heart pounded; her voice sounded
harsh, and I almost hung up.

My voice shook as my words poured out in a rush, "Hi, I'm fifteen years old and I want to meet some other girls who like girls. Can you tell me what I should do, where I should go, who I can talk to?" I inhaled and held my breath, glancing out the window to make sure Mom's car hadn't arrived.

"Well, honey, you're in a tough spot." The gruff voice softened. "Most women meet others in bars, but you're underage. There aren't any organizations or places to meet for young women like you. You'll just have to wait till you're older, I'm afraid."

My shoulders slumped as I exhaled. "Are there any books or magazines I can read till then?"

"Sure, I can send you our magazine, *The Ladder*. It comes in a plain brown envelope with no return address."

I asked her to please send it.

I intercepted the mail for days before Mom came home from work. I couldn't let my parents find it and my heart raced as I rushed to the mailbox. When the plain brown envelope arrived, I ran into the house, tore it open, and scanned the magazine. On the cover was a hand reaching for another hand. There were short stories about lesbians and poetry that was clearly romantic. One article urged lesbians to dress conventionally as women to pass as straight. I learned up to ten percent of women might be lesbians or bisexual. *Where are they? They must all be in San Francisco.*

I hid *The Ladder* in the back of my underwear drawer.

I'd thought then I would make my way to San Francisco and find other women like me. But that was before Mom found *The Ladder* and confronted Aileen—and I saw the looks on their faces.

CHAPTER TWO

I n high school, I became aware of the power my youthful body had to attract male attention but managed to keep it at bay. With trouble at home, school was my refuge, and I focused on my studies with only a few girlfriends and no romantic attachments. Then I met someone who forced me to confront the truth I'd resisted.

Senior year, my classes bored me, and I leaped at the opportunity to enroll in some courses at Phoenix Community College. I had to switch high schools and leave my few friends behind.

Waiting around for Mom to come pick me up one day in the student union, I caught sight of a tall, dark Hispanic man a few years older than me with expressive brown eyes, long lashes, and even white teeth contrasting with his brown skin. He noticed me looking at him and came over to my table.

"Are you saving this chair for anyone?" he asked.

I looked up, not meeting his eyes. "No," I answered. I thought he wanted to borrow the chair and take it away, but he sat in one fluid motion. He put his elbows on the table and regarded me in silence for a moment while I fidgeted. He wore pressed black slacks, and his broad shoulders strained his crisp white shirt, open at the neck.

"So, what are you studying?" he asked.

"Computer Programming 101," I answered and then stopped, not knowing how to make small talk. I looked down and re-arranged my notebook on the table.

"I took that class," he said. "Let me know if you need help." He smiled at me.

I didn't need any help; in fact, I was sailing through my classes. But he enlivened my day by telling me about his studies in math and physics, and his ambition to become a physicist. I enjoyed talking with him and as the minutes passed, I opened up and became less monosyllabic.

After an hour, I told him, "Gotta go. Mom's picking me up."

"I'll walk you out to the front," he said, getting up.

I could tell he was interested in me, but I wasn't sure what I wanted. "No," I said, "that's okay. Thanks, see ya!"

"I'm Ernesto," he said. "And you?"

"Patricia." I dashed away, not wanting Mom to see me with a Hispanic man. She'd always denied having an ethnic bias, but I suspected otherwise.

After that first meeting, I saw Ernesto several more times around campus. He was twenty-one and supporting himself through college by working as a server at a fancy downtown hotel. I couldn't imagine working and taking such demanding science classes at the same time.

One day, after we had been meeting for a few weeks, Ernesto told me about a science fiction story he was reading. A group of people had gone to an alternate universe where they discovered their exact clones living life in a future we had not yet imagined.

"I'm going to figure out how to enter another universe," he claimed. "One might be here, alongside us, in a different dimension of time and space we just can't perceive yet." He gazed off into the distance of his imagination.

I thought Ernesto was a little odd, but vibrant, handsome, engaging, and his brown skin beautiful. He'd smile at me and tell me I was like a rare, delicate desert flower that only bloomed in the shade but was lovely, and I'd blush.

Soon, Ernesto wanted to take me out to a drive-in movie.

Maybe I should go. I thought. *See if I can feel romantic.* For that to happen, I would have to introduce him to Mom.

At the appointed time, Ernesto arrived at our house—in his usual smart attire, a rhubarb pie held in his upturned palm. I had clued him in that Mom loved rhubarb. She smiled in surprise.

I had also told him she was proud of her flower garden, so before we took off, he asked to see her lovingly-tended rose bushes in the backyard. Through the kitchen window, I noticed they were smiling and chatting. Knowing Mom was warming up to him, I relaxed.

We went to see *The Graduate*. As unsympathetic a character as Mrs. Robinson was, I had found Anne Bancroft sexy ever since I'd seen her in *The Miracle Worker*. I don't know if it was seeing her in bed, or Ernesto's soft lips, smooth skin, and hairless face —or the insistent way he kept kissing me during the movie—but I felt light-headed and breathless as his hands roamed my body and the windows fogged up.

Even though I enjoyed his kissing, I didn't want him to go any further, and I stopped his roaming hands. The movie ended and the surrounding cars started up their motors and began drifting away. Ernesto sighed and started the car.

He drove me home in silence while I sat contemplating this experience. I'd felt something kissing Ernesto. Maybe I was not a lesbian after all.

For at least a few more weeks after the drive-in, I kept Ernesto at bay, confining his attentions to kissing and fondling when we weren't talking about his fantasies of alternate universes and curving space-time. When it was my turn, I told him I wanted to be a zoologist and travel the world studying animals in their natural habitat.

"Then why are you taking computer programming and accounting?"

"In case I have to support myself in business instead," I said, then added, "because I might not get married."

"You *are* an odd woman," he said.

I didn't want to be considered an "odd woman." Why was it odd to want independence—to avoid a loveless marriage like my mother had?

Christmas was approaching, and my father—ill again with severe, debilitating depression—was in the hospital at a VA facility near Los Angeles, as he was a retired Air Force major. It was a dreary place, so Mom decided she, my sister, and I should go to LA and take my father out for Christmas dinner.

When I told Ernesto about this plan, he asked if he could ride with us to LA—his family lived there. I had some trepidation about the idea, but I told him I would ask Mom. She agreed to have him come along.

While Mom and Ernesto chatted in the front seat, I sat with my sister in the back and gazed out the window at the passing desert landscapes. I thought about my father, Ernesto, his family, and whether we would have any time alone—and whether I wanted that.

Along the way, Ernesto suggested I should stay a couple of extra days with him and his family before we both took the bus back to Phoenix. I rubbed the back of my neck. *What does he have in mind?* But Christmas with a large "normal" family, so unlike my own, sounded like it might be fun, so I voiced enthusiasm for the idea and my mother gave her permission.

When it came time to meet Ernesto's family, the house was buzzing with the chatter of his five siblings. Set up in a living room corner was a nativity scene alongside an enormous Christmas tree. His father was tall, handsome, and beardless, like Ernesto; his mother was short and plump, with a protruding belly under her apron. She spoke little English, but she smiled at me often and invited me to stay for dinner.

But it was Ernesto's younger sister Maria who grabbed my full attention. Petite and slim, with long black hair, hooded dark eyes, and the same long lashes as Ernesto, it was hard not to stare at her sitting next to me at the dinner table. She smiled at me warmly and conversation with her flowed as if I'd known her for years. Maria reached over and put her hand on my arm, producing a flutter in the pit of my stomach. I hesitated, my fork halfway to my mouth.

"Eat up, chica, you're too thin," she said.

I did my best not to choke.

That evening, I stayed with Mom and Terri in the motel, but when they left the next day, Mom dropped me off at Ernesto's.

After an early dinner of green corn tamales and a walk in Granada Park where Ernesto and I held hands and kissed on a bench under a large oak tree, we came back to his house.

"You'll be sharing a bed with Maria," Ernesto announced.

My stomach dropped.

The room was small, barely enough space for a bed, dresser, and chair. We had to take turns getting into our nightgowns. Maria chatted away while she undressed, making no effort to hide her naked body. As I sat on the chair, I tried not to stare at her round, full breasts, flawless skin, and womanly curves. That she stood only inches from me made my heart race. I wondered what it would be like to touch her, but I pushed the thought away as she slipped a silky nightgown over her head.

I turned away from her to undress, then got into bed beside her. After we talked for a few minutes, Maria drifted off to sleep; I, meanwhile, remained rigidly awake, trying not to touch her as I lay on my left side with my back to her, my heart pounding against the bed.

When I was twelve, I shared a bed with my much older cousin, who had dark hair and eyes, fine bone structure, and a dimple near her mouth when she smiled. Awake before her, I'd prop myself up on one elbow and stare at her lovely face and think she was the most beautiful creature I'd ever seen—until Maria.

Maria stirred from time to time, her hair brushing my shoulder. At one point, she turned on her side, facing me. I rolled onto my back and felt her breath on my skin. My heart raced, my breathing increased, and sleep was impossible. I wondered what it would be like if I moved closer, so her breasts touched my arm. I closed my eyes, envisioning what it would feel like to turn over and fold Maria into my arms, to put my face in her hair, to kiss her.

My heart pounded in my ears, and I could lie still no longer. I jumped up and stumbled down the hall in the dark to the bathroom.

I had another reason for anxiety. That evening in the park, Ernesto and I had hatched a plan to tell the family our bus left earlier than it did so we could get a motel room for a few hours. We'd had weeks of making out and heavy necking, but I was still ambivalent and anxious about this next step. Several of my friends had already had sex with their boyfriends, and this would be my opportunity to prove to myself I wasn't a lesbian. I'd agreed, my body tense, my thoughts whirring. Ernesto had called to make a reservation. Now, though, I wondered if he'd obtained any protection. I worried about getting pregnant—about having to marry Ernesto, who would no doubt feel obligated.

That night seemed endless. When dawn came, Maria and I again took turns dressing, and a well-rested Maria asked me how I'd slept. I told her I'd slept fine, not revealing I was by then so tired and anxious I thought I might throw up.

"You look a little pale," she said.

I supposed with her lovely brown skin in comparison, I looked pale to her all the time.

"I'm fine," I lied, and accepted one of the cups of coffee

17

Ernesto had brought the two of us, looking all bright and shiny and well-rested himself.

We had a hurried breakfast, which I hardly touched. After lengthy goodbyes with his parents and siblings, Ernesto and I walked out of the house with our small bags, ostensibly to catch a city bus to our other long-distance bus for the trip to Phoenix.

Ernesto broke the silence. "Are you okay?"

"Yeah," I said with little enthusiasm. I wanted to want this. I wanted to be normal. But my mouth was dry, my palms sweaty. I could not shake the memory of the feelings I'd had when lying next to Maria.

At the motel, the queen-size bed dominated the room. After we'd gotten settled and Ernesto began undressing me, my muscles tensed, and I found it difficult to take a deep breath.

"Did you bring any protection?" I asked, pushing his wandering hands to his sides.

"Yes." He pulled a wrapped condom out of his pocket. "But first I want to feel you without it."

That did it. This terrified me. I didn't trust him. Visions of pregnancy, and babies, and going to Mass flashed through my mind.

"Ernesto, I'm not sure we should do this," I told him, panic rising in my voice.

Ernesto looked at me open-mouthed, his brow furrowed, and for a moment I thought he would overpower me and force me to follow through with what we'd planned. Then his face relaxed. "Okay, let's just lie here for a while. Close your eyes and rest. We can keep our clothes on."

We lay down on the bed together and I closed my eyes—but after a few minutes, Ernesto was on top of me, kissing me. I raised my arms and pushed against his chest, turning my head away from him. "Ernesto, stop. I can't."

The hurt in his eyes quickly turned to anger. He rolled off me, got up, and paced the small room. "You're not just odd, you're crazy," he spat at me. "Why did you come here with me?"

"Because I really like you. You're handsome and smart and I enjoy being with you. I thought I could be with you in that way, but I just can't. I don't know why." But of course, I did know why. It had to do with how I'd responded lying next to Maria. Bringing to light again something I'd known about myself but tried to resist.

Ernesto stopped and stared at me for a moment, his face red and contorted with anger. Then he grabbed his stuff and stormed out of the room and down the street without me.

I hurried to catch up, since he had our bus tickets. Ernesto was not speaking to me, his face closed tight. When we got on the bus to Phoenix, he took the single seat next to two occupied ones, so I would have to sit alone.

I slid into place across the aisle from him and turned my face toward the window so he couldn't see my tears.

Ernesto never spoke to me again. Months later, I heard through the grapevine at the college he had gotten some girl pregnant and married her. I thanked God it wasn't me.

CHAPTER THREE

I t worried me to not have the right feelings for men and to have what society told me were the wrong feelings for women. But it was about to get so much worse.

One afternoon, a few weeks after the breakup with Ernesto, a clean-shaven, middle-aged man with a full head of silver-blond hair approached the bench where I sat at a park near the Phoenix College campus. He asked if he could sit down.

I said "okay," but moved to the edge.

He sat with his legs apart in a typical man-spread, with his belly hanging over his belt, looking out over the pond, clearing his throat from time to time and disturbing my reverie. In profile, he had a square jaw and aquiline nose, and when he turned to look at me, I saw folds of skin drooping low from his upper lids, partially obscuring his blue eyes.

"Mind if I smoke?" he asked and pulled out a hand-rolled cigarette.

"Yes," I said, fidgeting, rubbing my arms as if I were cold, wishing he would leave.

He put his cigarette away but continued sitting on my bench. "What brings you here on this beautiful afternoon?"

It was indeed a lovely day, warm for January. Red-winged blackbirds were giving their characteristic *oh-ka-lee* calls in the tall grasses by the pond.

"I'm waiting for Mom to pick me up after work," I said,

though it was none of his business. I looked away at the pond where ducks swam lazily.

"Where does your mother work?" he asked.

"Phoenix Union High School." I picked up my books and notebook and held them tight against my chest.

"Really?" His face lit up with a lopsided smile, making him look a decade younger. "I work there, too, teaching shop. My name's Chuck."

I didn't care what his name was. I got up, said I had to meet my mother, and headed back to the college, not wanting to spend more effort fending him off.

For the next couple of weeks, when I went to Encanto Park, Chuck was often there. There was a school bus parked nearby, and when I saw him appear from it one day, I realized it belonged to him.

Is he living in a bus?

He saw me eyeing it. "Do you wanna have a look inside?" he asked.

"Sure." I had fantasies of running away from home and traveling the country in an RV with my dog.

"Be my guest," he said, smiling, then climbed the stairs after me.

I stopped at the top of the steps. He had a couch on one side, a sink, a stovetop, and a fold-out table on the other side. Farther along was a closet and a small bathroom. In back was a queen-size bed. He had punched a hole in the roof for a skylight.

"You live here!" I exclaimed.

"Yes," he said. "I have everything I need. I have to move

around because I can't park on the street in one place for more than three days."

A constant change of scenery. How perfect.

He showed me how his table folded out. He'd built in the plumbing for his sink and finished the cabinetry for his shelving and storage areas in the shop at the high school. Then he brushed against my arm, and I realized he was standing too close —so close I could smell the cigarettes on his breath, and the hair lifted on the back of my neck.

I whirled around, squeezed past him, and bolted out the door.

He came after me.

"Hey, I'm not going to do anything. You don't need to be scared," he assured me even as he walked briskly alongside me, not letting me escape.

"I have to pick up a book at the library," I said, to get rid of him.

"Okay, see you later this week, maybe." He smiled his lopsided smile and turned away.

As I walked in the library's direction, I saw Ernesto coming out of the science building. I raised my hand to wave, but he looked down and strode toward the parking lot. My shoulders slumped. I missed his friendship.

I continued going to the park because I enjoyed the tranquility of sitting in the willow's shade by the pond. I wanted to avoid being shunned by Ernesto, which was more likely to happen if I hung around campus after my classes. Chuck was often there with his bus and always came over to talk with me.

I soon learned he was forty-two, was from Pennsylvania, and had a daughter about my age. He had abandoned her and her mother, whom he never married. I often felt like an outsider with my height, my lack of a normal family, and what I'd been told were unnatural feelings for women. Chuck was an outsider as well—unmarried, living in a bus, perhaps a kindred spirit. His lifestyle, his unencumbered freedom, intrigued me.

Over time, I felt more comfortable in his presence. I told him Mom worked in administration at the high school, but she and I didn't get along. I didn't want to live at home anymore and wanted to travel. What I didn't tell him was my mother had so often denied my reality and my feelings that, for several years, I repressed them and stopped talking with her about anything deeply personal.

"What about your father?" he asked, rolling a cigarette.

I frowned, and he put it away.

"He's depressed most of the time. He used to be my buddy. When I was younger, he took me horseback riding in the desert and let me gallop. One time we took a trip together to the Grand Canyon. He played classical piano in the lodge. It was so beautiful, and I'd never heard him play before." I sighed, remembering how his hands danced along the keyboard.

"The next day, we stopped at a farmhouse where I rode bareback, chasing the dairy cows around the meadow, pretending to be a cowboy. He joked I made them produce buttermilk. He let me wear jeans and do things Mom would never allow." I looked off into the distance, feeling wistful.

"When did he get sick?" he asked.

"I guess he always had depression off and on. When I was about nine, he started on medication that made him stiff and tired. He began making weird grimaces he couldn't control and stayed in bed all day. We didn't do things together anymore. He's been in and out of the hospital, mostly in."

We sat in silence for a while. Chuck looked thoughtful, rolling his unlit cigarette back and forth in his fingers. Then he put his arm around my shoulders.

I stiffened, and he took it down.

"After my daughter was born, I had a vasectomy so I couldn't have any more children," he said.

I turned and stared at him. *Why is he telling me this?* I cringed with distaste for his middle-aged body with his paunch and cigarette-stained fingers, although his face suggested he'd once been handsome. My thoughts churned. Sex with him would pose no risk of pregnancy. I could try it with him to see if it worked as I was told it should. Perhaps the act itself, without the fear of pregnancy, would provoke a magical transformation in me—flip a switch that would make me feel desire for a man closer to my age.

I could not bring myself to get inside the bus with Chuck for several weeks. He continued to show up in the park, to open his cooler to give me a Mountain Dew, my favorite soft drink, and to tell me stories about his vagabond life while we sat in the willow's shade on the bench by the pond.

One afternoon, he shifted to face me. "You know, you really are lovely. It would thrill any man to have you."

I gripped the edge of the bench until my knuckles turned white. *Now is the time.* "You can," I whispered.

A few days later, we had sex in the back of his bus. Chuck was slow and gentle. I didn't experience the magical transformation I'd hoped for. I tried several more times, but because I never experienced arousal with him, intercourse was painful; I just stared at the ceiling and felt worse and worse about myself. Chuck tried every way he knew to make me come—to no avail, since the act lacked the essential ingredient of desire.

Mom suspected something nefarious was going on when I started disappearing for a couple of hours in the early evening.

"Where've you been?" she demanded one spring evening as I walked through the front door.

"Out with a friend," I said, before hurrying down the hall to my bedroom and slamming the door.

I could never tell her I was having sex with some forty-two-year-old guy who worked at Phoenix Union High School—in the back of his bus.

My father was disengaged and depressed, but Mom worried enough to investigate. With her long, shapely legs, flawless white skin, and Dolly Parton breasts, she had experienced her share of sexual harassment in her life. She wasn't about to let that happen to her daughter.

One chilly February evening, Chuck parked his bus a few blocks from my house, and I snuck out to meet him. I was on the verge of telling him I didn't think we should have sex anymore. Just as I got up the nerve to do so, Mom drove up behind the bus and laid on the horn. My chest constricted, my breathing grew short, and my ears rang as I stumbled to the bed in the back. Chuck leaped into the driver's seat, popped the bus into gear, and sped away. Mom followed close behind, still laying on the horn.

Shaking, I parted the curtains and peeked out the back window. I thought I would die of shame and embarrassment, but then we sped through a yellow traffic light that turned red just as Mom reached the intersection. She stopped, and we escaped.

When I skulked into the house an hour later, Mom was apoplectic, screaming at me I was a whore. I sat there looking down at my hands, letting my hair fall over my eyes, unable to rally any defense and accepting the shame as mine. When I looked up and saw her face had become blotchily crimson, I squeezed my eyes shut, sorry I'd caused her so much grief.

My father, home from the hospital, remained in his bedroom, ignorant of what was going on.

My sister, only twelve, emerged to ask, "What's happening?"

"Oh, shut up!" Mom snapped, and Terri returned to her room.

The next day, Mom dropped into the district superintendent's office to let him know Chuck was molesting her underage daughter, enrolled at Phoenix Union High School where he taught shop. I thought nothing would come of it, but to my surprise, they fired him.

Over the next couple of weeks, my outward attitude toward Mom was sullen anger, and I barely spoke to her. I couldn't meet her eyes. Not only had I been screwing this old guy, but sex with him had not diminished my attraction to girls.

Three weeks after Mom chased down Chuck's bus, I turned eighteen. No longer underage, I moved out of my parents' house in late spring and into an apartment in downtown Phoenix with Chuck—who, despite his faults, I considered my ally.

Mom thought she'd lost me.

For a month, I didn't contact her. Chuck cooked all our meals and paid for everything, though he didn't have a new job yet. We rarely had sex. Once, he looked at me with his sad eyes afterward and said, "It feels like you don't want me to be in there." It was the most perceptive thing he ever said.

Despite this upset in my personal life, I remained confident and goal oriented in my studies. I graduated from high school with honors, and Arizona State University awarded me a generous scholarship and grant to attend in the fall. This ability to compartmentalize, honed in childhood, was my salvation.

Thinking he would follow me to university, Chuck got a room near State's campus and helped me move my stuff into the dorm.

"I will be too busy with classes to see you," I told him, cringing at the thought of dragging my shameful past into my healthier life at the university. I didn't want anyone to know I'd been screwing this paunchy old guy.

Especially my new friend.

CHAPTER FOUR

Nearing the end of my move, I carried a box of my things down the hall to my dorm room on the tenth floor of the tallest building on campus and almost ran into one of the most gorgeous women I'd ever seen. She was an olive-skinned, tawny-eyed beauty with long, flowing auburn hair and a smile just like Sophia Loren's. I came to a dead stop and stared, balancing the container on my hip.

"Hi," she said. "I'm Amal. Do you need any help?"

"Uh . . . no, well . . . yeah," I managed before my brain kicked into gear and I said, "yes, absolutely, thank you." She took the box I was holding as I glanced down at her low-cut blouse and then into her tawny eyes, holding her gaze. My insides buzzed.

She helped me haul up a couple more boxes from the lobby. When we finished, she said, "Wanna come down to my car and smoke a joint?"

I hesitated because I didn't want to run into Chuck, but I decided he'd left by then, so I agreed.

Her car was a late-model, white Lincoln Continental, everything plush and top of the line. I wondered if she was rich.

"Come on, get in," she said. "You better get out of the sun, with skin like that."

Inside, she stuck an unlit joint in my mouth and then leaned over to light it—her long hair brushing my arm, her face inches from mine. I nearly choked on inhalation. She leaned back and smiled, revealing straight, gleaming white teeth, as she took the joint from my fingers, touching me lightly so my stomach jumped. Then she put it to her sensuous lips and inhaled deeply—an accomplished smoker.

She told me she was born in Syria to a poor Bedouin family with too many kids. At age eight they gave her to a childless, rich uncle and aunt who ran an import business in El Paso, Texas. She had agreed to come to university to get away from them. But she had no idea what she wanted to study.

"Do you have a boyfriend?" I asked, hoping to God she'd say no.

"Yes, his name is Mark."

The air sputtered out of the balloon of my hopes. Of course she did. She would have the same effect on men she had on me.

I was getting a contact high, not from the weed, as I studied her and held her gaze.

"I'm thinking of participating in rush week for the sororities," she said. "Wanna join me?" She gave me a dazzling smile.

I had no desire to join a sorority and go through the pretense of being straight, but I was already in her thrall. "Sure," I said, then wondered how I would survive having to wear dresses, drink tea, and pretend to be "normal."

"Wonderful!" she exclaimed, putting her hand on my arm, sending an electric shock through me. "I just knew we were going to be friends."

I followed Amal to interviews, teas, and other functions designed to let sororities and prospective sisters assess one another to decide if they were a good fit. I found I enjoyed the women I met in the Jewish sorority—and they liked me, perhaps because I was a serious student—but I was not Jewish, so even there I wasn't a good fit.

After these events, Amal and I would sit in her car, smoke a joint, and laugh about our encounters, knowing we were both outsiders. None of the sororities invited either of us to join, confirming for me once again that I didn't belong to the sisterhood of normal women. But neither did Amal, so I was okay with it.

That fall, Chuck took to hanging around outside my dorm, waiting for me to return from classes. Thinking I would die if Amal saw me with him, I tried avoiding him by coming into the dorm the back way. One afternoon he caught me sneaking in the back door, and rather than risk anyone seeing me with him out in the open, I followed him to his car, parked a couple of blocks away.

He stared out the windshield, then turned to me with his sad blue eyes. "Don't you love me anymore?"

"I've never loved you." I fidgeted, wanting to leave.

He was quiet for a few moments. "Come have dinner with me. I'll make the spaghetti you like."

I looked at him sideways and sighed. He was alone in that dingy little room, alienated from his family, rootless and drifting. It was Mom, after all, who had made sure the Phoenix school system would never hire him again.

I agreed to dinner.

That night he told me the story about his daughter, who he had abandoned as an infant. She'd tracked him down when she turned eighteen. He built a raft and planned to float down the Mississippi River from Minnesota to the Gulf of Mexico. She'd hung around so persistently that he invited her to go with him.

It sounded a bit like the novel *Adventures of Huckleberry Finn*, and I thought it was sweet he'd been able to reconnect with his daughter.

He smiled at the memory. "We became close; she'd climb into my sleeping bag with me at night to keep warm. Soon, we became lovers."

I choked on my mouthful of spaghetti. *He fucked his daughter?* I stared at him, eyes wide with horror.

Oblivious to my reaction, he told me they were so in love she wanted to have a baby with him. He consulted a doctor to see if he could get his vasectomy reversed.

I bolted from the table and ran outside. The food rose in the back of my throat, and I threw up. Overcome with dizziness, I stumbled home. I stopped on the sidewalk, clutching my stomach, and doubling over with one searing thought: *I've been fucking this old guy who's fucked his own daughter.*

Shame washed over me as I stood there, gulping the night air.

I stayed out late, walking around, looking up at the light in Amal's dorm room, not able to get my breath. I could never tell her about this. There were so many things I could not share with anyone. It set me even farther apart from other girls.

I woke up the next morning after a night of fitful sleep, desperate to rid myself of Chuck and to find a suitable boyfriend to double-date with Amal and Mark.

Victor—a single engineer in his early thirties who came to the dorm cafeteria most evenings to eat dinner and pick up college girls—manifested a couple of weeks later. We met when he sat at the table with Amal and me. He was tall and tan, with dark hair worn long on top so a lock nearly fell into his eyes. He'd run across the Hungarian border to freedom, dodging a hail of bullets when he was just a child. Smooth and sophisticated, he dressed in an elegant, European sort of way and showed an interest in me.

Chuck would not go away. On one of my early dates with Victor, we passed close by Chuck sitting in his car. I avoided looking at him, but out of the corner of my eye I saw he saw us.

A few days later, Chuck tracked me down on campus.

"Who's the guy?" he asked.

I kept my voice low. "That's Victor. He's fantastic in bed. I'm going to marry him and have lots of his babies."

This was a lie, of course, but I could see in Chuck's sad blue eyes I had hurt him. I never saw him again.

CHAPTER FIVE

That fall and winter, if Amal wanted to smoke weed in her Lincoln Continental, I was there with her. If she wanted to go out to a bar and dance until three in the morning, I'd go, even if I had to get up for an 8 a.m. class. If she wanted to drive out into the desert with the stereo playing full blast and lip sync to "Born to Be Wild," I'd sing along with her, ecstatic that she chose me to be her friend. She could come to my room day or night, and I'd drop whatever I was doing. We'd lie on my bed and I'd listen to her tales, problems, and dreams, and wish I could touch her.

Alone in my dorm room, I'd put Barbra Streisand on the record player—"How Does the Wine Taste?" Just beyond her fingertips, just out of reach, she saw so much, she could not reach, she mustn't touch. What might the fruit be like? Would it be lovely? A little frightening? I wondered too.

As beautiful as Amal was, she chose Mark, which I could never understand. He was not good looking, plied Amal with marijuana, alcohol, and LSD, and one time called her a bitch in my presence. My arm muscles twitched with the desire to deck him. But despite my distaste, I spent time with him and Victor so I could be with Amal. Often, Mark would be shit-faced drunk and out of it in a smoke-filled bar while Amal and I carried on a conversation and Victor surveyed the scene for potential new women to pick up. This didn't bother me, as I delighted in having Amal to myself.

This foursome thing continued for months.

One January evening, I was in Amal's dorm room when Mark arrived, having eluded the dorm monitors. He was drunk and loud and kissing her in front of me. I rose abruptly and said I was going to my room. Amal had earlier offered to let me borrow her car to do errands the following morning. As she reached to hand me the keys, Mark snatched them from her hand.

"Come and get them," he sneered, and dropped them into her cleavage.

Amal looked embarrassed. Heat rushed to my face, and I wanted to hit him or claw his eyes out. "Forget it," I said, turned on my heel and walked out.

Not long after that, she invited me to drop mescaline with her and Mark in a motel room she'd rented. I'd never considered using psychedelic drugs, but Amal wanted us to do it together, and I wanted to be with her. We sat in the dim light of the bedside lamp on one of the queen beds, three in a row, and consumed the mescaline buttons. An hour later, I felt nothing and thought the drugs must be fake.

Then Mark grabbed Amal right in front of me, pushed her down on the other bed, unbuttoned her blouse, and fondled her breasts. He raised his head and looked at me with a leering grin, as if he wanted me to join in. I sat with my arms crossed, hands balled into fists, sweat breaking out on my forehead. Amal threw me an apologetic look.

I'd seen enough. I jumped up, stormed into the bathroom, and locked the door. Wishing it were me alone with Amal out there on the bed, I spent a miserable night locked in the bathroom. When daylight arrived, I walked out without speaking to either of them as they lay together, passed out.

As Mark was so often out somewhere getting high, Amal and I had plenty of time alone. One evening, as we lay on my bed in the dorm, she told me how much she admired me, that I was strong and wise and had a perfect body. I didn't believe this, but from her, I wanted to. I rolled over and looked into her eyes, vibrating with desire, wishing it meant she wanted me. But the moment passed, and I did nothing, afraid to risk our friendship.

Still wanting to be normal, I had sex with Victor. Unlike Chuck, he was darkly handsome and had a lean, muscular body. He was sensuous for a man, enjoying long, hot showers, fluffy towels, high-thread-count sheets, silk shirts, and lots of foreplay. If I'd been straight, it would have turned me on.

But I wasn't, and by now, I was sure of it despite the lengths I'd gone to prove otherwise. It was Amal I wanted.

On my nineteenth birthday in March 1969, I blew up my life. Victor had decided we would go to a swanky restaurant to celebrate. I wore a flattering dress for the occasion and heels. Victor showed amorous behavior throughout dinner, asking me about my classes and my thoughts on various issues, and telling me how smart I was. He ordered everything expensive, plying me with wine I was not used to drinking, and putting his hand on my leg under the table.

Afterward, as soon as we stepped through the door of his apartment, he jumped on me. By then I was drunk and didn't resist. With Victor in a lather, we barely made it to the bedroom before he entered me—with no protection.

It took several weeks for me to come to the terrifying realization I was pregnant. When I missed my very regular period and counted backward to my birthday, I doubled over and sobbed. *Only one time without protection, and I'm pregnant?*

The only person I could tell was Amal. Lying on my bed in the dorm, she hugged me to her breast and stroked my hair while I cried.

Her holding me like that made me want to stay there forever, but I was still pregnant.

"Don't worry, we'll figure this out," she said, giving me a squeeze.

It was final exam week. I managed to get through the week and maintain a straight-A average.

When I told Victor I was pregnant—sitting in his car in the parking lot of the dorm, tears dripping into my lap—he didn't appear as shocked and panicked as I was; in fact, he didn't appear upset at all. The next day he made an appointment with a gynecologist friend to confirm the diagnosis.

I could not keep my pregnancy a secret for long. The semester ended, and I went home for the summer. At the kitchen table, I sat wringing my napkin in my hands, and waited until after my father and sister had left the room. Mom got up to clear the dishes.

I took deep, steadying breaths, but tears had already started. With no way to soft-pedal it, I blurted out, "Mom, I'm pregnant."

She whirled around, nearly dropping the plates. "Oh Patricia, how could you be so dumb!"

I sat mutely, looking at my lap, twisting the napkin, letting her see my tears. *I have ruined my life.*

Two days later, Mom came with me to the gynecologist. In the waiting room, Victor turned to Mom and said, "Sometimes I think I should just cut it off."

Mom laughed, but I didn't, consumed as I was with fear. And when the doctor confirmed my pregnancy, I thought I should cut it off for him. Especially because he'd arranged for this doctor of his choice to tell me Victor's sperm count was too low to have fathered a child. He insisted the baby wasn't his.

My pregnancy was a complete disaster and wake-up call. Not only was I pregnant, but I was lesbian—and in love with Amal.

Amal invited me to her adoptive parents' home in El Paso for a few weeks. Her room was spacious, with dark mahogany furnishings and a large Persian rug, but had almost no personal items, no photos or posters of rock stars; it was barren, like her relationship with her parents. She hardly spoke to them, and we stayed in her room.

We sat side by side on the uncomfortable antique couch. She took a drag on her joint, blew the smoke to the side, and regarded me. "Maybe you should just have this baby. It'll likely be smart, and I can help you raise it." She paused, took another drag, and exhaled slowly. "Or do you want to marry Victor?"

"Of course not!" I said, a bit more sharply than I'd intended.

I didn't love him. I never wanted to see him again. He would make a terrible partner and father. He was a self-centered philanderer. I didn't know or care what he wanted. *Is she actually offering to co-parent a child with me?* A buzz of excitement penetrated my gloom.

Soon, however, reality replaced excitement. Even with Amal helping me raise it, a child required more than I could give. I'd have to drop out of university. I would never become a zoologist and travel the world studying animals. My belly would bloat up like Ernesto's mother's; I would have stretch marks. I might die in childbirth. Amal depended on her wealthy parents for support. I had no money, and my parents were barely getting by.

A heaviness came over me as I sank further into a sea of despair. "I don't think I can go through with it."

"Then we must find a doctor who isn't a butcher," she said, taking another drag on her cigarette.

I thought of all the stories I'd heard about botched back-alley abortions—women bleeding to death or dying of raging infections—and a hard knot formed in my stomach.

"You'll need to do it soon." She looked worried. "I don't know anyone."

Time pressed forward, and I still didn't feel pregnant, even though I was at almost ten weeks. As lovely as it had been to have Amal's undivided attention, the destruction of my future loomed before me. I left her and returned to Phoenix alone.

I couldn't go to a regular doctor or family planning clinic; it was 1969, and abortion was illegal. Though I thought my life was at risk, others might not think so. How could I find someone who wouldn't leave me bleeding in the street? I tracked down an acquaintance to ask if she knew of any reputable doctors who would perform an illegal abortion. She didn't, but she did put me in touch with a girlfriend who gave me the name of a medical doctor in Nogales, Mexico, and offered to contact him for me.

That evening, after my dad and sister left the table, Mom and I remained. There was a deafening silence, except for the clock ticking. It was bad enough she knew I was pregnant. I could not also tell her I was now certain I was a lesbian.

"Mom, I found a doctor who will perform the abortion, but he's in Mexico. My friend contacted him, but I would have to go this weekend. It will cost four hundred dollars." I sat hugging myself and rocking back and forth. It was an enormous sum I didn't have. Victor, who was still claiming he wasn't the father, hadn't offered to pay.

Mom exhaled and reached for my hand across the table. "I'm so glad you found a doctor, honey. We'll find the money somewhere, and I'll come with you."

Tears of relief welled up in my eyes. I wouldn't have to face this dangerous ordeal alone.

When Mom and I arrived that Saturday night at the designated location in Nogales, Mexico, a driver picked us up and drove for half an hour through many twisting back streets and alleys with no street signs. The houses were wood and clay one-story buildings with flat roofs, often with derelict cars out front. Groups of young men spilled onto the road, sometimes shouting at us in Spanish, as we maneuvered our way past them.

We had no idea where we were in the city. The hand that held Mom's was sweaty with our combined fear. My heart pounded, my mouth was dry, and I could only imagine the terror Mom felt as she sat by my side, gripping my hand. In her purse was the four hundred US dollars in small bills.

I hadn't been religious for some time, but I prayed, *God, please don't let me die. Forgive me for aborting this fetus so I can live.*

We arrived at a small adobe house. Before we knocked, the door opened and a Mexican woman in a white apron, her graying hair in a bun, ushered us down a hallway and into a small room. A naked light bulb hung from the ceiling. Taking up most of the space was a table covered in clean sheets. She told Mom to wait outside.

Shaking, I undressed and sat on the edge of the table, rubbing my arms and looking around. *Is this sterile? Will I get an infection?*

The woman came back and told me, in part Spanish, part English, to lie down and put my feet in the makeshift wooden stirrups as she placed another sheet over me and patted my shoulder. When she left, I lay with my heart pounding, looking at the ceiling and wondering if it would be my last sight before I died.

I jumped when a doctor entered the room, his face covered with a surgical mask. Without speaking, and before I could ask questions or change my mind, he placed a black rubber mask over my nose and mouth, and I lost consciousness.

When I awoke, Mom was holding my hand, looking down at me, her expression soft and loving.

I am alive! And no longer pregnant!

In my woozy post-anesthetic state, I murmured to Mom, "He's such a good man," referring to the doctor whose face I'd not

seen before losing consciousness. I never saw him after the procedure. I'd wanted to ask him questions. How big was the fetus?
What sex was it? No one would tell me, and I decided it was best
not to know.

As soon as I could stand, the woman in the apron, now
blood-stained, ushered us into the night and the waiting taxi.

In the wee hours of the morning, Mom and I crossed the US border into Nogales, Arizona. I was hungry, crampy, and happy to be
alive. We stopped at the International House of Pancakes for an
early breakfast. Gratitude filled me for the network of women
who had helped me find the Mexican doctor, and to Mom, who'd
stood by me through it all. It never occurred to me I might someday regret having an abortion, or that I might become a woman
emotionally and financially equipped to raise a child.

As we drove back to Phoenix, the sun rose over the Sonoran
Desert, glinting off the shoulders of saguaros, their arms raised,
some of them twisted. Staring out the car window, I contemplated
my future. Pretending to be straight was not working for me. Still
imagining I was the only lesbian in Arizona, I resolved to go to
San Francisco. To find out how the wine tastes.

CHAPTER SIX

"I'm alive and doing well," I told Amal when I called her in El Paso after the abortion. *Should I tell her I'm a lesbian? That I have always loved her?* The words caught in my throat. I just couldn't risk it. I lowered my voice so Mom couldn't hear.

"I'm going to San Francisco for the summer, maybe longer. I might not return to Arizona State in the fall."

"Oh . . . I'll miss you," she said.

Mom came through on the abortion, but I was floundering. Unable to talk with anyone about my attraction to other women, or the grim future foretold by the literature of the era should I act on it. Despite my proclivities, and because of Mom's emphasis on the right appearance, I looked and dressed like most women of the day. I had none of the insouciant swagger, haircut, masculine dress, or attitude of a butch lesbian, though I sometimes felt that way internally. Other lesbians, if there were any in Arizona, wouldn't have recognized me as a sister.

Tortured with feelings of not belonging, not having the right feelings for men, and having the wrong feelings for women, I didn't know what to do with my life.

The abortion was a wake-up call for me. I could have died pretending to be what I was not. Despite what I'd heard about the twisted sickness of lesbians, despite reading being gay meant I'd have an unhappy, lonely life, and despite having to leave home and travel to a strange city on my own, I had to go. I had to. It was not a lifestyle choice. I was choosing to live the life for which I was born.

I borrowed money from an elderly family friend, told Mom I was going to visit my mother's cousin, Pearlie, in Berkeley, and booked my flight to San Francisco.

Pearlie ran a boarding house for sailors. She was a fabulous cook, tempting me to stay, but I needed my own apartment, especially because I wanted to meet other lesbians. Soon, I found an apartment—in Berkeley, as San Francisco was too expensive. It was one room with a double bed, a beat-up old dresser with a cracked mirror, a bathroom, and only one window facing a brick wall across the alley. It was temporary, and I could afford it on my borrowed funds.

After transferring my meager belongings to my dismal apartment and hooking up a phone line, I took the bus to San Francisco and went straight to Maud's, a lesbian bar I remembered from *The Ladder*.

I walked into the dimly lit space in the late afternoon and ordered a beer. An overweight woman in jeans and a ducktail haircut sauntered up to me and laid her hand on my arm.

"Let's see your ID, honey," she said, her voice raspy and unpleasant.

"I left my wallet at home," I stammered.

She smirked and jerked her thumb toward the door. "Outta here or we lose our license."

Clearly, I needed a different strategy for meeting women. On the bus back to Berkeley, I hatched an alternative plan: a personal ad in the *Berkeley Barb*, the local counterculture newspaper.

～

The next afternoon, I found the office of the newspaper and bought a personal ad. It read something like: "Attractive woman, age nineteen, wishes to meet same for romance and friendship. No crazies or men." I gave my phone number, but no address.

I left the Berkeley Barb and proceeded along Telegraph Avenue in the direction of pounding drums. The odor of incense wafted from the shops, and multiracial crowds of people strolled up and down in their rainbow-colored, loose-fitting shirts, bell bottoms, and sandals.

I loved drums, and on this day, a group of Black guys, some with dreadlocks or afros, were playing African drums on the UC Berkeley campus, accompanied by a couple of white guys with bongos. A small crowd gathered around them. I swayed to the rhythms. The summer breeze warmed my bare arms. I smiled, pleased with my resourcefulness, hopeful I would soon be overwhelmed with phone calls from beautiful women.

A young Black person watched me from across the drumming circle. They dressed in tight distressed blue jeans and a yellow and orange sleeveless vest, had very short, cropped hair, and were swaying to the music. I suspected she was a woman when she smiled at me. I smiled back.

She strolled over to my side of the circle and stood next to me, doing some subtle jive dancing to the drumming. A jolt of excitement coursed through me. *Is she coming on to me?* I stood in my spot, doing my own little dance, and slipping shy glances at her, noticing the subtle mounds on her chest. Definitely a woman.

After a while, she grinned at me. "I see you like drums."

She is coming on to me! It took a moment to find my voice.

"Uh-huh," I managed, dancing with more enthusiasm.

After we exchanged a few words, she said, "Wanna go get somethin' to eat?"

I agreed, and we strolled down Telegraph, the sound of the drums and incense wafting after us.

Sitting at an outdoor burger joint, we drank our Cokes on the high stools, dangling our legs and sharing our french fries. Her name was Quisha; she was twenty, lived at home, and worked part-time in her brother's print shop. She loved music, played saxophone, and hoped to play in an all-women's band. Her friendly smile made her white teeth seem to glow against her dark skin. She lifted the cuff of her jeans to show me she had a knife strapped to her leg.

I gasped and drew back. *Is she safe?*

She put her hand on my arm and leaned in. "For protection," she said. "Don't be scared." I noticed a pleasurable tingling of my skin where she touched me.

Soon it was evening, and I wasn't sure what to do. Should I invite her to my apartment? I'd decided she was no danger to me.

I took a deep breath, then exhaled. "Do you wanna come see my place?"

"I was hoping you'd ask," she said, smiling.

Quisha took my hand, a little sweaty with anxious anticipation, and we walked the few blocks to my apartment. *Am I going to kiss a girl?*

I unlocked the door, and we stepped inside. She took her time looking around. "Wow, this is nice. You live here alone?"

I didn't think it was at all nice, but before I could say anything further, she took me in her arms and kissed me, pressing her hard body against mine. She was six inches shorter and

45

tipped her head back and stood on tiptoe. Her lips were full, soft, and a bit chapped. I ran my hand over her short-cropped hair, breathing in the clean clay-like smell of talcum powder.

My skin tingled with heat. I didn't know what I should do next.

"You've never kissed a woman before?" Quisha asked, smiling up at me.

"You're the first."

She pulled me down onto my bed and began unbuttoning my shirt.

It was all so new to me, and my heart raced. Clearly, Quisha had been with a woman before, because she undressed me and ran her rough hands over my body, languidly—until I relaxed and the wild thumping of my heart slowed. It was like running outside naked through a warm rain. I stopped thinking, and my body responded to her touching me in ways previously forbidden.

But when she undressed and pressed her hard, sinewy body against mine, I recoiled. It felt like a man. She didn't push me, and for most of the evening we just lay side by side, her caressing me with her powerful hands and kissing me with her soft lips. For such a butch-looking woman, she was reassuringly gentle.

At some point, I fell asleep, and Quisha rose to leave early the next morning. Still groggy, I murmured something about getting together again, but we didn't make any arrangements.

But wow! I'd kissed a girl! And my ad had not even hit the paper yet.

My ad campaign got off to a rocky start. The first woman I met was a dark-eyed beauty from the Midwest. She said she was curious and had never kissed a girl before.

After we met a few times, we lay on the bed in my apartment talking. I rolled over and bent to kiss her. She grabbed my head and pulled me in for a passionate kiss that went on for several minutes. Then she pushed me away, sobbing.

"Why are you crying?" I asked, swallowing hard and thinking, *Did I do something wrong?* She'd appeared very enthusiastic.

She rolled away, her back to me. "I never thought I'd be able to do this," she sobbed. "I don't know how I can live with myself now."

Oh God, she must've swallowed the lies about lesbians being sick.

I leaned over her and put my arm around her. "It's okay. We just kissed. It's not life-threatening." I hoped we could do it again.

She pushed away my arm and sat up. I didn't dare touch her.

"Maybe not to you. But my family is very religious. They'd kill me."

Tears streamed down her cheeks. I struggled to find something to say to comfort her.

"But they're not here." I nervously rubbed the back of my neck.

"They're here in my head." She leaped up from the bed, grabbed her purse, and hurried out the door, leaving me sitting alone, clasping my knees under my chin, thinking.

There are worse things than family and societal disapproval: denying who you are.

The next woman had light brown hair to her waist and was in her late twenties She wore tight hip huggers to accentuate her womanly hips, thighs, and narrow waist. Braless, her large, soft breasts moved freely under her loose, flowing blouse. She was a wonderful kisser.

47

We did little beyond kissing and fondling, but there were problems with her too. She'd become agitated and undecided about whether I was too young, or too uncommitted, or too transient, and pull away in the middle of kissing me. Just when I was getting started. She was too melodramatic and confusing, and I stopped seeing her.

Disappointed in my initial encounters, I stood in my dingy apartment and looked in the cracked mirror at my sullen face. I had no job and was running out of money. I was young and healthy and at least some women found me attractive. I'd finally kissed a woman—several in fact—but why wasn't I happy?

The phone rang. It was a woman named Susan. She sounded refreshingly normal. Her opening line was, "I had to find out what sort of young woman put that ad in the paper."

We talked for over an hour. I still did not know whether she was gay or straight, but I knew I wanted to keep talking to her.

Chatting on the phone with Susan became a daily habit. She was a night owl. When I came home from an evening out, I could usually find her awake and ready to talk.

After weeks of phone calls, she agreed to meet me at the local International House of Pancakes. "I'm a little overweight," she said, as if that might disappoint me.

In her late twenties, Susan had long, glossy dark hair and intelligent brown eyes that saw through any pretense. She wore a loose, shapeless dress and sandals. Her deep-throated, infectious laugh let me know she found the stories of my encounters with women amusing. She never told me whether she was a lesbian and appeared to only want my friendship. That was fine by me. She gave me the sense she saw and understood me, that I wasn't alone. That was more important to me than sex.

By late July, I was broke, so I found a job selling encyclopedias. Seeing that I was shy and quiet, my employers' expectations for my sales were low.

My second week, a group of us piled into a van and our leader drove us hundreds of miles to Burbank, California, where we disgorged into a suburban neighborhood to sell our books door-to-door. It was dangerous going alone into people's homes, no one knowing where we were. I had one young man reach across my wares and kiss me, but he bought the encyclopedias.

I won the contest for the most encyclopedias sold on that trip. Some people I sold books to were lonely, and I was a patient listener, interested in their stories. Once I had enough money to move to a better apartment, I quit.

My new place was a room on the first floor of a multistoried, cedar shake, former single-family house chopped up into apartments on the corner of College and Haste in Berkeley, one block from People's Park. I arrived only a few months after hippies, radicals, and street people had cleared an abandoned lot, laid sod, planted flowers, shrubs, and trees. They built a winding path and amphitheater, and declared it a park of the people. Violent clashes with Police and National Guard, sent by Governor Ronald Reagan, ensued over the takeover of the park. But it was quiet that August when I moved in, and I loved it.

A week later, I joined thousands marching down Telegraph Avenue singing and swaying to the Hare Krishna mantra until we all converged on People's Park. We were served a meal of Indian-style basmati rice dished from plastic garbage cans by Hare Krishna monks in orange robes and with shaved heads. It felt like I was part of something grand.

Another month passed before a woman named Judith answered my ad. She was older (late twenties again), a podiatrist just beginning her practice. Though serious and accomplished, she could also be funny, regaling me with stories about a lesbian couple she had befriended whom she referred to as the "Chubby Bunnies."

We went to a drive-in movie together, and I held her hand, which I found erotic—a strong, squarish surgeon's hand. I sat next to her, hoping she would kiss me but afraid to make any move toward her because she'd told me she had a girlfriend back East. She talked about her girlfriend a lot—but then, she'd also answered my ad.

Judith drank scotch. I drank little, and I didn't take drugs (except for the little pot smoking I'd done with Amal), but sometimes with Judith I had a shot of her favorite scotch, Macallan. One night, after we'd been seeing each other for a few weeks, we sat on her living room floor, drinking, and looking over one of her photo albums. She reached over and pulled me to her for a long, passionate kiss. My breath came in quick gasps as I kissed her back.

"I shouldn't be doing this, but you turn me on," she said, her voice husky, as she fumbled with the buttons on my blouse and kissed my neck. I arched my back and made a little sound of pleasure. This only spurred her on.

The room spun, and I was dizzy with the alchemy of spirits and passion. I wasn't used to drinking scotch, and it had loosened my inhibitions; her touch on my bare skin made me want to feel her everywhere.

When I ran my hand down her leg, I encountered something hard, like plastic, and caught my breath. Confused at first, I realized it was a lower-leg prosthesis she kept well hidden under her pants leg.

She drew back and waited for my reaction.

"That might explain why you became a podiatrist," I said, hoping she would not become self-conscious and stop turning me on.

"Yes," she said. She provided no further explanation and was all over me again.

By the time she pulled me into her bed, I wished I weren't so drunk. She lay on top running her beautiful hands over my body in a way I would have liked to savor in a less inebriated state, breathless and eager though I was.

Afterward, in the wee hours of the morning, I looked over at the pile of medical journals next to Judith's bed, pulled one out, and flipped through the pages. I ran my hand over the glossy anatomical illustrations and said, "I love science and medicine."

Maybe it was her I loved. But then I remembered she had a girlfriend.

As the effect of the scotch wore off and Judith slept next to me, I thought of becoming a doctor like her instead of a zoologist. I'd often heard stories of my grandfather, a kind, slow-talking man who put himself through medical school waiting tables. He traveled by horseback up the Wynoochee River in Washington to deliver a baby or treat the mangled body of a fallen logger and was beloved by his patients. During the Great Depression, he often treated patients for no charge or in return for a chicken or a basket of garden vegetables. How satisfying it would be, I mused, to help others as he did.

I ran my fingertips over Judith's face, tracing the outline of her cheekbones, and she stirred, mumbled something, and gathered me into her arms.

A few weeks later, I ran out of money again. I applied for a job I knew would be temporary with "Ma Bell," a behemoth of a corporation. During the interview, the personnel director told me I was overqualified, but hired me as a long-distance operator, anyway.

To make the job more bearable, I listened in on the conversations of soldiers stationed in Vietnam, though it was against company policy. It wasn't long before my supervisor caught on and she fired me.

That night, I called Susan to meet me at IHOP. It was nearly midnight, but she agreed. After we'd ordered our food and taken our first bites, I put down my fork and said, "Remember the woman I met through my ad a few weeks ago? That I decided was a little too weird for me?"

"Not really," she said, taking a big bite of her Swedish pancakes. "It's hard to keep them all straight."

I ignored that and kept on. "She showed up at my door last night at 2 a.m., out of her mind, raving, obviously having a bad trip."

"What did you do?"

"I didn't let her in, but I got the phone number of her parents in Ohio out of her. I called and told them they'd better come get her."

We ate our pancakes in silence for a few minutes. Somehow, this incident had upset me more than being fired. I was adrift in my life, without purpose. Was I as lost as that woman outside my door? I missed the structure of university, the pleasure of learning, having goals, and doing something well. Since that night in Judith's bed, the possibility of becoming a doctor had been fermenting in my mind.

As if she could read my thoughts, Susan put down her fork and looked me in the eye. "So, what are you doing with your life, Patricia? Are you just going to drift around wasting your intellect and your opportunity to realize your dream of becoming a biologist?"

"Actually, I think I want to be a doctor like my maternal grandfather." I smiled, remembering Mom's stories and her admiration and love for him. "And Judith is a doctor," I added.

Susan held my gaze. "Well, you won't become a doctor working for Ma Bell."

I laughed. "They fired me today. I guess I should just go back to school."

The very next day, with new resolve and Susan's encouragement, I called Arizona State University and asked if I could get the second half of my scholarship and grant back to start college again in January. Given my straight-A academic record, they agreed. I felt lighter than I had for months as I boarded the plane home.

After my return to Phoenix, I stayed at my friend Margaret's house rather than going home to Mom and having to tell her I was a lesbian.

Three days later, I was sobbing on Margaret's bed. Susan had disconnected her phone. I couldn't believe she would cut me off like that; I had no address, no last name for her. My daily calls to Susan had anchored me. I'd trusted her. I feared I might never see or speak to her again.

Margaret listened sympathetically at first. Then she gave me a sharp look. "Did you meet any men while you were in San Francisco?"

Uh-oh. "Yes, a few." I looked away, tears streaming, and blew my nose. I might as well be the only lesbian in Arizona.

I called Mom the next day. Confused and hurt I hadn't returned to the family home after my foray into San Francisco, she demanded some explanation. It was time for me to confirm one of her worst fears.

I asked her to meet me at Mary Coyle's, a soda shop where we'd once had happier times. My chest tight with anxiety, I took several deep breaths before saying, "Mom, I'm a lesbian. I went to San Francisco to find other women like me." Then I sucked my root beer and melted ice cream through my straw and waited, heart pounding, for the sky to fall.

Mom slowly put down her soda and turned to stare at me. She opened her mouth to speak, then shut it and looked away. After glancing around the shop to see if any other customers were paying attention to us, she closed her eyes, her pulse throbbing in her temple, her hands clasped in her lap. I worried, aware she had high blood pressure, fearful she might have a stroke, wishing in that moment I could be what she wanted me to be.

Mom opened her eyes and looked into mine. "Yes. I've known that for a long time."

CHAPTER SEVEN

The medical hierarchy in 1970 was male-dominated, and men tightly controlled admission to the club. Still, there were ways to work within—and sometimes actively resist—something as powerful as a long-established boys' club. The way I looked at it, I might as well try. I had practice at not doing—and not being—what society expected of me. Why not go for it? Why not become a doctor? Coming out as a lesbian gave me the confidence I needed.

I met Mark in January 1970, while standing in line to register for spring semester at Arizona State University after my return from San Francisco. Tall, swarthy, handsome, and sporting a handlebar mustache, he was from Chicago majoring in political science. The line was interminable and had moved little for half an hour. Mark passed the time asking me questions and had already learned I was pre-med and had taken the first semester off to go to Berkeley.

"What dorm are you in?" he asked.

"I don't have a place to live yet," I admitted. Returning to the high-rise dorm of my freshman year did not appeal, and I had little money.

"My friend Ace and I rented a house near campus and are looking for a roommate," he told me. "The rent is cheap."

This sounded interesting, but was he coming on to me?

"I'm a lesbian," I told him.

He didn't so much as blink. In fact, he looked even more interested. "That's okay. Do you wanna come see it? You could have a private bedroom."

I drove Mom's car to the one-story ranch house in Tempe to see the large bedroom Mark said could be mine. Three days later, I moved in with my bookcase, futon, and plank-and-cinderblock makeshift desk—which was, it seemed, a sound decision. Mom, for once, was pleased I was back in school, studying pre-med, and with male friends, though I kept some distance from Mark and Ace. I often ate on campus, put a lock on my bedroom door, and buried myself in the study of physics, chemistry, and zoology.

I missed the company of women. I'd lost track of Amal after going to San Francisco. I contacted her parents when I returned to Phoenix, but they said she had dropped out of school and gone to San Francisco with her deadbeat boyfriend with no forwarding address. They hadn't heard from her in months. Chilled by this news, I feared for her future.

Over time, I made one good friend on campus: Gabrielle, a Greek American woman who was also a serious student, and straight. Beyond that, I occasionally emerged from my room to converse with my roommates. My stories of mass gatherings at People's Park in Berkeley and Hari Krishna marches down Telegraph Avenue intrigued Mark and Ace. Even if I didn't quite have everything I wanted, because I was focused and busy, I wasn't lonely. But when Mark suggested at the end of the semester that the three of us hitchhike from Phoenix to San Francisco, I was all in.

∽

It was harder than we'd imagined getting a ride to the Bay Area. Standing along I-10, thumbs hopeful in the air, cars whizzed by without stopping—not surprising, since Ace sported a thick black beard and Mark was shirtless with a sheathed knife attached to his belt. I was wearing a multicolored tie-dye T-shirt, bell-bottom jeans, and a wide-brimmed straw hat. It was 110 degrees.

Sweaty, hot, and cranky, Mark said, "Patricia, you thumb for a ride; Ace and I will wait over by the gas station until someone stops."

We were getting desperate, and I didn't mind being put forward as bait. "Mark, hide the knife," I said.

Soon, a VW van—painted with swirly bright colors and half full of hippies—picked us up. They welcomed us by passing around joints and chocolate-chip cookies. Later, we rode in the back of a pickup and in a long-haul truck.

When we hit Oakland, I parted ways with the guys. I had my agenda—to find a woman.

I called Judith, but her girlfriend had swooped in from the East Coast to claim her. Susan was lost to me, so I was on my own. I planned to stay again at Cousin Pearlie's boarding house in Berkeley.

Soon after arrival, I headed to Maud's, wearing a hippie outfit I'd had made the previous summer because I was too tall to buy anything off the rack. The top was a multicolored paisley, rayon material in a swashbuckling style, with balloon sleeves and a sash tied around the waist. Worn over bell bottoms of the same silky fabric in electric blue, it was enough to send an acid-head tripping.

Before anyone threw me out for being underage, I approached the bar and stood next to an attractive, trim Asian woman conservatively dressed in black slacks and a cream-colored silk blouse.

The woman swiveled on her stool to look me over: six feet tall and wearing that outrageous outfit. No longer shy about my height, which I found some women liked, I towered over her.

"I haven't seen you here before," she said. "I surely would've noticed you."

"I just got into town. But they're going to throw me out any minute."

It was only seconds before a tough-looking dyke with slicked-back hair came over and asked for my ID.

After the bouncer asked me to leave, the woman—whose name, I learned, was Cecilia—followed me out.

"Do you want to go for a walk? Grab some coffee?" she asked.

What luck! Of course, I agreed. A zing of excitement rippled through me as we walked to Henry's House of Coffee and sat outside, a sea breeze ruffling our hair.

It was still light out, and I could see her clearly now. She was eight inches shorter than me, with long, dark hair that fell over one eye and full, sensuous lips. She looked close to my age, so it shocked me when she told me she was thirty.

Cecilia was intelligent and observant, with a teasing, sardonic manner. She lived at home with her parents because she'd become despondent, unable to work, after going through a nasty breakup with a woman. Her older sister had come to her aid and suggested she move in with her parents, who'd made it conditional on her return to school. She had some soul-sucking, part-time job, but she had recently started taking classes at San Francisco State. Her dark eyes became animated when she spoke of her love of the "Moon Song" in Dvorak's opera *Rusalka*.

Hours later, long after we'd finished our coffee, I took a chance. "Would you like to come home with me? Well, not 'home,' really. It's a boarding house for sailors. I'm staying there with a relative who runs the place." I knew it was forward of me, but my time in San Francisco was limited and she intrigued me.

"Sure," she said. "But let's grab something to eat along the way."

Giddy with success, I grinned. Then had a worrying thought.

"There's one problem though. I'm sleeping on a cot in the kitchen. All the rooms are full."

Cecilia laughed. "That'll be different."

By the time we took a bus to the boarding house, it was late. The kitchen was deserted. I opened a closet, took out my cot, and set it up. It was a flimsy canvas and aluminum affair, and my feet hung over the end. An inebriated sailor was likely to stumble up the stairs and through the kitchen during the night.

We sat on the edge of the cot, talking, and Cecilia moved closer to me. She touched her hand to my face as I looked into her dark eyes. I trembled inside when she lifted her chin and her lips parted. We kissed, and I forgot about the dingy cot, the drunken sailors . . . there was only the feel of her lips on mine, her arms around me.

The gray light of dawn was creeping in before Cecilia left.

After that first night, we were together for the next two weeks—exploring San Francisco, buying flowers in Union Square, and kissing during stolen moments of privacy at the Presidio or at her parents' house when they weren't there. Cecilia was older, more worldly, and experienced.

One day, when her parents were out, we sat on the floor in the living room, cross-legged and making out. As Cecilia's kisses became more insistent, my breath became more rapid and my entire body started tingling. Then we heard the lock turn in the front door. Her body tensed and we jerked apart, putting an end to my growing lusty intentions. Not wanting her to stop, I pulled her up off the floor and we ascended the stairs to her room. She locked the door, undressed me, and pulled me down on the bed.

Effortlessly and stone sober, I came within minutes overwhelmed with the ecstatic release that had been missing from all my other sexual encounters.

That evening, glowing in the aftermath, Cecilia treated me to my first meal of lobster tail and melted butter. I loved it and would keep the shell for years afterward. We talked of literature, poetry, and music. Bright and witty, with a quirky sense of humor, she teased me about my appetites for new foods, new ideas, and new carnal pleasures. More than pure lust drew me to her. During those two weeks, I discovered a love for dim sum, the smell of gardenias, and Cecilia.

CHAPTER EIGHT

I tore myself away from Cecilia to return to Phoenix for summer school. I couldn't postpone biochemistry any longer and planned to take both semesters of it during the summer—a tough challenge. The professor garnered a reputation for being harsh and demanding. This class was infamous for weeding out those who would not make it through pre-med.

After I left San Francisco, Cecilia sent me a dozen roses with a card and a poem by Djuna Barnes called "Serenade." I smiled, hopeful we might continue our romance, despite the distance.

This was one of many poems arriving by mail—part of my education in the fine arts, she told me. I often looked up from my biochemistry book that July and stared out the window, daydreaming and remembering our two weeks together.

During the middle of the scorching desert summer, Cecilia came to visit, sharing my narrow futon on the floor. On the third day, I rode home from class on my bike. After arriving tired and sweaty, I showered, changed, and flopped down on the futon, pressured to study for an exam. The air conditioner kicked on outside the window, and Cecilia laid her head in my lap. I ran my free hand through her long, dark hair while poring over my notes, imbued with a profound sense of contentment. *This is how it should be: me working hard on my goals, a supportive woman by my side.* Although I was reading feminist literature, the only relationship model I knew was a traditional, heteronormative one—and in that framework, I saw myself as the breadwinner and Cecilia as the supportive "wife."

A few days later, I came home from class to the sound of voices and laughter coming from the back porch. I found Cecilia wearing a dress with a short miniskirt I'd never seen before and sitting with her legs crossed, drinking iced tea with Mark and Ace. *What are they doing chatting up my girlfriend? What is she doing wearing a miniskirt?*

Jealousy bubbled up in me. I wasn't about to let my male roommates horn in on my woman. "What's up with this?"

"I thought we could go out to eat," Cecilia said.

I ushered her into my room and closed the door, my cheeks flushed, my thoughts in a jumble. She stood on her tiptoes and kissed me, running her hands over my shoulders and under my shirt. In seconds, everything else fell away. I reached over and locked the door. We forgot about dinner.

The first semester of biochemistry had been brutal, and a B+ marred my straight-A average. To ensure this didn't happen again, I postponed further visits from Cecilia, stopped relaxing in the evenings with Mark and Ace, and doubled down hard on my studies.

It paid off: I finished with an A.

Whereas we'd started out with an easy camaraderie, tension developed between me and the guys. I'd read halfway through *Sisterhood is Powerful*, an anthology by Robin Morgan, as well as

Sexual Politics by Kate Millet. Feminist theory provided a framework for the resentment I'd long felt for male privilege and ease of access to power and opportunity. I began seeing my roommates as oppressors of women and chafed when they left their dirty dishes in the sink for me to clear up. In protest, I left mine. If they thought having a female housemate would relieve them of household chores, they had chosen the wrong woman. I rarely cooked at home, just grabbed meals on campus or popped TV dinners in the oven. I told them I was too busy to help regularly with the housecleaning; I was studying pre-med, and they seemed to have much more free time.

Our relationship crumbled. By the fall, they'd asked me to move out.

I moved into the oldest dormitory for women on campus and jumped at the opportunity to claim what had been the janitor's supply closet as my dorm room to avoid having a roommate. It was long and narrow, smelling faintly of bleach. A window at one end looked out over the courtyard. I put my desk in front of it and could just fit a twin bed behind. I had a room of my own, like the book Cecilia sent me by Virginia Woolf. Relishing my solitude, the tension I'd felt over the past few months drained from my body. I flung open the window and inhaled the scent of rain in the desert.

Even with a full scholarship, I had little money to live on, so I couldn't afford a full meal ticket to eat in one of the dorm cafeterias. Mom drove the thirty miles from north Phoenix to campus to bring me home-cooked dinners twice a week. It would have been cheaper to give me money for food, so it was clear she made the trips because she missed me and approved of my return to university.

With the ordeal of biochemistry behind me, I underwent a political awakening. When not immersed in physics and botany, I read all the feminist and progressive literature I could get my hands on in Arizona. Angered by the futility of the Vietnam War and the duplicity of our country's leaders, I joined several other students in wearing black armbands and occupying the ROTC Building until campus police routed us out.

One afternoon, a librarian asked me to leave the library when I argued with another student about the war. I had a similar confrontation with Mom, hovering halfway out of her car while she told me the war was necessary to curb the spread of communism.

"By dropping napalm on innocent villagers—women and babies—and destroying the environment with Agent Orange?" I shot back as I got out and slammed the door.

Despite my full life, I missed Cecilia. We continued to write but had few long-distance calls, as they were expensive. That fall, when she visited, we made love in the twin bed in my janitor's closet.

The next evening, brazen with lust, we made out on the lawn outside the science building on campus. As our kisses became heated, a car drove by, then turned around and drove by again, shining its headlights on us. In 1970, in Arizona, girls did not make out in public.

"What are you two girls doin'?"

The gruff voice made me jump. We stood up, and I jammed my hands into my armpits, my chin lifted, as I made eye contact with the older of the two campus cops standing before us.

He took me aside while the fresh-faced younger cop slouched against a tree nearby, chatting with Cecilia. My hands felt clammy, but I kept eye contact. He asked me several questions; I answered truthfully, while he jotted down some notes. He stared at me, rubbed his chin, and frowned. "What're you thinking? A serious student like you. Keep this up and you'll be in real trouble."

Cecilia and I walked away holding hands, shaken but defiant. I didn't want to hide my love, and I didn't believe I was sick and deranged or that being a lesbian doomed me to an unhappy life. The feminist literature I was reading asserted anything was possible. Women were working out alternative ways of being in relationship that were neither exploitative nor oppressive—ways that would allow us to express our full potential. I failed to recognize the incongruity of those ideas with my secret longing to have a supportive "wife" and receive the same benefits men enjoyed, as I embarked on the long uphill slog to become a doctor.

At the end of the semester, the administration informed me that because of a change in eligibility requirements, I no longer qualified for a college grant. This appalled my mother.

"How can the daughter of a 100 percent disabled veteran, who has maintained a nearly straight-A average, no longer qualify for educational assistance?" she groused.

"I don't know," I told her. "But I can't work and keep a straight-A average in pre-med at the same time. I'm going to apply to medical school early."

"I don't think you'll get in without finishing college, but I'll support you, honey," she said.

Given my six-month hiatus in San Francisco, I was just beginning my junior year. Still, I took the Medical College Admission Test and got a top score. In my applications I wrote: "I would like to ease some of the arbitrary and unnecessary injustices people must bear, whether brought on by bodily malfunction or the social environment. I don't plan to marry and have children." I thought the men deciding on admissions would want to hear that. Little did they know how much I meant it.

A few days later, I called Judith in San Francisco to tell her I applied to medical school, since she was part of my inspiration to become a doctor. When I found her number disconnected, my skin went cold. I called the women Judith referred to as the Chubby Bunnies to ask if they knew where she was.

"I'm so sorry, hon," Diane said. "She's dead."

Her words punched me in the stomach, and I held on to the counter for support. "What happened?"

"She and her girlfriend took off for a sail after dinner. They'd had too much to drink. I tried to stop them. They found the boat and their bodies under the Golden Gate Bridge in the morning."

With my head buzzing, the right words eluded me. "I'm sorry. I need to get off the phone," I choked. After hanging up, I stumbled around my room, unable to focus.

For months afterward, I thought of Judith—of our brief time together, of our talks, and her inspiration. I had never had someone close to me die. It made me want to move forward with my life with new urgency.

༉

Cecilia came to visit me again in the spring. The desert was in full bloom: ocotillo trees sporting a spray of crimson blossoms on whiplike canes, magenta flowers sprouting from barrel cacti. Despite the odds, we talked of me getting into UC San Francisco and moving there. With my encouragement, she had become more serious about her studies and decided she wanted to pursue a graduate degree in English with a focus on linguistics at UC Berkeley.

Although these dreams glimmered tantalizingly in the future, Mom was not enchanted with the reality of my having a lesbian lover and how it might affect my career goals. She begrudgingly agreed to have Cecilia and me stay with her for a few days during spring break. The three of us, along with my sister, took a driving trip to explore the ghost town of Jerome at the base of Mingus Mountain in the Verde Valley.

Despite her initial reserve, by the end of the outing, Mom and Cecilia were chatting together with ease about their favorite things to do and see in San Francisco.

Afterward, back on campus, Cecilia and I sat on the rim of the fountain in the main square. It was deserted for spring break —no one around except for an occasional professor or maintenance person—and quiet but for the calls of scrappy great-tailed grackles flying overhead.

"Let's meet again at this spot in ten years, no matter what happens," Cecilia said, moving close to me and taking my hand.

"Okay," I agreed, certain we would still be together.

༉

The future, however, never quite agrees with one's plans. In May, I received the letter from the University of Utah that would change my life.

Lucky for me, 1971 was the only year the University of Utah engaged in an experimental program to allow a select group of promising students to enter medical school without our having completed a college degree. When I got the acceptance letter, I turned up Rod Stewart's "Maggie May" on my record player full blast and danced around my janitor's closet. Then, more soberly, I considered what life would be like for a lesbian in Salt Lake City —in the heart of strait-laced Mormon culture.

When I told Cecilia, she wasn't pleased. "Now it's even more likely we won't ever live together," she said with a deep sigh, and for a moment her pessimism brought me down from my euphoria.

Ever the young optimist, I assured her we would keep in touch and visit each other often. I would apply to do my internship and residency in San Francisco. But first, I had to get through a summer science internship and four years of medical school.

The summer before I started medical school, I lived with a dozen bright future scientists from all over the US and Canada in a coed dormitory at the University of California, Riverside. The research internship director assigned me to work in a botany laboratory investigating the metabolism of algae—not my top choice.

In my free time, I read feminist literature. Angela Davis—the political activist, philosopher, and academic—was my personal hero. Articles in *The Furies* and *Off Our Backs* advocated that lesbian separatists should only relate to women who cut their ties to male privilege. Those who still benefited from heterosexuality and received its privileges and security, they said, would at some point betray their lesbian sisters. Yet I was about to join a nearly all-male class of medical students in one of the most conservative cities in the country.

My feminist brooding reached new heights after encountering George, a fellow science intern. He was huge—not only tall but overweight—and a biochemistry graduate from McGill University. Bright and charismatic, he enticed the other interns—all male—to follow him around like disciples. He tried wooing me with his intelligence, telling me how brilliantly he was solving his research problems. When I was unimpressed, he began making disparaging comments such as, "Are women even capable of critical scientific thinking?" When I ignored him, leaving him to shadow box with himself, he became aggressive.

A couple of weeks after my arrival, George invited me into his dorm room, where he and six of his disciples were drinking beer. He said he wanted me to explain to him why I thought the sexes should live separately, after a comment I'd made at dinner. I told him about the desire of some women to create their own culture independent of men. It had already begun to happen on the coasts.

George became sullen and the mood in the room grew tense.

"Why did you eat brussels sprouts for dinner?" he sneered. "They should have repulsed you, since they are about the size of your breasts."

The other guys tittered. My jaw clenched and heat rose to my face as I leaped from my chair.

"You're a chauvinist pig!" I exclaimed and stormed out.

Thereafter, I ate alone and kept my distance from the guys.

࿊

As soon as my research internship ended, Cecilia came to pick me up in her old VW and drove me to San Francisco, where we lunched in outdoor cafés in Sausalito and walked along the waterfront near the Golden Gate Bridge.

Even as I enjoyed my time with her, worries about my future in Salt Lake City nagged at me. I wondered how I would deal with male harassment in medical school. Would I have to isolate, as I had in Riverside that summer, ignoring macho dickheads like George, and just get on with my studies? Or would I become the stereotypical aggressive, domineering woman who must overachieve, always have the last word, and leave them reeling with a witty retort (as I'd heard from Mom my cigarette-smoking, gun-toting grandmother had)? Would I be able to claim my place at the table in medical school? And would I have any allies?

Maybe it would be like playing Red Rover with the boys when I was a child. I'd just put my head down and run full speed into the opposing line until I broke through.

PART II

MEDICAL SCHOOL

☙

"Through others, we become ourselves."
—LEV VYGOTSKY

CHAPTER NINE

In 1971, strict sex quotas limited my medical school class at the University of Utah to five women in a class of one hundred.

During the summer, looking for housing, I found only one other woman classmate and I were non-Mormon. As we were both from out of state, we decided, without ever meeting in person, to share an apartment in the twelve-story Medical Towers apartment building located only a couple of hundred yards from the medical school.

By the time I arrived, Arlis had already moved in. Looking with trepidation at the *Smile, God Loves You* needlepoint she'd hung on the living room wall, I whipped out my much larger Angela Davis poster with her big afro and fist in the air and hung it on the opposite wall. Then I went to dinner with my parents, who had driven me up from Arizona.

Anxious about being an outsider in so many ways—a woman, non-Mormon, unmarried, lesbian, and younger than most of my future classmates—I picked at my food at dinner.

Mom looked at me with concern. "Are you feeling okay?"

"Yes," I insisted. But I knew when they left, I would feel very alone.

Once classes began, our anatomy professor introduced us to the cadavers we'd be dissecting over the next nine months.

The anatomy lab was in the basement and smelled strongly of formaldehyde, which made my sinuses tingle and my stomach roil. Twenty corpses zipped up in white body bags and laid out on steel tables around a large room confronted us. My chest tightened when I realized they'd once been people like us, with lives and loves and families. But there was little time for reflection. The anatomy professor assigned us five to a body and told us we would all unzip the bags at the same time.

My heart pounded. I would see a dead person for the first time.

In my group, one of my male classmates unzipped the bag to reveal the pale, waxy face of a fifty-three-year-old woman. Wiping my sweaty palms on my lab coat, I stared down at her, so dizzy I had to lean against the table. I excused myself, muttering something about getting a drink, and rushed out of the lab.

In the hallway, I thrust my head down to the drinking fountain and pretended to drink until the dizziness cleared.

The voice of the anatomy professor made me jump. "Are you all right?"

"Yes," I said. "I'm fine."

Willing myself to return, I joined my colleagues for the first cut. One of the guys picked up a scalpel and sliced a bloodless line down the front of the woman's chest, between her breasts, as I took deep, steadying breaths.

I struggled to regard the woman we'd unzipped as an object, not a person, though the mental shift was incomplete. Sometimes, I would look around the room and the corpses would come alive in my imagination. I'd have to shake my head to rid myself of the images. That day, and for months thereafter, my lab coat, anatomy book, and notebook reeked of formaldehyde.

I didn't discuss my reaction to the anatomy lab with Arlis. She had a stern facial expression which often looked like she was frowning. I felt she disapproved of me. Sometimes, when I attempted conversation, she would roll her eyes or let out a derisive snort. We were not great buddies early on. To combat my loneliness, I threw myself into my studies.

One evening early on, I made my position clear I thought religion was a fabrication designed to enforce male power. This raised her hackles. She stopped speaking to me, threw me disdainful looks as we downed our cereal the next morning, and strode ahead of me on the way to class.

When I had the opportunity on our next phone call, I complained about it to Cecilia.

"You sometimes forget other people have feelings," she warned. "You're shocked when people respond defensively to some of your actions or words, which can be offensive, however innocent you might think they are."

Really? I knew I could be direct, blunt, and assertive. Though necessary in the male environment of the classroom, it didn't go over well at home.

A few months later, while Arlis and I were walking from our apartment to the anatomy lab, several of our Mormon classmates caught up and walked beside us. Looking over their lab coats, clean and pressed by their wives, I became uncomfortably aware of mine: greasy and wrinkled and reeking of formaldehyde. Muttering to no one and half joking, I lamented, "I need a wife."

Arlis heard me and said loudly, "What about that woman in San Francisco?"

Oh, no! This was Utah in 1971. I hadn't known until this moment Arlis was on to me. I questioned her motives. We were both competitive. If it became known to my professors I was a lesbian, they could make it even harder for me in medical school.

My face burned, and I said nothing—just pulled my greasy lab coat tighter around me and walked on in silence. I detected a faint smirk on Arlis's face.

That morning, I decided I'd better find a more compatible roommate and better cover. I'd begun getting to know David, one of the other ten non-Mormons. We often had friendly conversations between classes. He was short and compact, with a scruffy little beard, unruly hair, and a deep baritone. He'd gone to Harvard as an undergraduate, majoring in economics.

At first, I'd noticed nothing; but that day, when I walked behind David down the hall before class, I detected a slight swish and wondered if he was gay.

The next afternoon, as we headed for the medical tower apartments, I caught up with him.

"David, I was thinking—I know you don't care for your roommate much. Would you like to share an apartment with me?"

David's eyes widened, and he tipped his head to look up at me. He cleared his throat running his hands through his wild hair.

"Strictly as friends," I reassured him.

"Sure, we can talk about it," he said, eyeing me with some skepticism.

We went to dinner that night. Tense and quiet at first, I awaited his response.

Before the entre arrived, he'd agreed.

This was a bold move. People would assume we were in a romantic relationship; in Utah, we would be a scandalous couple living together in assumed sin. But at least I wouldn't be in danger of being ostracized for being a lesbian.

The apartment David and I shared was on the twelfth floor of the South Medical Towers building. Only a short walk from our classrooms and the medical center, the twin towers perched on the rise of the foothills of the Wasatch Mountain Range on the eastern edge of Salt Lake City. David and I had our private bedrooms and a fabulous view of the city to the west, especially at night. We could see downtown to the spires of the Mormon temple and the tidy grid of city buildings. To the south, our living room had a sweeping view of the Wasatch Range.

Neither of us had much furniture, just a battered couch, a record player, and a long row of vinyl records on a cinderblock-and-board table. My bedroom had a twin mattress on the floor and a desk and bookcase made of boards over cinder blocks. David had a proper bed with box springs.

After a month of our living together, I decided to tell David I was a lesbian. I'd been making secretive phone calls to San Francisco, and Cecilia would arrive for a visit soon. It would be impossible to conceal that we would share my twin bed.

"I think it's time I let you know Cecilia and I are lovers," I told him as we sat cross-legged on the living room floor with our morning coffees. To my surprise, he looked at me with his mouth agape. I couldn't believe he didn't know or suspect.

David blurted out, "But you don't look like a lesbian!"

Does he mean I don't look butch? Even in jeans, I wore feminine blouses, lipstick, and earrings—even a dress on occasion. I was my mother's daughter, after all.

"How long have you been a lesbian?" he asked.

"My entire life," I replied. "Even though I tried hard to be straight."

David sat wordlessly staring at me as I held my breath, worried I'd upset him. Then he grinned. "Well, that explains those late-night phone calls in your room."

I let out my breath and leaned back against the couch. At least one person in Salt Lake City knew who I truly was.

Although David provided companionship and cover, I yearned to live with a woman in a loving, supportive relationship. I hoped Cecilia and I could eventually make a life together, although I knew of no other lesbians who had done this. Films portraying women loving women, like *The Fox*, which came out in 1967, made sure the women came to a tragic end. In this movie a tree fell on one of them. In *The Conformist*, men hunted one woman like an animal as she ran through the forest in the snow, a haunting image that would stay with me for months. No film portraying lesbians ever had a happy ending.

Cecilia and I visited each other every couple of months, wrote letters, and talked on the phone at least every two weeks. Near the end of that first year of medical school, she flew out to see me.

After a sleepless night in my twin bed on the floor, we hiked to Horsetail Falls, one of the many lovely trails in Little Cottonwood Canyon. David wanted to come along.

The first quarter mile of the hike was rocky and exposed, but soon we were amid the pines and aspens, dappled sunlight shining through the trees. After the first mile, we came to a small meadow, and I realized Cecilia was not with us.

I ran back down the trail where I found her huffing her way up.

"Where have you been?" I asked, then wished I hadn't because of the look on her face.

"Trying to keep up with you two," she said. "You and your long legs."

"Sorry," I said and gave her my hand.

The rest of the way was relentlessly uphill, but I remained by her side.

After a while, Cecilia asked me about my experience as one of only five women in my class. "Was it as bad as you thought it'd be?"

"Well, in the first anatomy class, Dr. Hashimoto put up a slide of a woman's bare breasts from *Playboy*. The guys laughed and thought it was great. I was uncomfortable."

"You didn't like it?" she asked in a teasing tone.

"Not in that context."

Walking on for a few more moments, I thought of the fear of not belonging I had when I'd first started medical school. Most Mormon men were older and married, having gone on missions for two years before medical school. Many already had children and lived off-campus. I had no more in common with the three Mormon women in my class than I did the men. It was not until I'd exchanged Arlis for David as my roommate, and found my tribe of single non-Mormons in the Medical Towers to make meals and study with, that my loneliness abated. Regardless of our backgrounds, we were all in this together, imbued with purpose, spending hours in the tiered rows and hard seats of Classroom A, stuffing our heads with knowledge, much of which we wouldn't remember in a few years. Even Arlis and I became more friendly, and several of the men and I exchanged banter in class. That day, I looked up at the speckled sunlight through the trees, filled my lungs with fresh mountain air, and realized I was happy.

That last week of school, when exams loomed, it was hard to focus. It thrilled me to have Cecilia there, walking me to class, studying with her on the couch—me at one end and her at the other, our legs entwined in the middle—then falling into bed together at night. Both of us dressed conventionally as women and were never affectionate in public. No one other than David, and possibly Arlis, knew we were lovers.

Cecilia and I were sitting across a table from each other in a secluded corner of the medical library. I tried to focus on neuroanatomy, but images of our previous night together kept intruding.

I read, "The sacral segments of the spinal cord occupy the conus medullaris." *Her tongue caressing my nipple.*

"Preganglionic fibers descend in the cauda equina within the ventral nerve roots." *Her hips in my hands.*

"Upon emerging from the pelvic sacra foramina, the fibers separate out as the pelvic splanchnic nerve." *Our bodies undulating, my fingers in her wetness.*

I looked up at her across the table, leaning forward, her long, dark hair falling over half her face, her eyes downcast, reading. *Her hair falling on my breast as she moves down my body.*

Cecilia looked up. She picked up on something in my face and smiled.

I was having a problem with my own neuroanatomy: an ache in my pelvis. She looked back down at her book as I fidgeted and crossed my legs, which only made the ache worse. I gripped my book hard and tried to read.

"Postganglionic fibers of the sympathetic and parasympathetic systems form the neuroeffector junctions."

When I looked up again, Cecilia was gazing at me, her lips parted in a half smile. We locked eyes. Hers were very dark, tender, loving. I squeezed my thighs together and came.

Cecilia resented David's ubiquitous presence in our apartment and his desire to join us on our excursions. Our time alone was precious. After my exams were over, we slipped away for a drive up Mill Creek Canyon to Log Haven for their amazing pancakes. Afterward, we took a hike. We walked until it began to get dark, and we had to hurry back down the rocky trail. Aware of her shorter legs, I reduced my stride and carried her across a rushing creek on my back.

That day, we talked about our future. Cecilia appreciated my agency and dogged determination to become a doctor. She still had a tough time motivating herself to achieve specific goals in her studies. It was up in the air whether she would land at UC Berkeley or UCLA for her graduate work, but she was intent on pursuing a career in academia.

She couldn't picture herself coming to conservative Salt Lake

City. We hoped to have both career and a stable home life together somewhere on the West Coast. This was my dream. I would prove to myself and Mom the dire predictions I had read and absorbed from the culture were wrong—love relationships between women were not doomed to failure.

But when Cecilia returned to California and chose to study linguistics in graduate school, I was not enthusiastic. *Linguistics?* It seemed an arcane, dull subject. But it was her life—her choice, not mine—and I wanted her to be happy.

Cecilia once said my lack of interest in language was because I belonged to the dominant social class. The real reason was I resented that her graduate studies occupied increasingly more of her time and energy and took her away from me. I wanted her to be available and supportive of my career, to go with me wherever it took me after Salt Lake City. I worried our ambitions put us on a collision course and were incompatible with my wanting a supportive wife—my feminism out of sync with my heart's desire.

CHAPTER TEN

Ironically, during those years of medical school, I realized my ideal of a coequal, supportive relationship with David—platonic though it was. While I would throw a frozen dinner in the oven during the week, David enjoyed cooking for us. On the weekends, we'd make meals together in between marathon study sessions and hikes in the mountains. I nicknamed him "Beauf," French for beef, after I punched him playfully in the arm one day and found it hard and muscular. I teased him about his hairy legs and suggested he keep them covered up, to which he retorted, "Hair is beautiful," as he pranced across the living room in his red-striped shorts.

In response, David nicknamed me "Patroosk," his derivation of Patruschka, a Russian ballet, just because he liked the sound of it. His friendship was my buffer with the straight, white, male world we inhabited, and it made the stretches between visits with Cecilia more tolerable.

One morning, during our second year, we were sitting on the floor in the living room, listening to Elton John's "Bennie and the Jets." When the song finished, David sat looking at his hands. He raised his head.

"Do you think about how marvelous it is to be alive?" His blue eyes were sparkling, his head cocked to one side.

I gazed at him, thinking.

"Really," he said. "Sometimes I'm overwhelmed with gratitude that I'm me and I'm alive!"

David's intensity compelled me to join him in that moment of gratitude—especially after we'd spent so much of our time the past year contemplating disease and death. I would remember this moment later when illness threatened his life.

Our lives continued to intersect in the third year. The chief of medicine hand-picked us both for the internal medicine honors program. This medical school held internal medicine in high regard, and many of the smartest people in the class intended to go into it for their residency training. I felt honored to be chosen but obligated as well. It was now expected I would choose internal medicine as my specialty.

A requirement of the honors program was that we engage in a research project. David and I chose one together. Animal research was in vogue and ours involved a young spider monkey. We were investigating his kidney function following the administration of a drug. It required putting a catheter in his penis and inserting an intravenous line.

"You do it," David said, wrinkling his nose and closing his eyes.

My hands shook, and it took too long for me to slip the catheter into him. The monkey squirmed and whimpered, and I grimaced, feeling his pain and terror. By the time we finished putting in the IV, holding him down and trying to ignore his cries, I was in tears.

"I'm never going to hurt an animal in the name of science again," I told David, whose face also revealed distress. Not all men were indifferent to the suffering of animals.

Afterward, we enjoyed the first of many compensatory prime rib dinners at the Balsam Embers.

Over wine, David asked me, "Do you think animals have souls?"

"Of course they do," I said, still upset.

Cecilia and I had difficulty finding a place to be alone together. When I visited her in San Francisco in the fall of my third year, she called upon an old girlfriend, Jennifer, for a place to stay.

To return the favor, Cecilia made fondue one night for Jennifer and her lover, Jane. As we sat cross-legged on cushions around the plywood table on cinder blocks, Cecilia and Jane chatted together as it got later and later. Jennifer and I remained silent, drinking too much wine.

Our time together was rare and precious. I was losing patience, but I could not get Cecilia's attention to communicate my wish to end the conversation in which neither Jennifer nor I were included. The muscles on the back of my neck tightened, and I fidgeted. I tried to engage Jennifer in small talk, but she also seemed annoyed by what was happening.

I'd had enough. I reached over Cecilia's lap, picked up her full water glass, and drizzled the liquid into her crotch.

Jane stared at me, her eyes wide. "What are you *doing*?"

I knew my actions were inappropriate, but in that moment, impulse rather than good judgment ruled.

Cecilia was more surprised than angry, and I later apologized to everyone. But Jennifer did not invite us back.

When it came time to do my psychiatric rotation that fall, we had a combination of didactics and clinical time with a professor of psychiatry, Dr. Nyla Cole. She was a masculine-looking woman with short-cropped silvery hair and a severe, angular face. *Like a vampire*, I thought. I found her intimidating, yet I spoke up with my observations of patients, often ahead of my classmates.

At the end of the rotation, she called me into her office for my assessment.

"How do you think you're doing?"

"I'm doing well," I answered, never one to downplay my achievements.

"Why do you think you are so competitive?" Her eyes bored into mine.

My shoulders tensed. "How else would I have gotten into medical school?"

To my astonishment, given her butch appearance, she said, "You should soften your manner. Don't be so aggressive and competitive. It's very unbecoming for a woman. People won't like you."

I didn't hear the rest. I clenched my jaw, gathered my things, and stormed out of her office. She no doubt admired the same qualities in a man. *Why isn't she helping me to succeed instead of giving me this offensive advice?* A couple of decades older than me, she'd likely internalized the misogyny and homophobia even more prevalent in her day.

"She's homophobic and projecting her fears onto you," David said when I told him what she'd said.

David's sympathetic response tempted me to inquire about his own proclivities. "Have you ever found yourself attracted to men?" I probed. I'd noticed the way he looked with obvious longing at one of our handsome male classmates.

"I've had sexual feelings for guys," he admitted, looking away and clearing his throat. "When I wrestled with my male friend as a teenager, I became aroused. But I could never act on it." He fiddled with his fingernails, a habit when he was nervous.

For the time being, I let the matter drop. However, I hoped to help him accept and act on his sexual feelings—when the time was right.

During our semiweekly phone call, Mom mentioned my father's behavior had changed. Rather than spending most of the day in bed, he was getting up early and had taken up tennis. He took the bus to the library most days and brought home stacks of books he never read because he could not sit still long enough. He invited my mother to go out dancing which he had not done for years. When Mom passed him the phone, he told me jokes and laughed, filling me with hopeful excitement.

Is Dad crawling out of his chronic depression? Now in his late fifties, I thought I might see the return of the father of my early childhood—at least until the next episode of depression.

Two weeks later, there was a knock at my door. I opened it to find Dad standing there with a big grin. He had no luggage, just a small fanny pack around his waist.

"Hi Dad. I didn't know you were coming. Come in. Does Mom know you're here?"

"I took the bus by myself to Luke Air Force Base and flew standby." He told me he'd gotten a ride from Hill Air Force Base to Salt Lake City, then walked almost four miles, much of it uphill, to my apartment. Stunned, I listened with wide eyes. He talked nonstop, insisting he was finished with doctors and treatments. He described his last residential stay, how he often could not sleep because his roommate brought in prostitutes and was up most of the night having sex.

"Stop, Dad. Take a breath. I need to call Mom." My surprise had turned to alarm. This was not a return to normal.

On the phone, my mother broke down in tears. "He is making me crazy, up all hours of the night, taking taxis all over town, out dancing, and strange women have been calling the house. I'm worried he will drain our bank account. He is irritable and angry. I've called his doctor at the VA, but they do nothing. I'm scared."

Fresh off my psychiatry rotation, I realized my father's chronic depression had swung wildly into mania, his brain flooded with excitatory neurotransmitters. This was new.

When I first spoke to his doctor at the Phoenix VA, he resisted my diagnosis of mania. "He is too old to develop mania all of a sudden."

Lithium had recently been approved in the US for treatment of bipolar disorder. I insisted my father be prescribed it right away and carefully detailed his behavior.

With the help of one of my professors (not the vampire), I got my father stabilized and on the plane to Phoenix. His doctor at the Phoenix VA relented and put him on lithium.

This was the beginning of my medical advocacy for my parents, the reversal of our roles. Though alarmed by my father's sudden onset of mania, my ability to handle his illness, to help my parents—instead of being a victim of their difficult circumstances as in childhood—was gratifying. I could not cure my father's illness, but I was no longer a helpless bystander bobbing in its wake.

CHAPTER ELEVEN

That same year, just before Christmas, Cecilia rented a room in a large house near the University of California Berkeley where she was in her first year of graduate school. I arrived after two months of separation, full of lust and anticipation. We were in bed, naked and making love in the dark, when she saw movement behind me, jerked away, and screamed.

I turned to find a knife reflecting the light from the clock radio. A gruff man's voice said, "Do y'all got any drugs?"

Cecilia screamed again, but I said in a low, calm voice, "There're people just down the hall." I tried sitting up, but he held the knife to my throat. I struggled to keep the shaking out of my voice. "They'll hear us and be here soon. We don't have any drugs."

He lowered the knife. In the glow from the streetlamp, he could see we were both naked in a twin bed. "You two together, you lovers . . . tha's cool sisters, tha's cool," he said as he backed away.

In a flash, he leaped through the open window and vanished into the night.

Once he left, I slammed the window shut and sat on the bed, shaking. Cecilia hugged me.

"You saved us," she said.

I put my arm around her. "I hope we can find a place and a time we can live together—safely."

"What did one sagging boob say to the other sagging boob?" the surgery professor began during a didactic session in third year. "We better perk up and get support or people will think we're nuts."

The ribald, sexist jokes our professors sometimes used to lighten up the lectures often fell flat with me, but I'd decided not to let it get me down.

Many of my professors supported my learning, but not always. In January of the third year, on surgery rotation, students got the opportunity to intubate a patient or to assist in a surgery. Not me. The surgeons, all male, left me holding retractors for hours, unable to see what was going on, while my male classmate got to suture the wound closed. When I asked questions, they often ignored me, leaving me shaking with anger.

Obstetrics was similar. That spring, Dr. G, the chair of Gynecology at University Hospital, assigned me to Latter Day Saints Hospital. Even in obstetrics, there were no women physicians on staff.

After a week of twenty-four hours on at the hospital, followed by twenty-four hours off, my only assignment was catching the afterbirth in a bowl. Never did I get the chance to help position the baby or slice the tissue near the vagina to make more room, or to suture it afterward. Just as in surgery, the message they gave me was women couldn't be trusted to deliver a baby or suture a wound —although we'd been delivering each other's babies since we'd become *homo sapiens*.

By the end of the first week, hot, angry tears rolled into my mask. I left the birthing room, plopped the placenta into the utility sink with a *thwack*, ripped off my mask, and stomped into the doctor's lounge.

"I'm not learning anything here," I said to the doctor whose patient had just given birth. He just looked at me, shrugged, and swiveled around in his chair with his back to me. I turned on my heel, changed out of my scrubs, and strode out of that hospital, intending never to return.

At the university hospital, Dr. G listened to my plight with a thoughtful expression. As a Jew in the land of Mormons, he'd likely experienced discrimination himself. He knew I was an excellent student near the top of my class.

"You can work with me doing gynecology for the rest of your rotation," he offered.

Over the next three weeks on gynecology, I discovered women often feel a special connection with their female physicians. One of my first patients was a Mormon woman, Mrs. Morrison, who had given birth to five children. Now pregnant with her sixth child, she was distraught—she did not want another child. In her early forties and overweight, she had a couple of golf ball—size fibroids in her uterus. Doctors often performed hysterectomies for fibroids and Dr. G scheduled her for a medically-necessary hysterectomy, knowing she was at least seven weeks pregnant.

Mrs. Morrison hadn't told her husband about the pregnancy. It was 1973, and *Roe v. Wade* had just made abortion legal, but in Utah, change did not come quickly.

Assigned to assist in the surgery, I examined her belly pre-operatively. She became tearful and turned her face away. I stopped my exam and took her hand.

"I know you feel bad, Mrs. Morrison. I understand. I had an abortion. I didn't feel good about it either, but I would've felt much worse having an unwanted child. It would've ruined my life. It's your body, not your husband's. *You* get to decide."

She turned to face me and managed a weak nod.

Dr. G let me do more than just hold a retractor; he explained what he was doing every step of the way and taught me how to suture the wound closed.

When I walked into Mrs. Morrison's room to check on her postoperatively, she smiled at me.

I took her hand. "It all went well," I said. "You made the right decision for you."

She looked into my eyes and squeezed my hand.

A couple of weeks later, when I arrived at University Hospital to start my cardiology rotation, the administrative assistant to the Dean stopped me in the hall.

"Someone left something for you," she said.

I followed her into her office. On the desk stood a foot-high papier-mâché doll: a woman in a white coat, a stethoscope around her neck, carrying a black bag with gold lettering that said, "Patricia Grayhall, MD." The note from Mrs. Morrison said, "Thank you."

I still had hope Cecilia and I might live together when she transferred to UCLA in the spring of my third year to complete her graduate studies. On my first visit to LA, we explored the city together; she hoped to entice me there for my internship when I graduated.

Cecilia's letters to me that spring and early summer assured me of her love, but they were also full of anxiety about her ability to complete her graduate program and uncertainty about her academic future. Unfortunately for both of us, I didn't take heed of her growing unhappiness and how it might affect our plans. I hoped my upcoming subinternship in San Francisco would facilitate my getting an internship there after graduation.

The subinternship at San Francisco General terrified and exhausted me. I often had the responsibility of a full-fledged medical doctor. One day I was alone in the emergency department with no medical supervision. An obese, sweaty man arrived by ambulance, complaining of chest pain and dizziness. His EKG revealed a dangerous type of heart attack. Despite hands shaking with anxiety, I put in an intravenous line and administered a drug to dilate the blood vessels in his heart. It took ages for a senior resident to arrive and direct operations—just as the patient suffered a cardiac arrest.

A week later, I caught a stress cold that spread to my chest. Still at work despite paroxysms of coughing, I dragged through the days. Cecilia was having problems of her own: living with her parents for the summer was a tense situation, and she expected a demanding postgraduate program at UCLA in the fall.

During that miserable summer, Cecilia mentioned meeting a woman, Nancy, in a bar. She was finishing a medical internship at Pacific Medical Center. That Nancy had time to go to a bar while an intern piqued my interest.

Struggling through the subinternship, I worked especially hard, hoping if I made a good enough impression, UCSF would accept me into their internship in internal medicine. I thought I might also consider Pacific Medical Center for an internship. It might be less stressful and give me more time with Cecilia.

It was not until I returned to SLC at the end of the subinternship that I could reach Nancy by phone. I quizzed her for several minutes about her experience as an intern. Her answers were short and curt.

"Sometimes," I said, sighing, "I think I should just get an internship in LA when I graduate so Cecilia and I can get a jump on us living together."

"Oh." Her voice was cold. "I wouldn't do that."

"Why not?" I asked, puzzled.

"Because she and I are lovers," she said matter-of-factly.

My breath fled my body, as if she had punched me in the chest. *Did I hear her correctly?* When we hung up, I sat immobilized, staring at the wall of my bedroom for several minutes. The room spun. The earth seemed to move under my feet. *Cecilia and I were monogamous—committed. How could she? And with a doctor?*

Sitting in my darkening room, turning these questions over in my mind, I did what I usually did when I received upsetting news: I sprang into action.

Within the hour, I had booked a flight to LA.

When I arrived at her apartment, Cecilia didn't appear overjoyed to see me, especially since I hadn't warned her I was coming.

Right away, I confronted her. "Are you and Nancy lovers?"

She crossed her arms, hugging herself. "Yes," she said, her voice barely audible. "I was so discouraged and unhappy. I didn't mean to hurt you. It just happened."

The knot in my chest hardened. *Betrayal doesn't just happen.*

Glancing around at her apartment, I noted she had a twin bed and a desk, but no chairs. She had piled her books in a corner and her suitcase was open on the bed. She was not at all settled.

Hot and restless, my stomach churning, I had to move. I couldn't believe this was happening. *We had plans.* I'd hoped to match in California for my internship. We would live together in San Francisco when she finished her graduate program.

"Let's go get a drink," I said, and she followed me out.

We walked in silence the short distance to a bar on Sunset Boulevard, dimly lit with lots of chrome. Sitting downstairs at a table with high-backed, dark wood chairs and plush leather cushions, we both ordered white wine. I downed mine quickly and ordered another.

Over and over, I asked her why she had gotten involved with Nancy. She didn't know. She could only say her life felt out of control, and she was unhappy.

Unable to make sense of her explanation, I thought of her sparsely furnished room and her lack of furniture. "Would you like one of these chairs?"

Cecilia didn't answer. As she looked on with mounting alarm, I rose from my chair and picked it up. As if it were the most normal thing in the world, I carried it up the stairs. No one spoke to me, so I continued out the door and down Sunset Boulevard.

Soon Cecilia caught up. I don't even know if she paid the bill.

"What are you *doing*?"

"I'm getting you a chair for your desk."

Can she not see the lengths I would go to take care of her? She should choose me.

Back at her apartment, the chair dwarfing her desk, we lay on the twin bed, and she pulled me into her arms. Tears rolled

97

down my cheeks into her dark hair. We just held each other, not speaking.

There was a knock on the door.

We both leaped off the bed and Cecilia opened the door. There stood Nancy, down from San Francisco to claim Cecilia. My chest constricted and I couldn't breathe. I leaned on the wall for support, unable to focus. *What will Cecilia do? She has to choose.*

Cecilia was talking. I was too stunned to make out what she was saying. I only heard she was taking Nancy to a motel—leaving me.

Then she was gone.

I collapsed onto the bed, depleted. My energy drained from my body like water from a bathtub.

Mom was right, I thought. *People like me cannot sustain a normal and happy life.* My dream of a long-term, committed relationship was in tatters; my love for women had doomed me to a lifetime of betrayal and unhappiness.

CHAPTER TWELVE

There is no loneliness lonelier than distrust. Shattered by Cecilia's betrayal, it seemed safer to hedge my bets, and to scatter my affections, than to fall in love again. The free-wheeling sexual revolution of the 1970s made that easier.

Overwhelmed with grief when I returned to SLC that fall of 1974, I sought solace from David. But rather than comfort me, he said, "I know this is bad timing, but maybe we shouldn't try to match together for our internships."

Not David, too. He wanted to match at a hospital in San Francisco, but I wanted to get as far away from the source of my pain as possible. With my head hurting and eyes swollen from crying, I said, "We'll talk about this later."

In the matching process, we listed our top choices of hospitals for our medical internship in order of priority. Teaching hospitals then listed their top choices of medical interns. Inevitably, David and I would choose an internal medicine internship and residency. The chief of medicine, who had national renown within the medical community, had written us both glowing recommendations. In mid-March of the following year—our last year of medical school—we would learn which of the hospitals we listed had chosen us.

David and I planned to do electives in Boston that fall. We both listed Boston internship programs in the same order of priority for the match, except David listed San Francisco General first. We submitted our choices, and a few days later, we flew to Boston.

A woman I'd met in San Francisco—during my 1969 summer of coming out—had a friend in Boston willing to put us up until we found a place of our own. She picked us up at the airport—and despite my fragile emotional state, I couldn't help but notice she was attractive, looking disturbingly hot in her rakish black hat and red scarf, draped around her long, elegant neck.

When we arrived at her apartment in Cambridge, it surprised me to find only one room with nothing more than a bed, a couch, and a small kitchen area. Gesturing toward the bed, she told me, "You can sleep with me, but the boy sleeps on the couch."

We couldn't object, not having anywhere else to stay.

Despite her obvious charms, it took me only minutes to fall into a deep sleep, and by the time I awoke the next morning, she was up and dressed. "I tried to cuddle up to you to keep warm," she told me. "But you kept moving away."

Really? I'd been aware of nothing.

As David stumbled out of bed in his tighty-whities, she appraised him with disapproval and announced, "You can stay, but the boy has to go."

Without a word, I watched David throw on his clothes, grab his suitcase, and walk out the door. I had two choices: I could stay and try to woo this beautiful woman in front of me, or I could stick with the best friend I'd ever had in my adult life.

I ran after David.

"Wait, let me get my stuff. I'm coming with you."

～

Our medical rotations started in just two days, and we had no place to live. This kept me from constantly thinking about my breakup with Cecilia. We sat in our cheap motel for hours, perusing the local papers.

We found an affordable furnished room in Sommerville. The problem was it only had one bed. I imagined all the skin cells, dust mites, and vermin left in the mattress by former inhabitants and insisted we cover it with several mattress covers. But we didn't have mattress covers—or sheets, or blankets, or towels, or the money to buy them.

At the motel, we darted into the open maid's closet and made off with the needed supplies promising each other we would return them when we left the apartment.

Our first elective was infectious disease at New England Medical Center with the famed Louis Weinstein. His teaching rounds were inspiring—full of powerful clinical stories. One of us would present a recent case; Weinstein would speak for sixty to ninety minutes on the history of an illness, its diagnosis, and its treatment. Then he'd light up a cigarette and take a deep drag.

With his vast clinical experience, Dr. Weinstein recounted memorable cases of diseases such as Hemophilus meningitis or gram-negative endocarditis, sharing pearls and pitfalls. David and I listened, spellbound, to his tales of caring for patients with infectious diseases before and after the introduction of antibiotics. Listening to his stories, the Anthony Fauci of his day, confirmed how right I'd been to choose internal medicine.

Maybe I would even go into the sub-specialty of infectious disease.

Energized by my elective during the day, and free of having to be on call, evenings found me wedged at the bar among women at the Saints, a tavern on Broad Street in downtown Boston. With high-backed booths, a large pool room, and a dance floor, it was open to both sexes by day, and to only women at night. Packed in the evenings, it was a great social equalizer: there, professionals, including doctors and lawyers, mixed with street vendors, political activists, potheads, and bikers. Well-known feminist authors dropped in, including Kate Millet.

Almost right away, after first arriving at the Saints, I met Coyote. She stood next to me at the bar, awaiting her turn at the pool table. She jostled into me and quipped, "Oh, did I bump your aaam?"

Loud and boisterous, she had shoulder-length blond hair, intense blue eyes, and a very thick Boston accent. Her wiry kinetic energy made me think she must be high. I moved away.

She followed me. So, we talked. Unemployed at age thirty-two, she was unattached and still trucking around Cambridge, following her whim, gathering inspiration from women's songs, marches, and lectures, and railing against capitalism, men, and the system. That night, though, there she was, showing up with her sarcasm, blue, blue eyes, and working-class Boston accent. Intriguing me.

Her name was Maryann, but because of all that wild energy, I nicknamed her Coyote. When she leaned close to me at the bar, I felt a buzz, but I was ambivalent about pursuing her. She seemed slightly unhinged.

When I left that evening—alone, I thought—to ride the T back to Cambridge, I heard her before I saw her. She admonished a young man in a loud voice, "Pick up ya gaaabage—ya think ya motha lives here?"

I turned my face to the window and didn't make eye contact. It seemed impossible to avoid her, as we both got off at Harvard Square.

She offered to walk me home. I accepted but didn't invite her in.

Soon after that, Coyote showed up at my apartment at odd moments. I wondered if she was stalking me. Once, noticing I had no gloves, she appeared with a fancy leather pair she said she had stolen from the Harvard Coop.

"Take them back," I demanded.

Coyote insisted it had been enough trouble to steal them. She wasn't taking them back.

Frowning, I handed the gloves back to her.

The intrigue of the women's community at the Saints kept me returning. One bustling evening that fall, I stood amidst the throngs next to a striking woman who seemed out of place.

The woman wore none of the traditional lesbian garb—jeans, flannel shirt, Fry boots—and looked with her silk scarf and cashmere sweater, as if she could be a housewife from the suburbs. She was tall, with long dark hair touched by a few gray streaks, high cheekbones, and lovely blue-gray eyes with laugh lines that crinkled when she smiled. *Interesting*, I thought.

I watched her for several minutes, sneaking in frequent sidelong glances, before she spoke to me. When she did, it surprised me she seemed so friendly and at ease.

"You do know this is a women's bar?" I asked.

"Of course," she said. "That's why I'm here."

"You don't look like a lesbian," I said—then winced at my stereotyping.

"Neither do you," she countered, gazing at me with her amazing blue-gray eyes—so long I had to look away. That evening I had come straight from the medical school, so I was still wearing work clothes: pressed navy-blue slacks, a white cotton blouse open at the neck, and a form-fitting navy jacket with a rolled collar.

Her name was Cass. She had a low, resonant voice and spoke with hesitation, sometimes searching for the right word, as she looked steadily into my eyes with her discomfiting gaze. I don't know who made the first move, or whether it occurred that night; I just know we soon became lovers.

Cass was thirty-three, had two daughters, and was separated from her husband. Her older daughter, Rebecca, lived with her father, while her younger daughter, Sara, age eight, lived with her in Peterborough, New Hampshire. Cass had an affair with a girl in her late teenage years. But the pressure to be "normal" had become too much, and she'd married a man.

While it thrilled me she'd chosen to be with women again—specifically me—we didn't have a place to be together in Boston as I was still sharing a room with David. Every weekend, I took the bus to Peterborough, even though Sara was there. I stared out the window, awed by the gold and reds of the maples turning in the fall, the white-steepled churches in every village, and the stately old multistoried homes, so different from the Southwest. The distances were small compared to the West; the region steeped in history.

My having met Cass piqued David's interest. How did I go about meeting women?

"You just decide who looks interesting and then walk up to them and make conversation," I explained, suggesting he find a gay bar and try it.

I made it sound simple. I struggled with small talk in that situation myself, but I wanted to encourage him.

Muddling his way through, David walked up to a couple of police officers on the street. "Excuse me, Sirs. Can you tell me where the male gay bars are in Boston?"

Definitely not what I'd have recommended.

They looked a bit surprised, he told me, but they were forth-coming with names. He checked out one place they mentioned once or twice but brought no one home.

If David's romances were developing slowly (or not at all), mine were moving right along. On weekends, when I went to New Hampshire, Cass would pick me up at the bus station. If Sara was visiting her friends, we'd often stop at the Hancock Inn for hot buttered rums by a crackling fire. If we were lucky, we'd arrive before Sara returned and make out on the couch, always keeping an ear out for the sound of Sara's footsteps on the stairs. It felt illicit—exciting, but also frustrating.

Once Sara was there, she demanded all of Cass's attention.

Cass was a devoted mother—patient, never raising her voice, helping Sara with her homework, assigning her small chores, and making dinner for us all. Conversation focused on Sara, her day at school, and her interactions with friends.

In the evening, I waited, almost too excited to contain it, for Sara to go to sleep so I could have Cass to myself—which was worth it. I'd never been with anyone like her. Not only was she beautiful, with a strong, womanly body, but she thrilled me with her skill in bed. At twenty-four, still undifferentiated in my preferences and desires, with her I got to experience everything.

Back in Boston, I had to contend with Coyote prowling around. Her home life was unstable—she shared an apartment or a house with several other lesbian feminists, along with their kids, dogs, and cats, and she seemed to always be looking for another. She complained about the capitalist pigs who'd jacked up the rent in Cambridge so that unemployed feminists on welfare couldn't find a decent place to live.

The Cambridge Women's Center was Coyote's anchor and daily source of inspiration. On International Women's Day, in March 1971, a large group of women had dramatized the need for dedicated women's spaces by occupying an underutilized, Harvard-owned building. They'd brought sleeping bags and food and set up camp inside. When arrests were imminent, they'd left. Susan Lyman donated five thousand dollars for the down payment on the purchase of the house.

It was Coyote who enticed me to my first Women's Liberation Meeting on a Thursday night in the crowded living room of the Cambridge Women's Center at 46 Pleasant Street. Women of all colors and ages sporting afros, shaved heads, long hippie hair, and conservative hairdos sat on chairs and couches, or cross-legged on the floor. The collective energy lifted me as they talked about overcoming male oppression, feminists creating their own culture, and efforts to get the Equal Rights Amendment to the US Constitution ratified.

Later that week, Coyote appeared at our apartment while I was reviewing some infectious disease articles for rounds the following morning.

"Holly Near is singing at a coffeehouse in Harvard Square," she told me. "You wanna go?"

"Nah," I said. "I need to read these articles."

Later, I would wish I'd gone, but the magic of the opportunity to see an icon of the feminist world in the intimate setting of a coffeehouse was lost on me that evening.

What was not lost on me was the energy of the feminist movement in those years. Much had happened since I'd read *Sisterhood Is Powerful*. Abortion was now legal, women's liberation groups were holding consciousness-raising sessions, and authors such as Susan Brownmiller were writing for mainstream publications like *Mademoiselle*. Women advocated for sexual liberation, and monogamy was passé.

Most of this activity had passed me by, so caught up was I in my medical studies and my long-distance relationship with Cecilia, but now, here in Boston, I found myself swept up in the sexual revolution.

CHAPTER THIRTEEN

When she was not ranting about politics, Coyote was getting to me on an intimate level. She didn't care that I saw Cass every weekend, and she appealed to my baser nature by filling in as my lover around the edges. I'd made no commitment of exclusivity to Cass, so I indulged my freedom to engage in what I regarded as casual sex.

Coyote reassured me by saying, "When I refer to you as my lover, don't take that expression seriously—actually, I call you the woman I relate to. 'My lover' sounds so common and trite. We are fellow Madonnas of the Grape, courting the carnal pleasures of life."

Okay. Bring it on.

One weekend, when we were engaged in hot sex in the middle of the afternoon, Cass arrived early from New Hampshire at the front door. Without a word, Coyote leaped up and fled out the rear window. I suppressed a stab of guilt as I opened the door to Cass.

The next week, Coyote was back again, undaunted.

I didn't tell Cass about Coyote, as I suspected she wouldn't approve of either Coyote as an individual, or of me having sex with her. Inappropriate though my dalliance with Coyote might be, it felt safer not to let Cass have my heart completely. With my intellect and libido fully engaged in the Boston experience, the pain of Cecilia's betrayal had faded some—but not entirely. I still found it difficult to trust.

That fall, still in Boston, I moved on to a radiology elective. I'd never been able to interpret x-rays well and thought this elective would help. I seethed with sexual energy, however, so it was hard to concentrate—so hard that when our instructor darkened the x-ray reading room to explain how to read x rays in three dimensions, I drifted into sexual fantasy.

Not all of life was about medicine and sex, though. As fall became winter, with the first snowfall, Cass decided I should learn how to cross-country ski. We visited a ski shop where I splurged with my meager funds and bought a beautiful pair of polished wooden skis. Cass was coordinated and athletic; I was neither, but she taught me how to wax my skis, put them on, stand up without falling over, and, eventually, glide along in her tracks. At every small hillock we encountered, I fell over, which often resulted in our throwing snow at each other and laughing at my pathetic state, tangled up in my extra-long skis.

Cass found me lacking in certain other skills—cooking, shopping for clothes, or doing anything mechanical—and often tried instructing me in those areas. So far, I'd done well without such knowledge. I preferred having her do the domestic chores or fix squeaky door hinges, all of which she could expertly handle. All I wanted was to focus on obtaining medical knowledge and skills, explore New England—and be with her.

Although Cass was beautiful and feminine, she had her unconventional side. In one photo I snapped of her that winter, she leaned against a railing, smoking a cigar, her eyes narrowed at the smoke. Cass beguiled me, and our romance sizzled, although I could not see beyond the present moment.

⌒

Tired of sharing a bed, David and I found better lodging in the home of a medical student we'd met during our infectious disease elective. Her parents lived elsewhere, and she let out rooms to several students. The large, multistoried, light-filled house was near Harvard Square in Cambridge, and we all had our separate rooms.

Now that I had more privacy, Cass could visit me when Sara was with her father and sister. David, Cass, and I would sit on the sun porch, the traffic bustling on the street below, and talk. David was attracted to Cass—"because she is a nice person with a good heart." The two hit it off, and my chest sometimes tightened with jealousy. I wondered if Cass liked David better, until she enticed me to my room alone and dispelled any such notions in bed.

It was so liberating to feel free and uninhibited in Boston. One weekend, Cass and I took a shower together in the bathroom in our house full of straight medical students; David stood guard while we ran down the hall, wrapped in our towels. Other times, I held her hand—and even kissed her on the mouth—in the middle of Harvard Square.

It was still dangerous to be out in much of the rest of the country though. In early November, as Cass and I drove up to Peterborough, we both were overcome by an inability to keep our hands off each other. When Cass decided she would rather do something else with her hands than drive, she pulled over to the side of the road.

We were into some heavy necking and in a partial state of

undress when an unmarked police vehicle pulled up behind us. A police officer sauntered over and shined his flashlight into the car while I buttoned my shirt. Cass rolled down the window.

"Is everything all right, ma'am?" he asked Cass.

"Yes, Officer. Everything's just fine. My friend's a doctor, and she was just examining a breast lump I was worried about."

Suspicious of male authority, I watched him for any signs of aggression and remained silent.

The officer smirked as he demanded her driver's license and car registration. Cass leaned over, grabbed the documents out of the glove box with one hand and rearranged her bra and blouse with the other.

The officer examined them for an eternity. Then he shined his flashlight on us again, leering down at Cass, who was holding her blouse together. My muscles tensed, my heart raced, and my perceptions descended into lizard brain. Worried he'd ask Cass to get out of the car, I balled my hands into fists. If he laid a hand on her, I would explode, regardless of the consequences. They might charge me with assaulting a police officer or engaging in public homosexual behavior in conservative New Hampshire. Neither would be career enhancing.

After a long, excruciating moment, he handed the documents back to Cass. He chuckled. "Next time you want to make out, get a room."

In stunned silence, we watched him saunter back to his car. I let out the breath I was holding, and we sat in mute relief until he pulled away.

"Good quick thinking, Cass," I said as we returned to the highway.

I mused how life can change in an instant. The officer might have charged us with a misdemeanor and Cass might lose custody of her daughters in her pending divorce case, all depending on the whim of a guy with a badge. We were white, and I was almost a doctor—privileged in many ways—but our love made us vulnerable.

Too soon, it was time for David and me to return to Salt Lake City to finish our fourth year of medical school. Cass and I fell into a routine of writing and calling whenever we could, but she was caught up in her divorce proceedings and trying to get a job. She often sounded stressed and distant on the phone.

Coyote didn't let me forget her and wrote me many letters. Despite a terrible snowstorm, she hitched a ride to the 1975 Gay Conference in Provincetown, where there were discussions of discrimination of gays against gays through dress codes, cover charges in bars, and high-ticket prices for gay events. At the conference, she encountered such notables as Elaine Noble, the first openly gay woman elected to the Massachusetts House of Representatives in January 1975. Called a racist by a Black woman who "I could only appease if I'd have prostrated myself in her esteemed presence," Coyote consoled herself by going to a dance where "sisters were just shining on."

Her letters made me smile, hopeful that the feminist wave sweeping the coasts might even make its way to Salt Lake City.

As usual, Coyote was having difficulty finding an apartment because of interpersonal difficulties—or, as she said, "I'm not used to explaining myself to others because I react on instinct, and how can you explain the actions of a bird, a creature of flight, to a logical, calculating human being?"

Later she had to sell her guitar, bike, and blues harp to pay rent and avoid eviction. Her roommate had "listened to the dictates of her feminist heart and the jingling of her Jewish pocketbook," and conceded to let her stay.

Coyote wrote, "If you come to Boston, I'd like very much for you to live with me. I mean for a place to live."

There was no chance of that happening. I was drawn to Coyote's impulsive, unbridled nature and occasional bursts of insight, but I couldn't imagine living with her in the chaos of her life. I'd left that kind of life behind in Berkeley.

CHAPTER FOURTEEN

Though once I'd hoped to find a woman to settle down with in a committed monogamous relationship, I found I wasn't so monogamous after all. Maybe I was polyamorous, blown about by desire like a leaf in the wind. It seemed in sync with the times, at least on the coasts. The closest thing I'd had to a stable home life as an adult was with David, my closeted gay male roommate, friend, and colleague.

Perhaps Cass and I could make a go of it, but she was still in the throes of divorce, going back to school, and raising two daughters in New Hampshire. Did I want to take that on? I didn't think so—at least not at age twenty-four, when the wide world of women was just opening to me. How does one determine what one wants as opposed to what one needs? Most of us are hard-wired for attachment, but how it would manifest in my life was still unclear.

By December, David and I had settled into our routines of internal medicine electives at the hospital, studying, cooking together, and socializing with our colleagues on the weekends. We were into the last stretch—only five more months and we'd get our MD degrees, along with our three-way stethoscopes and black bags with our names engraved on them, courtesy of pharmaceutical companies that were courting future doctors with gifts. Most of our elective rotations involved no night call. We were well rested and free to hike in the mountains when the snow melted and enjoy prime rib dinners at Balsam Embers.

I also had time to read books. I binged on Jane Rule's *Desert of the Heart*, *This is Not for You*, *Against the Season*, and *Lesbian Images*. Such literature, especially novels, had become more compelling to me than the feminist politics of my earlier years. I didn't want to be angry; I wanted to be in love.

In March, David and I nervously waited for the results of the internship match. After Cecilia's betrayal, I'd changed my top choices from San Francisco to Boston. Sitting in Classroom A with ninety-eight of our other classmates, we held our breath, and in unison tore open our envelopes and showed our results to each other.

I gasped and shouted my delight. "We matched together at Boston University Hospitals!" I turned to hug David.

Rather than elation, his face showed disappointment.

"I'm happy we'll be at the same hospital," he said as he hugged me back, perhaps more for comfort. "I'd just hoped to match in San Francisco."

His disappointment was understandable. It had been only a few months since David had finally come out, and San Francisco was the mecca for gay men.

Regardless of our pending move to Boston, we still had specialty rotations to finish up in Salt Lake City. In April, the medical school assigned me to Holy Cross Hospital for my pulmonary elective. Dr. Ted Nelson was a pulmonologist with an office on the first floor.

Slouching in his beige office, jiggling my foot up and down, and enduring a boring monologue on pulmonary sounds, I tried my best to stay awake. After all, I had committed to the internal medicine honors program track, and this was my last rotation before graduation.

As I was about to nod off, the office door opened abruptly and in walked Dee, head of the Respiratory Therapy Department—without even knocking. She was a short, slim, sharply dressed woman. She appeared to be in her early thirties, every hair in place, makeup perfect, with an imperious bearing, and intelligent brown eyes. Despite her feminine appearance, she bristled with confident butch energy. I snapped to attention; that alluring mixture of butch and femme piqued my interest.

"Mr. Jordan's blood gases are back, and his tidal volumes are inadequate. You need to change your order to wean him off his respirator today," she instructed her boss, thrusting the patient's chart toward him on the desk.

Wow, that's gutsy, I thought.

Dr. Nelson, however, seemed unperturbed; he nodded and signed the order she'd written for him. Then, he introduced me.

"Dee, this is Patricia Grayhall, a fourth-year medical student who will work with us for the next six weeks."

Dee looked me over quickly, and I felt self-conscious in my corduroy jeans, a shirt that had never seen an iron, hiking boots, and wrinkled white coat. If I'd known I was going to meet this interesting woman, I'd have taken more care dressing that morning.

"Hi," I greeted her, heat rising to my face.

Dr. Nelson waved his hand in my direction. "Dee, why don't you show Patricia the pulmonary lab and go over its functions the rest of the afternoon."

And spend the night with me, I thought, then checked myself.

Suddenly full of energy, I sprang from the chair to follow her as she strode out the door.

Over the next few weeks, I found every excuse possible to visit the pulmonary function lab or to accompany Dee on her rounds of patients on ventilators. Dr. Nelson was more than happy to turn me over to her.

Dee was teaching me an enormous amount about pulmonary physiology. In those days, even some of the cardiopulmonary surgeons didn't understand how to monitor their patients on a ventilator or to interpret blood gases and other measurements of pulmonary function. Dee intervened, made suggestions, and stood up to them, including Dr. Nelson, when she thought they were jeopardizing patient care. I was in awe of her.

One April morning, Dr. Maize, a cardiovascular surgeon, entered his post-op patient's room, turned various dials on the ventilator, and walked out. The alarm sounded, alerting Dee and me to return to the room. We found the patient thrashing around in his bed. Dr. Maize had already left the Intensive Care Unit (ICU).

Dee frowned. "No wonder he's agitated. Maize upped the pressure to 90!" She readjusted the dials to the proper setting.

I followed her around like a puppy, absorbing her knowledge and admiring her chutzpah in standing up to her superiors in the medical hierarchy. Sometimes we had lunch together. I was dying to find out about her personal life. Two weeks into the elective, I decided to probe.

"What do you like to do on your days off?" I asked, turning the saltshaker around and around on the table between us.

"Run up and down the hills on our snowmobiles, travel in our RV, play with the dogs," she said.

"Are you married?" I noticed she'd used the plural.

"No, but I share a house with Brenda," she told me pointedly. She rose and picked up her tray. "Shall we go upstairs and see how Mrs. Levin is doing?"

I mulled this over as we rounded on patients. I still had no straightforward answers. She lived with a woman—what did that mean? Was she interested in me? Or could she ever be?

That Friday, when I was leaving for the weekend, I ran into Dee going the opposite direction in the stairwell.

"I'm off," I said.

She paused, looking up at me. "Are you doing anything interesting this weekend?"

"I thought I'd try to find someone to ravish," I ventured—and at once cringed and shoved my hands in my pockets. That was not true. *What am I thinking?*

Dee grinned and without missing a beat said, "I'm sure you won't have any trouble."

My stomach flipped as she passed me on her way up the stairs, and when I got to the parking lot, I bounced into my '68 Ford Mustang, popped it into gear, and drove way too fast up the hill to my Medical Towers apartment with the radio blaring Joni Mitchell's, "Help Me."

The next time we sat down together for coffee, I took a deep breath, exhaled, and looked her straight in the eye.

"In case you didn't know already, I'm gay."

This was a bold admission in 1975, especially in conservative Salt Lake City, and she might well have taken offense or reported me—or worst of all, turned me back over to boring Dr. Nelson. I just had to trust my intuition she might be too.

Dee smiled at me. "Of course. I knew it the day I met you."

"And you don't mind?" I hoped she would say something about herself.

"No, not at all. I am too."

Bingo! My heart leaped. But I needed to keep myself in check. She lived with Brenda.

"Why're you living with David?" she asked, raising an eyebrow.

"Oh, David's gay," I assured her. "He just hasn't acted on it much yet." I winced, realizing I had outed him to Dee as well—but we were only a month from graduating, and I felt sure his secret was safe with her.

Dee looked at her watch and exclaimed we were late for rounds. We got up and put our coffee cups in the dish tray. I slam-dunked the remains of a donut into the trash. *Where might this be going?*

Over the next few weeks, I bounded out of bed, looking forward to rounds with Dee. I hardly ever saw Dr. Nelson anymore, though Dee was in touch with him about my progress. By then, I knew enough about the practice of medicine to know he was over-prescribing. He even ordered a laxative for a patient with a colostomy bag. Dee prevented him from making major malpractice blunders, and I wondered with some resentment how many male doctors were propped up and kept out of trouble by their lesser-paid female staff?

After my announcement about being gay, Dee suggested we go out to the Sun Tavern, a gay bar in town, after work that Friday. I was leery because I'd heard it was rough and in a high crime area of town—but I wanted to be with her, so I agreed.

I drove home to change first. I donned my usual Boston bar attire: jeans, a checked flannel shirt, a jean jacket, and hiking boots—and, for good measure, because of the neighborhood, I slipped a small kitchen knife in a sheath in my sock, as I had seen Quisha do in Berkeley several years earlier.

At the bar, I basked in Dee's attention as she chatted away with commentary about the other women and hospital gossip, but little about Brenda. Oblivious to the other women, I focused only on Dee. We danced together, though we couldn't decide who should lead, so we just danced free style.

When we were near to leaving, I lifted the cuff of my jeans to show her the knife in my sock.

Dee gasped. "What are you doing with that?"

"For protection in this neighborhood," I said matter-of-factly.

She laughed and touched my cheek with her hand, sending a frisson through me. "Oh, sweetie—obviously, you don't get out much."

Over the next week, we continued to see each other outside of the hospital. After work one evening, Dee stopped by my apartment for a cup of tea, and I noticed she had a Type 1 herpes fever blister on her lip. I'd recently treated a patient dying of herpes encephalitis and any potential exposure to the virus repelled me. After she finished drinking her tea, I walked behind the counter and threw the porcelain cup away—and she saw me. Her eyes widened.

"I'll have another cup of tea, please," she teased.

My face grew hot; clearly, she thought my medical student paranoia was over the top and it was. I hoped I'd not offended her.

That week, Dee talked more about her home life, working in the yard with Brenda, or going to visit family. I told her about Cass and my time with her in Boston.

Then on rounds, just before we entered a patient's room, Dee remarked, "It's difficult when you're living with someone to always be thinking about someone else."

Wow! I'd never lived with a woman in a romantic relationship, so I didn't know what it was like to be thinking of someone else. *Is that someone else me?* I remained silent, although my insides were buzzing.

Dee turned away and addressed the patient. "Hello, Mr. Turner."

When we sat together in her office the next day, Dee asked me why David had no lover.

"Lack of opportunity? Fear of being outed? I don't know," I admitted.

"Why don't we give him an opportunity? Rick, my employee, is gay, nice-looking, and single. We could set him up with David." She rose and headed for the door.

"Sure." It would be my chance to spend time with Dee. I hoped David would be amenable.

David was, and our plan materialized that Friday night. Dee arrived at our apartment in her white 240Z sports car, and Rick came in his own. The four of us sat around our living room for a few minutes, talking. I sat cross-legged on the floor because we didn't have enough furniture, while David and Rick sat on opposite ends of the old second-hand couch—and Dee hovered nearby.

"I think we need to go get some scotch to loosen them up," she whispered in my ear.

"Okay," I said, and rose in one swift motion. I slipped a cherry LifeSaver out of my pocket and popped it in my mouth. "Can I drive your car?"

"Sure," she said as she headed for the bathroom.

When she emerged a few minutes later, she took my hand and led me into my bedroom. She tilted her head up and whispered, "May I kiss you? I just brushed my teeth and hid the toothbrush in my bra."

With no hesitation, I leaned down and kissed her. The taste of cherry LifeSaver was overwhelming. I spit it into my hand and tossed it. Not wanting to waste any time, I kissed her again, more deeply.

She pulled away. "Wow," she said, smiling up at me. "We better go get that scotch before we change our minds."

I drove her 240Z to the state-run liquor store before it closed and bought a bottle of Johnny Walker Red for the boys. As we got in the car, she told me, "I don't want to be functional for the evening."

What does that mean? It thrilled me to be with her. This evening was as much about us as it was David and Rick. I suggested a detour: "Let's go out to Red Butte Canyon for a few minutes."

We decided it might take too long, so we stopped instead along the road to the Canyon in an isolated section. There was a manure pile nearby, pungent even in the open country air. She didn't let it deter her; she smiled at me and pulled out a bag of clothes. We got out, and she hid behind the car to change out of her gabardine slacks into jeans. She joined me, sitting on a log.

It was windy and cold, but I opened the Johnny Walker and we each took several swigs. Then she lit a cigarette—holding it away from me, because I'd told her I couldn't stand cigarette smoke. We swallowed a few more swigs of scotch as I regaled her with stories of my adventures in Boston. She was quiet, listening. Then noticing a light pressure on my shoulder. I glanced to my right to find her hand resting there, the tip of the cigarette glowing between her fingers.

"Turn," she commanded as she leaned in to kiss me. Confused, I hesitated a moment too long.

I noticed her jaw clench. She jumped up. "Okay, fine, you call the shots."

I shivered either from cold or excitement or both. I stood abruptly and grabbed her by the shoulders. "Let's get out of here. I want to kiss you, but it's freezing."

This time she drove, taking us farther up the Canyon so we could run the heater before parking. All the while, we passed the bottle back and forth. I began to feel light-headed.

Dee pulled over and turned to face me in her bucket seat. "I really don't know what I want."

I didn't understand what she meant or whether she still

wanted to kiss me. The taste of scotch was strong in my mouth, and I wasn't sure I liked it, but it had loosened my inhibitions. I moved toward her across the stick shift and kissed her softly at first, then more ardently as she pulled me in. Her bucket seat clicked back. We both were breathing hard. My head spun.

Aroused and smashed, I would have liked to carry on, but it was cold and cramped in the car and I'd left David to fend for himself. "We'd best get back. We've drunk most of the scotch, and Rick and David have probably done whatever they are going to do by now."

We arrived at my apartment with no major mishaps, but the door was locked, and I couldn't find my key. We knocked, and David opened the door in his briefs. Rick had already left.

Dee started in on David. "You're so cute," she crooned. "Did you and Rick get your pants down?"

Even in my inebriated state, I noticed his eyes widen and his face flush. Recognizing the need for damage control, I put my hand on her shoulder. "David needs to go to his room and think about things right now."

He looked at me gratefully, padded into his room, and closed the door.

"I should go," Dee said.

I could not let her go. I wanted to finish what we'd started. This opportunity might not come again. I pulled her down on the couch for yet another session of heated necking.

"This would be far better with our clothes off," she said.

We moved to my bedroom, and I stripped down to nothing. As I began undoing her bra, she stopped my hand.

"Since I've lost weight," she told me, "My bust line has gone down."

This insecurity seemed uncharacteristic, prompting a surge of tenderness. "I like small breasts," I told her as I continued undressing her.

I pulled her onto my mattress on the floor. She lay on top, her hands roaming my nakedness, but as much as I wanted her, my head was spinning. A wave of nausea swept over me.

"What can I do to satisfy you?" she asked.

I only groaned, fearing I might have to get up and puke. My earlier desire and the sensitivity the situation deserved deserted me. I sat up.

That did it.

"I should go," she said again. "I have a home."

Then she was up and dressed in her tweed jacket. I was still on the bed, struggling with another wave of nausea. When it passed, I pulled her onto the bed and hugged her from behind, feeling the roughness of her jacket against my breasts, willing her to stay.

"I think we'll never do this again," I told her.

"You're so sensuous," she said as she extracted herself from my embrace.

I rose with her, steadied myself against the wall, put on my bathrobe, and followed her to the door. She reached up and kissed me, pressing her body to mine.

"You look sexy in that robe," she mouthed against my lips—but she pulled away and left.

I staggered to bed and stared at the ceiling, trying to focus on the events of the evening.

Before I could close my eyes, there was a knock at the door.

Dee was back, undressed and lying on top of me, her hands on my breasts, her mouth on mine. But after several glorious minutes of pleasure, I was again beset with nausea and dizziness and urged her to stop. She rolled off me and almost immediately fell asleep.

I lay awake, trying to decide whether I needed to get up and puke.

After about an hour, I realized it was 2 a.m. and Brenda would be anxious, so I jostled Dee awake.

"Dee, you need to go—or call Brenda."

"How come I have to leave?" she mumbled, still half asleep. "I don't want to. Can't I just stay here?"

"You should at least call," I insisted.

She took her time getting up and dressed. At the door, I kissed her and asked that she call me when she arrived home.

She agreed, but I didn't hear from her until late the following morning. She told me she'd fallen asleep on the freeway but jerked awake when her tires hit the rough lines on the side. I winced, upset with myself for letting her drive, still impaired. I was relieved she was okay. I didn't ask her how Brenda had received her, and she didn't tell me.

That morning, as I stumbled around the apartment, wincing at the light, and holding my throbbing head, David made me coffee and baked eggs. I drank the coffee but couldn't stomach the eggs.

I quizzed him about his experience with Rick.

"Nothing much happened," he reported. "We kissed and groped a little, and then he left."

Despite our start-and-stop evening, and my getting smashed,

I remembered every detail of being with Dee. I hoped we might do it again sober.

I also wondered if David would ever find love, and whether I would ever find myself in a committed relationship. Were such relationships even possible for us?

The following week was my last one at Holy Cross Hospital. When Dee spoke to me at all, her voice sounded clipped and curt. I crumpled inside and responded with aloofness. I had powerful feelings for her, even love, but I would not admit that to her.

Over the next few days, Dee softened, and we talked again.

"I'm confused and disappointed in myself," she said over lunch.

I only wish I wasn't so smashed.

"I know you have a girlfriend. I also have a partner and a home with her."

My shoulders slumped. I hadn't allowed myself to think anything permanent could come of our affair. I didn't see beyond attraction and gratification of desire, not even with Cass. As for Dee—if she was living with Brenda, what was she doing in my bed? What did that mean about her commitment?

My exposure to the women's movement in Boston had taught me female eroticism was cause for celebration, but it had provided few models of sustaining relationship beyond desire. I didn't even know where to begin with that.

Dee looked troubled. I wanted to reach across the table and take her hand but reached for my water glass instead.

"Will you come to my graduation?" I asked. "I would like my parents and sister to meet you."

She smiled. "Of course I will, sweetie."

∽

When I called Mom before their visit, I asked her to bring up the only painting I'd ever done: an abstract oil of a tiny figure connected by a tendril to the brain of a much larger figure in profile looming overhead. I'd painted it after I'd returned to Phoenix and Susan had cut off all contact. In my grief, I'd needed an outlet to express her importance to me. I planned to give the painting to Dee upon my departure to show her she was important to me also—without using words.

Just before graduation, my entire medical school class—along with fourth-year students across the country—took the US Medical Licensing Examination. Despite my distracting personal life, I'd studied hard over the last few months. When we received our results, the chief of medicine and head of the Internal Medicine Honors Program stopped by my desk and put his hand on my shoulder. He was usually stern, but that day he smiled and said, "Congratulations, you got one of the highest scores in the country and the highest in the class."

When I looked at the breakdown of my scores, I saw it was my score in pulmonary medicine that helped push me into this rarefied stratum. Thanks to Dee.

I can't imagine Dee was an exception, though she was indeed exceptional. She served as a role model for holding my own with authoritative men. How many brilliant women like Dee were relegated by their sex to supporting roles, propping up physicians who were earning far more money? She should have had the title and authority of MD, in charge, making better decisions for patients than some of her physician superiors.

Through sheer determination, a bit of luck, and a propensity to go against the grain of social pressure, I would forge a different path.

CHAPTER FIFTEEN

When my parents and sister arrived for graduation, I couldn't wait for Mom to meet Dee, who fit her image of how a professional woman should look and act and was also a lesbian. While my father and sister left for a walk around Temple Square, Dee, Mom, and I met on the Thirteenth Floor, an upscale lounge on top of one of the downtown hotels overlooking the city.

As I knew she would, Dee arrived dressed to perfection in a silk blouse, scarf, skirt, hose, and high heels, with makeup on, and her hair blow-dried and perfect. She and my mom fell into an amiable exchange and soon became quite chummy.

We ordered drinks, and I had a scotch on the rocks, which caused Mom to raise an eyebrow. After my first few sips, I began tuning out the conversation.

My mother wore a turquoise dress with a draped neck, pearls, matching purse, and high-heeled shoes, despite how they hurt her feet. I snapped back to the conversation when Mom started in about my attire.

"Dee, you're a woman of good taste. Do you think you could influence Patricia to take more care of her appearance, especially since she's becoming a doctor?"

Dee smiled at me with a look of apology. I sat up straighter in my chair and braced for what might come next.

"Dressing well as a woman is important for my professional

image," Dee began, and Mom nodded her encouragement. "Besides, I enjoy looking good and it increases my confidence."

Mom took advantage of the opportunity. "Do you think you can convince Patricia to wear the dress I bought her for her graduation ceremony and dinner?"

I knew I had no choice of attire with Mom visiting and was eager to change the subject. "She doesn't have to convince me. I'll wear it."

I finished my scotch and ordered another. When it arrived, I took a few more gulps, ignoring Mom's look of disapproval. Now that she and Dee were in cahoots, chatting as if they were old friends, I proceeded to get drunk.

An hour later, Dee said she had to get home to feed the dogs. She and Mom gushed effusive goodbyes, and I leaped from my chair to walk out with her, leaving Mom sitting by herself at the table.

When the elevator arrived, it was empty, and I got in it with Dee. As the door closed, I pushed her up against the side wall and kissed her with lunging desperation. I didn't want to leave this city without her knowing I still wanted her. That our previous awkward evening together was not just a one-night fling for me.

"What are you *thinking*?" she asked, pushing me away as the doors opened into the lobby.

I followed her out to her car. When she arrived at the driver's side, she glanced nervously around and said, "Get in."

Of course, I complied, and as soon as we both shut our doors, I leaped on her. I was younger, taller, stronger, and more inebriated, and at first, she kissed me back. Then she pushed me away. "You're leaving this town in a few days, but I live and work here. I can't do this."

Not so drunk that her words didn't affect me, I backed off.

"Go back up there to your mother, drink lots of water, eat something, and I'll call you tomorrow."

Chagrined, I returned to the table, where my mom had ordered some potato skins for us. The server had replaced the scotch glass with one of ice water. *Perfect*, I thought.

I sipped the water, unable to look Mom in the eye. After a few silent moments, I took a deep breath and faced her disapproving look.

"Patricia, you should know better than to drink scotch," she said.

Indeed, I should.

Graduation day dawned. Mom put her arm around me in the kitchen. "Watching you get your diploma and becoming a Doctor of Medicine will be the proudest moment of my life."

As the proud moment approached, I stood poised to hear my full name called and cross the stage to receive my diploma and handshake from the Dean. He announced, "Patrick Grayhall."

Quickly he corrected himself, "Gosh, I can't even do a simple job correctly."

Though the audience chuckled, I was not amused. In fact, my face grew hot as I clutched my diploma. He'd masculinized my name and robbed me and my family of this solemn, proud moment.

Later, Mom would make light of his mistake, as if it didn't matter. But it mattered to me.

～

After the ceremony, David, Arlis, and I stood around in our caps and gowns with our classmates, smiling for pictures, diplomas in hand. Afterward, I donned the red and black dress Mom had bought for the occasion, along with pantyhose, heels, and earrings. David and I set off with our families for our joint graduation dinner.

The restaurant, Quail Run, was a rich golden stucco with a gabled roof set on twenty acres of private gardens and vineyards at the mouth of Little Cottonwood Canyon. The setting western sun cast a warm glow over the Wasatch Mountains, rising on each side of the Canyon to the east. Peacocks roamed the grounds fanning their brilliant tails, and ducks swam lazily in the pond near a small crescent bridge over the stream. Savoring the last rays of the sun, we strolled up the drive to the restaurant. The soft, warm breeze and the beauty of the valley evoked a bittersweet nostalgia in me for this fabulous city, so close to big nature, where I had spent the last, mostly happy, four years.

Mom had been busy setting everything up to perfection. There was a bouquet of fresh flowers on the table and place name cards. To the right of our plates, David and I each had a slim package tied with a red ribbon placed on top of a pile of note pads printed with our names, followed by "MD." We opened the boxes to reveal gold Cross pens, also inscribed with our names, followed by "MD."

David's father, quiet and sweet, smiled when we exclaimed how useful the pads would be, both of us aware he had printed them himself in his shop. David and Mom rose from the table and huddled in a small cubicle off the intimately lit dining room to purchase wine for the dinner—the custom in Mormon country.

As was her style, Mom had arranged the menu in advance. It was a multi-course Belgian-French meal with pear salad, escargot, rack of lamb, French potato purée, braised pearl onions, buttered carrots, and plenty of wine. I worried the entire dinner must have cost our parents a fortune; neither pair was well off. No one seemed troubled by it, though, and Mom chatted with David's mother and father, all three smiling and laughing. My father ate quietly with his private thoughts, a little zonked out on his newest medication, but stable. I knew he was proud of me.

I wondered if David's parents thought we were a couple and if he had told them he was gay. That night whatever their illusions, David and I enjoyed an interlude of happiness—a moment of calm and celebration of accomplishment before the storm to come.

Later that evening, we convened at the Thirteenth Floor lounge downtown. David and I danced the Bump to George McCrae's "Rock Your Baby" while Mom looked on with pleasure—no doubt happy to see me wearing a dress, dancing with a man, sober, and behaving "normally."

Years after David and I left Salt Lake City and lived on opposite sides of the country, the medical school would send mail, newsletters, and announcements of class reunions to David—addressed to both of us. They must have assumed we were a common-law heterosexual couple, unable as they were to conceive of any other arrangement outside the box, just as the Dean assumed my graduating class was all men.

The next afternoon, I slipped away from my family to say goodbye to Dee. We drove up one of the nearby canyons and stopped under a group of shady cottonwoods. I was still feeling sheepish about my behavior the last time we'd been together. I leaned back in my bucket seat and waited for her inevitable rebuke.

Dee reached over to take my hand. I stared at her hand, working out what to say.

"I'm sorry I was so aggressive and oblivious at the hotel."

For a moment, she remained quiet, looking serious, and a cold stab of fear gripped my chest that she didn't like me anymore.

"I think our friendship can withstand it—but," she warned, "that sort of insensitive behavior doesn't become you."

If I were a dog, I'd have hung my head, my eyes averted.

The following week, our last in Salt Lake City, I called a junk dealer to get rid of our furniture. David had already left to drive the Mustang cross-country with all our belongings. I stood in our empty apartment and gazed out over the city, nostalgic about leaving it behind. I had cocooned here with purpose and connection, yet I felt optimistic about my upcoming internship in Boston. David would be there, and Cass, too. I couldn't wait to see her.

In the early morning, I boarded the plane to Boston—with no idea of the hell awaiting me.

PART III

DOCTOR

"The very first requirement of a hospital is that it should
do the sick no harm."
—FLORENCE NIGHTINGALE

CHAPTER SIXTEEN

The only woman intern at Boston University Hospital, I'd just turned twenty-five. It was July 1975. Right away I plunged into the high-stress Cardiac Care Unit (CCU) with another medical intern, George, an affable man who often looked stunned. We were on call all night, every other night, thirty-six hours on and twelve off, seven days a week—for six weeks.

Ten days into this rotation, an elderly woman, Mrs. Federman, was admitted to the CCU with left-sided congestive heart failure. The unit staff was familiar with her. She had been admitted just a month earlier with a myocardial infarction—or heart attack.

Mrs. Federman was George's patient. Sick as she was, when I was on call, she would still try to engage me in conversation when I came to draw blood or check her intravenous line and urine output.

"You don't look like a doctor," she told me one day as I drew her blood.

I was used to people thinking all doctors were male; I just smiled.

"Do you have a boyfriend?" Her thinning hair was in disarray, but she had a disarming smile.

"No, too busy." I smiled, thinking about how scandalized she would be if she knew about Cass.

"Honey, you best get a husband before you are too old to have babies. A pretty girl like you should marry."

"Babies and marriage aren't on my agenda," I told her.

Despite her conservatism, I liked Mrs. Federman. She had a dry humor and a twinkle in her eye. She also had lots of concerned family coming in and out during visiting hours; I could often hear laughter spilling from her room—rare in the CCU.

Several days later, when I was on call again, Mrs. Federman was not her usual talkative self. She was nauseated and hadn't eaten her dinner. I looked at her cardiac monitor and noticed she was having frequent abnormal extra beats; her heart was not pumping as efficiently as it should. If that kept up, I'd have to page the senior resident.

Sitting at the central desk, I reviewed her admitting history and her initial medication orders. She was not on anything that would adversely interact with Compazine, a drug for nausea, so I ordered it administered rectally so she wouldn't throw it up. I also noticed George had discontinued her diuretic (water pill) a few days earlier.

Chronic congestive heart failure is tricky. If the blood volume is too high or too low, the weakened heart muscle does not work properly, blood backs up into the lungs, and the patient becomes short of breath. A diuretic can help with maintaining the right blood volume, but potassium—important for the electrical function of the heart—gets washed out with the water pill, so we often give it as a supplement.

A new admission interrupted me before I could finish reviewing Mrs. Federman's most recent medication history. I would have to come back later.

∽

When I returned to Mrs. Federman's chart and reviewed her lab values, I noticed the electrolytes I'd drawn earlier that evening showed a potassium value of 9.4 units and had been circled in red. *A value of 9.4 units? That would be incompatible with life.* Potassium should not be above 5.5 units, or it will interfere with the electrical circuitry and muscle contraction of the heart. *It must be an error*, I decided. She'd been sitting up and talking to me, after all.

As a medical student, I'd been taught that when you see a lab value that appears off the wall and incongruous with the rest of the patient's picture, you repeat the test. So, I walked into Mrs. Federman's room to redraw her electrolytes—but I couldn't find a vein.

"I'm so sorry, Mrs. Federman," I told her, laying my hand gently on her shoulder. "I'm going to draw blood from the femoral vein in your groin."

By then, she was very pale. As I prepared my equipment to draw her blood, she moaned, "Oy vey," and lay still.

I looked up at the cardiac monitor and saw her heart rate had dropped to thirty beats per minute, with wide ventricular complexes, showing she was in complete heart block. This was a serious electrical malfunction that would deprive her organs of oxygen. I shouted to the nurses to page the senior resident. Meanwhile, I put the head of her bed down flat, threw her pillow aside, made sure she was still breathing, and felt for her carotid pulse.

Her blood pressure had plummeted. She was unconscious. I called a Code Blue, CCU, Room 12.

The nurses rushed in with a crash cart to the bedside with

the cardiac defibrillator, IVs, cardiac medications, syringes, and an intubation kit. The senior medical resident, Dr. Sands, was paged over the loudspeaker and he sprinted to the CCU. Breathless, he turned to me for urgent details.

"Eighty-two-year-old woman admitted with congestive heart failure, post-myocardial infarction, many premature ventricular contractions earlier this evening, complaining of nausea, suddenly developed complete heart block and became unresponsive," I reported. I didn't mention the abnormal potassium value; I would wait until I had confirmed it with a repeat blood draw.

Following protocol, I moved in between the nurses and medical residents at the crowded bedside and drew electrolytes and blood gases from Mrs. Federman's femoral vessels. I sent them off with the nurse to the lab to be processed STAT and returned to Mrs. Federman.

She had gone into cardiac arrest. Everyone stood back while we applied the defibrillator paddles to her chest. With the discharge, her body jumped involuntarily, and the monitor showed the return of a very slow ventricular heart rate.

Because she wasn't breathing on her own, Dr. Sands intubated her and began preparing for the insertion of a temporary pacemaker through the subclavian vein in her upper chest. Sweating and swearing, he struggled with the procedure as blood seeped onto her neck and breast. I stood by, taking orders from him, and awaiting the results of the labs I had drawn. I looked around —tubes and packaging and equipment strewn everywhere, blood dripping from Mrs. Federman's chest onto the bed and my shoes.

Before Dr. Sands could get the emergency pacemaker in, Mrs. Federman again went into cardiac arrest.

"Shit, we're losing her. Stand back."

Once again, we shocked her, and this time the line on the cardiac monitor remained flat. We made several more attempts, but nothing.

"Okay, it's over," he pronounced. "Thank you, everyone."

I looked at my watch and noted the time.

The staff returned to what they were doing earlier as Dr. Sands and I stepped into the hall to debrief. A nurse walked up to us with the results of the STAT electrolytes. Mrs. Federman's potassium was 9.8 units.

Dr. Sands turned to me. "What the fuck?"

My gut clenched, and my voice quavered. "It was in the 9s earlier. I was just going to draw blood to repeat and confirm the test when she developed heart block."

He stood very close to me, his face contorted with anger. "And you didn't *tell* me?"

My mouth was dry; I was shaking. "It was so high. I thought it was a mistake."

"You as good as killed her!" he snapped at me, grabbing her chart.

I stood immobilized, my heart racing while he flipped through her records. Finally, he looked up. "Go! Clean her up. Get out of here."

Would he speak to me like that if I were a man?

I walked back into Mrs. Federman's room. There lay sweet Mrs. Federman, lifeless, a tube down her throat, IV lines still attached, a pacemaker kit open on the bed, a fresh gash in her upper chest and neck, and blood everywhere. *What a horrible way to die.* A lump formed in my throat and tears filled my eyes. I would have to fill out the death certificate and break the news to her loving family.

Fighting a wave of nausea, I pulled out her IV lines and urinary catheter, cleaned the blood off her neck and chest with a wet towel, and pulled the sheet up over her. I left the rest to the nurses. By the time I'd finished, the senior resident had gone.

I picked up Mrs. Federman's chart and thumbed through it. What I saw in the medication orders, and had been too busy to notice before, was that George had discontinued her diuretic a couple of days earlier but didn't discontinue her potassium replacement. Since her renal function was already compromised, this oversight had resulted in a sudden and dramatic rise in her blood potassium level. This caused the arrythmia of her heart and, ultimately, her death. I took some solace in knowing I had not killed her. I was only the last in this chain of unfortunate failures to detect this error. By then, it was too late.

All night, I thought about Mrs. Federman. I couldn't help feeling what had happened was all wrong. What do we want at the end of our lives? As doctors, we swore to do no harm. Were we improving the last days of these elderly people with our frenetic procedures and treatments? Didn't we sometimes do more harm than good? I'd aspired to become a doctor like my grandfather— kind, caring, and beloved by his patients but hospital practice was nothing like that. Did I really want to become an internist? How could I survive the year? And then what? More of the same? I shuddered at the thought.

༄

On rounds with the senior residents and attendings the next morning, I had to report what had happened. No one yelled at George. No one told him he had killed his patient. Nor had he had to watch Mrs. Federman die.

What the fuck? I get yelled at and he gets nothing?

I stood there, hands clenched around Mrs. Federman's chart, feeling light-headed. When everyone left, I sighed and sagged into the chair at the desk; I still had eight to ten hours to go before I could escape home.

The cumulative fatigue, the pressures of internship, the hostile politics of this hospital—how could I explain it to someone like Cass? No one outside of the crazy-demanding world of a medical intern could understand the hell I was going through. Given the brutal hours, lack of sleep, inability to eat regular meals, or exercise, how were we supposed to muster the concentration and empathy our patients deserved?

Although David didn't get thrown into boiling oil in the CCU/ICU—he never experienced being blamed for the death of a patient—David was going through the same grueling internship. Neither of us had the luxury to shop, cook, or do anything but sleep when home. I drank too much wine during my off shifts and wished I had someone to take care of me.

Exhausted and needy, I did not make a very satisfying girlfriend for Cass, a thirty-five-year-old woman struggling to go back to school, juggle several part-time jobs, and function as a single parent. She and I rarely had the time or energy to talk or share the experiences of our separate worlds. Neither did we speak of commitment, though Cass assumed since we were sleeping together, we were monogamous. I was too miserable to contemplate what I wanted.

Early in my internship, I had twelve hours off and Cass came to see me. The renovated townhouse David and I shared on East Springfield Street, a couple of blocks from the hospital, occupied two levels, with a bare brick wall in the living room and two large bedrooms downstairs with purple carpet.

Cass and I sat at our crude pine dining table eating Chinese takeout. I stopped talking mid-sentence and must have fallen into a few moments of micro-sleep because I awoke to Cass's hand on my arm. "Patricia, are you all right?"

"Just tired." I didn't want her to feel her visit was for naught. But after a bit of desultory conversation, I had to give in to fatigue. "Let's lie in bed and talk."

Once undressed and collapsed into bed, I experienced a brief surge of lust, pinned her to the mattress, and kissed her. When we came up for air, she started telling me about her classes and the problems of the clients she worked with in the WIC program, which provided food for low-income women and children.

I nodded off.

"Am I boring you?" she asked, with a hint of resentment in her voice.

The question startled me awake. "I want to talk and make love with you," I said, "but I just can't stay awake."

Along with the fatigue, an aching sadness swept over me—for the fragility of life, for the indignity of aging, for the inevitability of dying, and for the pain I inflicted with often useless treatments. I had no words to express the depths of my despair. I lay on my back, sobbing, the tears dripping into my ears.

Cass rolled me over, enfolded me in her arms, and spooned me until I fell asleep. When the alarm rang at 6:30 a.m., she could barely get me out of bed to start my next thirty-six-hour shift.

A month later, a nurse in the ICU paged me at 3 a.m. I had just arrived in the on-call room, hoping to sleep. No such luck. "Mr. Scott is fighting the ventilator," she told me. "You need to come up."

I sighed. "Okay, I'll be up."

I ascended the stairs to the ICU, where I sat under the fluorescent glare at the main desk across from Mr. Scott's pod. I could hear the steady whoosh and thump of his ventilator.

His nurse, a young blonde woman, stood over me, frowning. "He needs to be extubated." She demanded I take the tube out of his throat so he might breathe on his own.

"I need to review his medical history and orders before I see him," I reminded her, hoping she would go away and leave me in peace for a few moments. I was so tired and dehydrated. It had been hours since I'd last had anything to eat or drink.

The irritating nurse continued hovering over me. Through bleary eyes, I could discern Mr. Scott was a man in his sixties with severe chronic obstructive pulmonary disease and pneumonia. His earlier blood gases on oxygen weren't very good. I wondered if the nurse wanted me to extubate him just because he was annoying her, fighting the ventilator, causing her to have to come to his bedside every time the alarm sounded.

I got up and rummaged in the supply cart for a syringe to draw blood gases. Regardless of what that nurse requested, extubating should only occur when backup was available, in case he needed to have the tube re-inserted.

When I entered Mr. Scott's pod, he was thrashing around in bed. When I called his name, his eyes fluttered open for just a few seconds.

"Hello, Mr. Scott," I introduced myself. "I'm Dr. Grayhall,

and I'm going to get some blood gases from the artery in your wrist."

This would allow me to measure his lung function. With a breathing tube down his throat, he couldn't object.

Fortunately for both of us, it was an easy draw, and I sent the samples off STAT for immediate analysis.

While waiting for the results, I put my elbows on the desk, rested my head in my hands, and closed my eyes.

The blond nurse appeared again, hovering like a mosquito. "Are you going to extubate him?"

"I'm waiting for the blood gases," I answered, weary and despondent.

No matter the result, I didn't want to extubate him. It was 4 a.m. The hospital was almost at capacity—bursting with new patients—and I might not have an experienced resident available to back me up if I pulled out his breathing tube and he could not breathe on his own. He was obese and had a thick neck. Re-intubation would be difficult. Plus, I'd never intubated a patient before. When I was a medical student on surgical rotation, the surgeons had not given me an opportunity to practice, unlike my male classmates. I expected I'd learn it on the job as an intern, but only with an experienced doctor standing by. I wondered why she thought she could pressure me into doing something I knew was medically wrong.

The blood gas results arrived. Not good. I adjusted the ventilator and shuffled to the on-call room to catch a few minutes of sleep.

Before I could close my eyes, the nurse paged me again. *Can't you just let me sleep half an hour?* I called the ICU.

"Mr. Scott is fighting the respirator again."

"Give him two milligrams of Valium IV," I instructed and hung up, banging the phone down a bit too hard.

Immediately, it seemed, my pager beeped again. My eyes snapped open. *Fuck!*

"Can you come up?" the nurse asked. "He's agitated, and I've already given him the sedative."

My jaw clenched as I dragged myself up the stairs. I resolved to stand my ground and trust my own judgment.

As soon as I arrived in the ICU, the blond nurse appeared at my side. "You have to extubate Mr. Scott—*now*." Then with her tone more aggressive, "Call a male doctor if you can't do it."

I snapped at her. "I am not extubating him at 4:30 a.m. with no medical backup."

"Yes, you are," she insisted.

What do you say to an imperious nurse who is acting beyond her station? *Fuck you* came to mind, but I held my tongue. "No." I said, then picked up the phone to answer another page and left the ICU.

I was on the floor below, putting a catheter in a male patient's penis—the hospital staff required the interns do this because they assumed all interns were male—when the ICU paged me again, I could not ignore the page. It could involve a different patient or problem. I stopped mid-procedure and picked up the nearest phone. "Dr. Grayhall."

It was her again. "You're getting no sleep until you extubate Mr. Scott."

The muscles in my neck were tight and aching, my head pounding. Did she just get off on harassing interns while we

149

were low in the hierarchy—before we became the ones lording our power over her? Or was this because she truly believed her patient was suffering with the tube down his throat and he needed to try breathing on his own?

"No way." I slammed down the phone.

This tug-of-war continued until 7:30 a.m., when the nurses switched shifts. But I noticed she didn't leave. Was she doing a double? Or was she there to heckle me, now on my twenty-sixth hour at the hospital with at least eight more to go?

When the attending doctor arrived for rounds, we both gave an update. "Mr. Scott was fighting the ventilator," she explained, "trying to breathe on his own, but Dr. Grayhall refused to extubate him." She smirked at me from the other side of the patient's bed. I shuffled my feet and stared at the floor, my stomach roiling from no breakfast, preparing to defend my decision.

The attending doctor looked at her, then at me. "That's okay," he said. "Dr. Grayhall's decision to wait until morning was correct. We'll extubate him together after rounds if his blood gasses are okay."

He bent over the patient with his stethoscope in his ears to listen to Mr. Scott's chest. The others were all looking at Mr. Scott, except for the blond nurse, who watched me with hostility. Vindicated, I smiled at her. Her eyes shot daggers at me.

Sometimes that year I felt like a child throwing a tantrum—kicking and screaming on the floor, unable to express the fear, hurt, and rage in words. The rage would haunt me for years, erupting at seemingly minor provocation. But despite it all, I was learning to trust myself as a doctor and not let the hostile work environment undermine my confidence.

Eight hours later, when I changed out of my scrubs in the

on-call room, I leaned against the wall for a moment, too tired to feel angry, tears welling up. *I don't know if I can survive this*, I thought, before I jammed my scrubs into the bin. But as the only woman intern, I could let no one see me cry.

In October, I drove up to see Cass in Peterborough. I had another stress cold and arrived in my Mustang with a thick book: *Magic Mountain* by Thomas Mann. I lay in Cass's bed all day, lost in the snowy world of Mann's Swiss tuberculosis sanatorium. Cass looked after me with hot tea laced with honey and rum and other ministrations to my body. Though I was ill, I enjoyed a brief two days of contentment and care.

When I got home, David was on call and the refrigerator was empty. It was unusual for us to be home on a weekend together, but when we were, we sometimes ventured out to the Magic Pan on Newbury Street in downtown Boston, with its country French decor, for savory crepes, wine, and commiseration. Other than these rare forays into civilized life, we had no time to shop for fresh food and ate our meals at the hospital or scavenged off discarded patient trays.

Sleep was so vital that when the opportunity arose, I slept like the dead, not hearing the phone or David coming in. The week after my return from New Hampshire, still ill, I fell into bed after another thirty-six-hour shift and fell asleep right away, without dinner. In the morning, after dragging myself out of a dreamless slumber, downing a bowl of cereal, and rushing to leave for rounds at the hospital, I discovered the house next door had burned to the ground overnight. No doubt fire engines had arrived with sirens blaring, but I'd slept through it all.

CHAPTER SEVENTEEN

One reason I wanted to be a doctor was to be present during some of the most challenging and intimate moments of other people's lives—when they had to make major decisions for themselves or their loved ones, when they were struggling to survive, or when they were dying. As an intern, I experienced a few such occasions when a patient spoke to me with complete honesty.

On rotation in the oncology unit, I entered the private room of an elderly woman, Mrs. Jordan. She'd been cross with me earlier for asking all the same questions during her admission others had asked her dozens of times before. It was a ritual we had to endure, and she knew it. She'd been admitted many times for treatment of her chronic lymphocytic leukemia, now out of control with enlargement of her lymph nodes, liver, and spleen.

"I'm sorry I was short with you earlier," she said.

I'd read all her previous chart notes by then and was aware she was the mother of a famous documentary film producer. She had suffered through multiple chemotherapy treatments and was now in the last stages of her disease. I smiled at her. "No problem. I know how tedious it must be for you, especially when you're ill."

As I performed the obligatory admission physical exam, I put my arm behind her, gently lifted her into a sitting position, and placed my cold stethoscope on her back to listen to her breath sounds. As I laid her on the pillow, she looked into my eyes and said, "I'm not afraid to die, you know."

I contemplated this. Why had she been admitted to this hospital if she didn't want us to perform every test, every procedure, every conceivable medical treatment to save her life? I paused my examination. "Why did you come to a teaching hospital?"

"My son wanted me to. He's afraid I might die." She smiled wanly and sighed in resignation.

I knew if she spiked a fever, as she was likely to do with almost no functioning white blood cells to fight infection, I would have to rush in and draw her blood at least six times for cultures. Even my examination of her might introduce harmful bacteria to her compromised immune system.

"Given what you just told me, do you want me to designate you DNR?"

"Let me talk to my son."

On the oncology unit, I'd treated many people in the last stages of dying. This was a Boston teaching hospital, and even when there was no hope, the attendings and senior staff urged us to do procedures on patients just so we could learn. In this macho culture, my male colleagues vied for the opportunity to put a central line in the jugular vein in the neck, a large-bore needle into a distended abdomen to tap off excess fluid awash with cancer cells, or into the chest to drain bloody fluid in the pleural sac between lung and chest wall. Sometimes these procedures relieved suffering, but in dying cancer patients they often just added to it. I would steel myself and do what they ordered me to do.

Afterward, I would go into the supply closet and bang my fist on a blanket or cry a few tears in frustration. I questioned the rationale for some of these invasions with the senior residents when it felt unnecessary and wrong.

That night, Mrs. Jordan spiked a fever. Her son had objected to her being designated DNR, so I had to do a complete workup. She sat up in bed, short of breath, her face flushed. With my stethoscope, I listened to her lungs—they were rattling, full of fluid.

I hustled to the supply closet to pick up six bottles containing culture medium and returned to her room.

She knew the drill. "Don't do this," she pleaded.

My pager beeped. I could leave her in peace for a few more minutes.

The senior resident passed me at the nurses' station and asked, "Have you drawn a CBC and the blood cultures on Mrs. Jordan yet?"

I shook my head no and returned to her room, reluctant to put her through this uncomfortable procedure.

"I'm sorry, Mrs. Jordan, but I have to draw blood for cultures to find the source of your infection."

She grimaced as I lifted her right arm, tied an elastic tourniquet around her upper arm and began looking and feeling for a vein. There were none. I moved the tourniquet and tried her hand. Nothing. I tried the same procedure on the other arm. Nothing again. I found a tiny blue vein in her left hand. I put the needle through her skin, but the vein rolled away.

I poked her several more times before I said, "Sorry, Mrs. Jordan, but I am going to draw blood from your groin."

To whose benefit was all this? She was becoming listless and though she didn't object, her face contorted in pain when I entered her femoral vein. I filled all six cough-medicine–size bottles and two tubes with the right amount of blood.

I needed to transport the blood to the lab in another building across a sky bridge that spanned Newton Street. My stomach tightened into an angry knot. As I reached the double doors, three culture containers in each hand, I kicked open the doors and let them slam against the wall. *Why did I have to do this?* Mrs. Jordan didn't want it. She wasn't afraid to die. She would die soon, anyway. It was easy for the senior resident to order me to jab her with needles for no logical benefit, except perhaps to reassure her son we were doing all we could. I was the one who had to witness her anguish and couldn't turn away.

To me, "doing all we could" would have been to leave her in peace and keep her comfortable while we let nature take its course.

The next time the residents asked me to do a spinal tap and draw blood cultures on a terminally ill patient who spiked a fever, I slow-walked it, taking care of other patients first.

The next morning on rounds, I stopped by to see a patient with bladder cancer, Janice Dodson. She was in her early sixties—unmarried, but another woman about the same age was often sitting by her bedside, holding her hand, helping her eat, or arranging her pillows. I wanted to linger and talk with them, but every time I tried, my pager beeped, and I had to leave for some other crisis.

When I arrived, the bed had been stripped and housekeeping was cleaning the room. I rushed to the nurse's desk. "Where's Janice Dodson?"

"She was transferred to the fifth floor an hour ago," a nurse told me.

My jaw clenched. Why hadn't the nurses notified me? She was my patient. I hadn't had a moment to talk with her, to hear her story, to discover what the woman who was always there meant to her.

Too often, I was too busy to get to know my patients as people—to establish the essential bond of empathy, the way my grandfather had.

With anger as my coping strategy and constant companion, I was often in conflict with my senior resident and the medical director of the residency program. I resented being singled out as the only female intern for harsher treatment than my male colleagues, especially when I questioned and balked at some of the senseless procedures my superiors ordered me to perform. Hospital internal medicine was inherently stressful. Most of the time we could do little to help the patients in our care. Everyone—the patients, the nurses, and the house staff who had to cope with disease and death throughout their shifts—suffered in their own ways. Across town, a physician wrote a book called *The House of God,* a scathing satirical account of the dehumanizing effect of medical internship. But it would be decades before reforms.

Two of the thirteen medical interns in my group succumbed to the harsh conditions. One had a nervous breakdown and was hospitalized on the psychiatric ward. Another developed a serious case of pneumonia and required hospital care. The rest of us had to pick up the slack. I no longer cared about excelling or even learning, my sense of purpose gone. I just wanted to survive.

Though he was overworked and sleep-deprived, David seemed to slog through his medical internship without the conflict

I experienced. This irritated me. It may sound mean, but I changed his nickname to Weasel, although I said it with affection. He was my ally, not my competitor—my only friend in a sea of misery. But his personality caused him to acquiesce, while mine compelled me to rebel. Perhaps I had developed this trait in part to cope with Mom's controlling anger during my childhood, but it wasn't serving me well in my internship.

During those first months, I had little time for reflection—no opportunity to discover what I wanted or needed other than sleep and a decent meal. It was not surprising, therefore, that I had an affair with a fourth-year medical student late that fall—just because she was there.

Anna was from New York and doing a rotation on the endocrine metabolic unit where I worked as an intern. She was of Russian descent, and in the artificial light of the hospital I noted she had deep-set eyes, a delicate mouth, and scarring from acne. She had a handsome beauty but sometimes a hard look in her eyes.

Just before Thanksgiving, I walked by a patient's room and found her lying on the bed with an IV in her arm. *Is she ill?*

She motioned for me to enter.

"I signed up for this experiment because it pays well," she said, "but it requires me to lie here for three days with no one to talk to. Come sit for a minute. Tell me about yourself."

"I can't right now," I said. "I just admitted a patient in ketoacidosis and have to get him stabilized." The way she looked at me caused me to wonder if she might be a dyke. Given my working conditions, lack of free time, and the necessity of being closeted at work, it had been impossible to meet any other lesbians for love or friendship since my move to Boston. "But as you're stuck here, I'll come by later," I promised.

For the next three days, I stopped by Anna's room when I had a minute. I didn't even have to talk much, as she rattled on with her stories about growing up in New York, her medical school experiences, her recipes, her observations of the house staff— whatever came into her head.

On the second day, just before I left her room, she looked me in the eye and said, "I think you might be gay. Am I right?"

I was impressed with her gaydar, since I appeared straight in my white coat and conventional hospital garb, although one day I'd worn jeans. "Yes, you're right."

"We have that secret in common," she said, smiling.

I left her room with a bounce in my step, pleased to have a sister in the house.

On the third day of my visits to Anna, she appraised me with a skeptical look. "Why should I like you, huh? Why should you be my friend? Just 'cause you're cute and have curly hair? 'Cause you're smart? 'Cause you look good in your jeans?"

I smiled and shrugged. But I might've said, "Because I'm lonely, and stressed, and want to get laid."

Which happened soon enough when I spent my next thirty-six-hour break going to New York rather than to see Cass—for no good reason other than the novelty of it.

Since we both loved to eat, Anna and I dined all over New

York City. We ate beef and bean curd with noodles and brown sauce for brunch, black beans, oranges, tongue, and rice at a Vietnamese-Puerto Rican restaurant for a later meal, then Indian food for an even later dinner. The following day, we had a Spanish omelet for breakfast, a gyro sandwich for a snack, and soul food with greens, yams, and pigs' knuckles for lunch.

I ate and Anna talked. And talked and talked. We ended up that evening at Mother Courage, a feminist restaurant. Regulars included Susan Brownmiller, Kate Millett, and Jill Johnston, well-known feminist writers of the day. Servers poured the wine for women to taste first and gave women seating priority. We washed down our food with plenty of their fine wine.

We slept together that weekend. No fireworks, though.

I took the last train back to Boston late Sunday night and barely arrived before rounds on Monday morning. I had no time for an update on my patients from the intern on call.

My chief resident was not the only one upset with me.

"Where have you been?" Cass demanded when she called that week. "I'd hoped you would come up last weekend."

I slumped in the chair, my guilt undeniable. "I was in New York with Anna," I admitted.

There was a painful silence. Then I realized she was crying.

I had no good explanation. I told her I was sorry; she was the one I loved. But my actions held more weight than my words, and she refused to see me the next weekend I had off.

〜

Over the next few months, I tried to woo Cass back, calling her and sending her letters, but she was still reluctant to start our affair again. I missed her and even thought of moving to New Hampshire, since there was no way she could uproot and come to Boston.

"I can't bear the thought of two more miserable years at Boston University Hospital," I told her one evening on the phone. To become a board-certified internal medicine specialist, as I had originally intended, I would have to follow my internship with two years of residency.

"Maybe I can take a year off and do general practice in New Hampshire."

There was a pause on the line. "Maybe," she said, noncommittal.

Am I forgiven yet? I wondered.

In early March, during one of my weekend thirty-six hours off, I set up an evening meeting with a doctor advertising for another physician in a town near Keene, New Hampshire, where Cass had moved. After a delicious dinner of pot roast at the doctor's home, we talked long enough for me to know I didn't feel adequately equipped to take on a small-community practice. I didn't even know how to deliver a baby.

It was late when I arrived at Cass's, and she was already asleep. It was a frigid, snowy night; she never had the heat on very high to save money. But we hadn't slept together since I'd gone to New York in early December, so I was unsure if I was welcome in her bed. She didn't lay sheets and blankets out on the couch, though she expected me. A good sign. I crept into her bed and curled up around her, her back to my front, to keep warm.

She woke up and moved her hips against me. A zing of excitement rushed through me, and I turned her over. The flame of desire became a four-alarm fire as we both dissipated our pent-up need, losing ourselves in each other.

Lying next to her, languid in the post-orgasm glow, I mused I would be happy anywhere, doing anything as long as I could make love with Cass. But of course, life was more complicated than that.

In the morning, I wondered again if she'd forgiven me for my affair with Anna. I was back in Cass's bed—but was I back in her life?

A few days later, still looking for options other than to continue with another two years of internal medicine residency, I drank an entire bottle of Mateus—a cheap Portuguese rosé—and wrote a letter to the Harvard School of Public Health. People walked by my window, their boots crunching in the snow. I jiggled my pen and stared at the wall, trying to express my thoughts. In my inebriated state, I scrawled my displeasure at the way medicine spent the bulk of its resources on dying patients in the last few months of their lives with little positive impact. "I want to investigate the environmental causes of cancer and other diseases and work to prevent them," I wrote.

Over the next two days, I edited my letter and sent it.

A couple of weeks later, while on duty and admitting a patient in the emergency department, I was paged for a call from Dr. John Peters at the Harvard School of Public Health.

"I liked your letter," he said, "and I agree with you."

"Thank you; I was sincere." My pager beeped, but I ignored it.

"I'm calling you because the Harvard School of Public Health has just received a grant from the National Institutes of Health to start an occupational medicine program."

I stood up straighter and pressed the phone to my ear. He now had my complete attention.

"The emphasis will be on epidemiology, toxicology, biostatistics, and prevention of cancer and other chronic diseases. It may be just what you're looking for."

"Absolutely!" I answered, my senses fully alert despite having gotten no sleep the night before. Was he offering me a position?

"Would you like to be our first resident in occupational and environmental medicine? You can get a Master of Public Health degree at the same time."

It was as if the sun burst through the clouds, light flooding my world. *This could be my escape.*

Then caution crept in, dimming my enthusiasm. "I'm not sure I can afford Harvard tuition."

"Not to worry," he said, his voice friendly and smooth. "The grant will cover the tuition and you'll be given an annual $18,000 stipend."

In 1976, that was a vast amount of money. If he'd been in the room, I'd have thrown my arms around his neck and kissed him. Of course, I said yes.

"It might interest you to know occupational medicine was first established in this country by a woman, Alice Hamilton, who also was the first woman physician appointed to the faculty at Harvard."

Even better. This offer would change the course of my life.

Though I had my future lined up, David and I still had to complete the last stretch of our medical internships.

Then disaster struck. A young man David had admitted two weeks before—a drug addict who had a virulent form of hepatitis B, his liver no longer able to rid the blood of the toxins affecting his brain—leaped from his bed in his delirium and ripped out his IV. Contaminated blood splattered everywhere. As his intern, it was David's job to get him back into bed, reinsert his IV, and clean up the blood. These were the days before universal precautions and protective gear was lacking.

Six weeks later, I was doing a rotation at the Veterans Administration Hospital when I received the call from David. He felt nauseated and the whites of his eyes had turned yellow. A blood draw revealed a dangerous clotting deficiency—a bad prognostic sign in hepatitis.

"I'm being admitted to Beth Israel Hospital," he told me, his voice tremulous and weak. "Can you come?"

I was on duty that night with a senior resident who assigned me extra admissions and the patients requiring the most work. A sympathetic fellow intern agreed to take over my night call.

I described each of my patient's problems for him and what action or tests were pending before I called the operator and signed out. I gathered my belongings but before I could leave the house staff room, the senior resident blocked my exit standing in the doorway, his arms holding on to the door frame. "Where the hell do you think you're off to?" he barked.

"My friend is seriously ill with hepatitis he caught from a patient. I'm going to Beth Israel to be with him."

"Like hell you are." His lip curled in a sneer.

"I've signed over my patients to Dr. Evans and finished my

admission notes and orders." My chest tightened and my hands closed into fists as he continued blocking my exit. I had to get to David. He might be dying. He needed me. There was nothing else more important. "Get out of my way, you bastard!" I snapped.

He smirked as he stepped aside. "You're screwed."

I put on a paper gown and gloves and entered David's hospital room. He lay still, his eyeballs yellow, looking vulnerable and frightened. I couldn't even hold his hand. My stomach churned with anxiety as I spoke to his doctor, who shook his head and said, "Time will tell."

That very day, my senior medical resident at the VA informed the head of the residency program of my insubordination. The director convened a meeting with my all-male cast of supervisors—some of whom I'd rubbed the wrong way over the last year—to determine whether I would receive credit for my internship. I had only three days left.

Over several days, as I hovered by his side, David's health improved. His blood-clotting factors returned to normal. Although he continued to be very yellow and weak, he was well enough to leave the hospital and return home to recover.

I delayed opening the envelope, whose contents would tell me whether Boston University Hospitals would require I do my internship year all over again and busied myself looking after David.

A week later, sitting on the couch next to David in our barren, dreary living room, I took a deep breath and tore open the envelope. "Dear Dr. Grayhall," it read. "After careful consideration of your work ethic . . ."

They had given me credit for my internship, after all. They knew I was leaving for a residency at the Harvard School of Public Health. Despite my persistence in being a fierce advocate for what I believed needed to change in the way we cared for patients, my work that year had been good enough. Though I never learned who they were, some men took my side. I was grateful to them.

Perhaps times were changing.

After the call from Dr. Peters, it was clear I would stay in Boston. Moving to New Hampshire to be with Cass was no longer on the table. Over the summer, we drifted apart.

At the time such events are happening, it's hard to see their long-term implications, especially when you're young and rudderless, swept along by the next breaking wave. Cass and I lived in two different worlds: she, in her midthirties, lived in conservative New Hampshire, working, going to school, and responsibly parenting her daughters; I, in my midtwenties, preferred to stay in liberal Boston, a hotbed of feminism, living and working with a man, dating other women, following the dictates of desire, and training to be a doctor. I was bound to disappoint her.

Still, I would keep coming back to her again and again.

CHAPTER EIGHTEEN

That summer, after our internships ended, David and I traveled by train to New York for the Gay Pride Parade. It had been seven years since Stonewall. The 1969 riot in Greenwich Village erupted after police raided a gay bar in the city and the occupants resisted, jump-starting the gay rights movement.

That day, we waved jauntily to a busload of tourists from Kansas who were hanging out the windows and snapping pictures of us in our rainbow T-shirts and tiaras. The mood was upbeat and joyous, the attire outrageous and colorful. David and I were marching in front of a float full of drag queens in reflective mirrored sequins, huge speakers blaring Donna Summer's "Love to Love You Baby." We were swept up in the moment, singing along and laughing, gay and proud, our arms around each other's shoulders. Among the crowd, I saw smiling faces—people of all ages waving rainbow flags and giving us the thumbs-up.

Then David squeezed my shoulder. "Oh God, Patroosk, they're filming us for the TV news."

I flinched, remembering we had to hide our sexual orientation from our employers.

The year of the Stonewall uprising was the same year I came out of the closet as a lesbian in San Francisco. Then I had to hide in the closet in Salt Lake City, and again during my difficult internship. It had been challenging being in the minority as a woman, let alone as a lesbian, in the medical field.

For this one day, our first gay pride parade, we could freely announce to the world who we were, and revel with other gays and lesbians—with pride.

The hell with hiding. I stepped in front of the camera.

David and I stayed on in New York for the Bicentennial celebration on July Fourth. We drank wine on the balcony of one of David's acquaintances overlooking the Hudson River. Sixteen tall-masted ships, as well as a British schooner crewed by women, passed below us. Later, two thousand sailors and five brass bands blaring patriotic music marched up Broadway to city hall.

As the sun set on the warm day, fireworks lit the skies over Battery and Riverside Parks. I thought of the ancestors of both my parents. They'd arrived in North America before the US was even a country: farmers, pacifists, engineers, soldiers, doctors, teachers, mothers, and wives. I felt proud—to be both gay and American.

David and I returned to Boston in time to welcome Mom and Terri, who had driven over 2,600 miles from Phoenix in my sister's 1973 AMC Hornet. My father was in the hospital with agitated depression—yet again.

It amazed me that Mom, in her sixties, would embrace tent camping for an entire week along the way. When I heard that they'd dodged a tornado raging across Ohio, I was even more impressed. But the visit didn't start out smoothly.

Mom, Terri, David, and I were at lunch at Boston's Original

Oyster House. My mother brought up the subject of internship. "Was it as dreadful as you thought it would be?"

"Far worse." I launched into a rant about the inhumanity of it all for interns and patients. My face grew flushed and my chest tight.

Mom turned to David. "It wasn't really that bad, was it?"

David deferred in his diplomatic way, but I didn't hear the words. *She doesn't believe me*, I thought. She'd dismissed and denied the validity of my feelings, just as she often did when I was a child. When she told me I was just too sensitive, my feelings ridiculous.

I got up and left the table.

Later that day, in a calmer frame of mind, the four of us prepared to travel in the Hornet to Montreal for the Summer Olympics. We planned to camp during the entire trip.

The first night, I took Mom's arm and helped her crawl out of the tent. I walked with her to the restroom, shining the flashlight on the uneven path and steadying her on my arm.

"You're so sweet to look after me like this." She squeezed my hand.

Even as a kid, I strove to take care of her. When she was in tears, feeling trapped in her marriage with my depressed and nonfunctioning father, I was her confidant, though only a child. I urged her to get a job and earn her own money, which she did. As an adult, I dropped everything, no matter where I was or what I was doing, to fly to Phoenix when she needed me.

The Olympics topped off my summer of spectacle. On the way home, we stopped for lunch with Cass in New Hampshire. I was dying to be alone with her, but under the watchful eye of Mom, it wasn't possible. I wondered what Mom thought of her. Cass likely challenged my mother's stereotype of a dyke.

After we left, Mom didn't comment on Cass's attributes, but she had no negative comments, either. For Mom, it was the highest form of praise.

David was still struggling at Boston University Medical Center, now no longer an intern but a second-year resident. It was my job to find us a new place to live. The choice was limited. I settled on a third-floor unit in an old, renovated house that had been chopped up into apartments. It had two bedrooms, but David had to walk through my bedroom to get to the single bathroom or the kitchen, creating an awkward encounter if I brought anyone home. It was in Brookline, a pleasant neighborhood across from a park and within walking distance of Harvard Medical School and the School of Public Health, and I didn't need a car. I sold David my Ford Mustang so he could drive to the hospital. He promised to lend it to me sometimes.

In late August, I began working evenings at a women's clinic in Cambridge. Members of the Boston Women's Health Book Collective, the group that had written *Our Bodies, Ourselves*—a landmark book full of good medical information for women—were often on-site. I performed gynecological exams, prescribed birth control pills, and inserted IUDs.

Soon after my arrival, a member of the Collective stopped by the exam room and leaned against the door frame, her long, dark hair falling over one eye, her bell-bottom jeans torn at the knee. She informed me I was not to counsel the clients. Only women with the proper feminist perspective and training could do that.

"In fact, it's best if you hardly speak to them at all," she told me with a straight face.

I choked. *What? I am a woman, a lesbian, and a feminist, and she is telling me I can't talk with women about their bodies?*

Apparently, my being a medical doctor and thus a member of the patriarchal establishment trumped everything else. After that day, my work there became robotic and dull.

The summer was almost over. Cass was cool and distant on the phone. I just didn't know where I stood with her. I ventured out to meet some lesbians, at least for friendship. I dropped in at the Cambridge Women's Center—where Coyote had often hung out what seemed like ages ago. She had disappeared from the Boston area in the intervening years, and I'd lost track of her.

A consciousness-raising group was in progress. Most of the women sat cross-legged in a circle on the floor. I leaned against the doorframe, half in and half out, not sure I wanted to stay.

The topics were self-examination and children in the gay community. I recognized a few members of the Boston Women's Health Book Collective. A young woman had just finished showing how to use a speculum and mirror to examine her own vagina. "You can't trust female physicians," she admonished the group, "as they are part of the same patriarchal system as male doctors."

I fumed inwardly but said nothing.

Later, another woman with long blond hair and granny glasses announced women in Sweden could now produce children with their female lovers by fertilization of one egg with another. Nobody challenged her, and several nodded their agreement. This was too much. I snorted loud enough to be heard. *Where are the scientists? Didn't they realize one egg could not possibly fertilize another?*

"That's totally untrue!" I blurted out.

Several women turned and gave me disapproving looks.

As the group continued to speak on the topic, I became light-headed, the room closing in around me; I shook as I stood there in the doorway, unable to get my breath. *I don't belong here. I don't belong anywhere.* I took my pulse, and it was up to a hundred and twenty, a panic attack.

Counting my heart rate calmed me only a little. I feared I might pass out in this room full of women who I assumed wouldn't know what to do.

I left without speaking to anyone and trudged outside. The cool night air refreshed and calmed me as I headed over to the Citadel Bar, which was almost empty, then the Together Bar, which was also nearly empty. I didn't drink or talk to anybody at either bar.

I took the T home, slumped in my seat, feeling very much alone.

The next week, I quit my job at the Cambridge women's clinic.

Disappointed that Cass was too busy to see me, I traveled by train to New York to visit Anna. She was now a medical intern. At least we had that in common.

When I arrived at her apartment, she talked to me for only a few minutes before jumping me from behind and pushing me onto her waterbed for sex before dinner.

Still no fireworks.

That evening, we saw a Broadway play called *For Colored Girls*

Who Have Considered Suicide/When the Rainbow is Enuf. It told the story of seven women of color through poetry, song, and movement. The women, who had all considered suicide, talked about their lives. No matter how bad things got, and no matter how many times they suffered setbacks, the women were strong enough to rise again and not let darkness conquer them. Inspired, I thought about how I'd despaired trying to be straight, after my abortion, and again during my internship. Yet I'd salvaged my sanity by claiming my true identity, becoming a doctor, and snagging the residency at Harvard that better reflected my values.

That night Anna and I convened at Mother Courage with two of Anna's friends. Anna talked nonstop.

"Patricia likes to eat. She and I have been all over town to restaurants and it will be her fault if I put on several pounds; I like excellent food too, we don't get any at the hospital . . . Last week a priest came into the emergency department with maggots in his leg ulcers I had to clean. I could eat nothing that day . . . It took two hours for Patricia to try on every blouse on the rack at Bloomingdales before she found one long enough . . ."

Anna spoke in such a steady stream of consciousness I tuned her out, thinking her constant prattle would drive me nuts over time.

The next morning, I had a shower in Anna's bathtub and got water on the floor.

"You didn't clean it up, you slob," she carped, then socked me in the arm—hard.

I froze, brought my fist to my mouth, and turned away so she wouldn't see my tears. When she left, I had a silent cry as I mopped the bathroom floor with a towel.

I couldn't look at her until we were on the pavement outside. I still couldn't put into words the tightness gripping my chest.

"Oh, Patricia, stop pouting," she said, nudging me with her body.

Anna sighed. "Listen, I'm sorry I hit you. I get water on the floor sometimes, too."

But it wasn't enough. That she was also a doctor had drawn me to her at first. But after that weekend, I knew our affair was over.

I missed Cass and yearned to experience again the companionship and passion we'd shared. The fall leaves were turning yellow and gold and blowing along the ground when she agreed to a visit. I rode the bus from Boston, through picturesque little towns, on my way to Keene.

Cass and I spent most of Saturday together catching up on our lives. We made dinner, and I helped Sara with her math homework. I cast glances at Cass throughout the evening, remembering how exciting it had been to make love with her six months earlier—the soft curve of her back arching over me, her hands running down my body, my fingers inside her, her passionate kisses. Now she seemed very much in her own world of struggle and responsibility. Her eyes looked tired, and she sighed when she sat next to me on the couch. I massaged her tight shoulders and put my arm around her.

All evening I vibrated with desire. A ripple of excitement

coursed through me when she took my hand and led me to her bedroom.

Once we were in bed together, we began with tender caresses. My energy had been building for months, and I didn't want to dissipate it right away. But with passion mounting, and Cass knowing exactly what to do, I couldn't help myself as waves of orgasmic pleasure pulsed through me. The raw edge taken off, Cass and I took our time and savored the next rounds.

Awake most of the night making love, we slept in the following morning. I sat on the couch reading epidemiology for my upcoming class, while Cass prepared breakfast for Sara, who was soon off to visit with friends. Once Sara left, I slid behind Cass in the kitchen chair and nibbled the back of her neck, slipped my hands under her shirt, and cupped her breasts. We moved to the bedroom, and I barely made my bus to Boston.

But our lives were to diverge again. With no promises of forever or monogamy, I was to embark on a path that would lead me further away from Cass—but not completely, never completely.

CHAPTER NINETEEN

That fall, I again found myself at the Saints on a Saturday night, cruising. At twenty-six, it's easy to think if it doesn't work out with one person, there will always be another; infinite possibilities exist for finding our soul mate. It is not until we're older that we discover in a lifetime, there are only a few special people with whom we connect deeply.

Despite my height of six feet, and my androgynous bar attire, I leaned toward a feminine presentation. As a child, Mom told me I was beautiful, as if that were the most important thing in the world. This caused me to have an over-valued opinion of my looks. I showed up at the Saints, expecting to be noticed and hit on—but felt desolate and deflated if I wasn't. I rarely enjoyed the atmosphere of the bar, being assessed and having to make small talk. I worried about being "outed" in my professional life, so I revealed little about myself unless I thought someone was interesting and safe. I was drawn to women who "passed" as straight, like Cecilia, Cass, and Dee.

That night as I leaned against the bar, swilling my beer from the bottle, and glancing around, I caught the gaze of a woman across the room in the dim light who did not fit the mold of what I normally considered appealing. She was overweight, tucked her flannel shirt into her jeans, and wore stern-looking glasses. Though she had a butch swagger, there was something about her face—expressive and intelligent—I found appealing. Enough so that I left the bar, walked in her direction, and introduced my-self.

"I thought I would put myself down for the next game. Do you play?" I asked, figuring she was the type who would play pool. I was terrible at it.

"Sure," she said, peering at me over the rim of her glasses.

Her name was Maryann, and as I shot my cue ball into the side pockets over and over, she told me she had a Master of Fine Arts in English. Maryann had developed her own commercial cleaning business in Connecticut, where she grew up, then moved to Boston to teach English in a Catholic high school.

After we'd finished a game and Maryann was tactful enough not to comment on my lack of skill, she asked me, "So would you like to have dinner this week, somewhere quieter?"

I agreed.

Maryann and I met at Legal Seafoods in Cambridge. We sat across from each other on the high stools, peeling our shrimp and dip-ping them in the sauce, sawdust on the floor below us and a bottle of wine between us. Maryann inquired about my summer and if I was seeing anyone. I told her about my recent trips to New York and New Hampshire, leaving out any mention of rapturous sex with Cass.

"It must exhaust you servicing all the women on the East Coast," she said, dipping her shrimp in my pot.

I almost choked on my water but coughed back my surprise. Her brashness appealed to me, though I wasn't ready to make or accept any moves. When Maryann dropped me off at my apart-ment, I gave her a peck on the cheek.

"Do you wanna have breakfast with me and my brothers this weekend?" she asked.

Again, I agreed. I enjoyed her company.

It was mid-October, my favorite time of the year. Maryann's two younger brothers came up from Connecticut to see her. They were tall, blond, ruddy-faced young men who wolfed their food as we sat shoulder to shoulder in a booth at the International House of Pancakes. While Maryann engaged in lively banter with her siblings, she kept her hand on my knee, filling me with the warmth of inclusion. When they dropped me off that afternoon, I climbed the stairs to my lonely apartment—David was away on call—slumped down on the couch and stared out the window, already missing her.

One night over Thai takeout, I told Maryann about Cecilia—how I'd wanted to make a life with her, and how she'd betrayed me. Maryann put her arm around me on the sofa, regarded me with a thoughtful expression and said, "You had a rough go of it with her, but I want you to know I'm different."

Maryann exuded such self-confidence. Did she think we should become lovers? I wasn't sure. Perhaps I just needed a friend.

By the end of October, Maryann was dropping by Brookline Hospital, where I had a side job admitting patients at night. If I was working on a Saturday, she'd sneak into my on-call room to chat with me between admissions.

Sitting next to me on the bed one evening, she took my hand.

"I watched you for a long time at the bar the night we first met. I winked at you, but you ignored me. It surprised me when you talked to me."

I had nothing to say to that. I returned her gaze, wondering where this was going.

"The more I'm around you, the more I like you. We have a lot to look forward to," Maryann assured me. She appeared to be on a mission and it scared me.

That fall, Cass expressed a clear boundary: she would not be intimate with me if I would not be monogamous. I didn't blame her. I couldn't offer Cass the loyalty and stability she needed from a partner then, despite my love for her. I couldn't offer that to anyone.

In early November, Maryann came by my apartment after work. As she was pulling groceries out of the refrigerator to make dinner, she put the lettuce down and confessed, "Patricia, I feel my feelings are getting out of control. I want to experience what it feels like to be held by you. I think about you all the time."

I didn't know what to say. I liked Maryann's company and her attention, her hand on my knee at breakfast with her brothers, but was unsure whether I wanted her as a buddy or a lover. We'd never even kissed. I still had feelings for Cass, although I didn't see how we could make a life together. We rarely talked on the phone anymore, and when we did, she seemed stressed and preoccupied.

"Let's wait a bit," I said after a pause.

⤳

For the next month, Maryann became an integral part of my daily life. She told me I was a lousy cook and took over cooking all the meals we shared. She picked me up in Cambridge after my gym sessions and self-defense class. We did our laundry together, and she ran errands for me.

The night of the first snowfall, she sat on my bed in the on-call room. She leaned toward me, and I kissed her for the first time. She kissed me back hard and pushed me down on the bed.

"Whoa," I said, "not here."

But we'd started something, and soon we were having sex—lots of it.

To Maryann, it was a sign we were now a couple.

I wasn't so sure.

"I still might be attracted to other women," I warned her.

That didn't faze her.

At Thanksgiving, David was on call, so Maryann and I visited her family in Connecticut. As a union organizer, her father expressed interest in my work in occupational medicine and entertained me with stories and suggestions for my future research. Maryann's mother was a homemaker who liked her booze.

Maryann's rowdy, intact, traditional family sitting around the table at dinner filled me with warmth and longing for inclusion—though with a sense of caution. Maryann hadn't told them we were more than friends. I wondered if her parents would still be so friendly if they knew what I was doing with their daughter in bed.

179

At the end of November, Maryann's lease on her apartment was up. She was spending so much time with me, it felt natural for her to move in.

David worried about walking in on us at an awkward time, but with the demanding schedule of his internal medicine residency, he wasn't often home, anyway. The quality of the meals had improved, with Maryann assuming the role of dinner cook. Though disconcerted initially by Maryann's forthrightness, David had gotten used to her. I sometimes heard them laughing together in the living room while I studied. He agreed to have her move in.

I was lonely. Maryann took care of me while I dove into epidemiology, toxicology, and biostatistics at Harvard. All the while, I worked part-time at Brookline Hospital, attended plays and the Boston Symphony, read books other than medicine, took up jogging, and planned my research projects. Still traumatized from my internship when I needed such nurture and didn't have it, her caring was welcome—at first.

After Maryann had been living with us for three weeks, she and I traveled by train from Boston to Phoenix to visit my family for Christmas. Terri had graduated from college and was teaching in grade school. I told Terri when I was with Cecilia that I was a lesbian. After asking me a few questions about what women do in bed, she'd accepted it as one of the many puzzling characteristics about me she could not understand. Maryann and she got on very well. They had much to talk about since they were both teachers.

As I might've predicted, Mom didn't take to Maryann at all.

"She looks like a dyke," Mom said upon our arrival.

Mom had accepted that I was a lesbian, but she could not tolerate my flaunting it to the world with a girlfriend who couldn't pass as straight.

The painful visit dragged on. When Maryann was in the shower, Mom continued her tirade. "How could you bring her here and try to shove her down my throat?"

On a different day, she said, "She's a little nothing," and added that my liking her enough to live with her was my problem.

I flinched, knowing this time Maryann had heard her. Mom thought I could do better, but the way she expressed it was rude and cruel.

On the eighty-five-hour train ride back to Boston from Phoenix, Maryann was tearful, and I tried comforting her.

I cared for Maryann. Her disregard for passing as straight, and her assertive self-confidence were qualities I had grown to admire. But as much as I tried to resist it, Mom's words had an effect. I stepped back from Maryann emotionally and even wished at times that she hadn't moved in with David and me.

CHAPTER TWENTY

Over the next few months, Maryann, David, and I settled into a domestic rhythm. David and I enjoyed the improved quality of the meals and not having to cook. It was a major change living with a woman for the first time—sharing a bed, and not having any private space. Normally a light sleeper, I had to retire when Maryann did, and rise earlier than I'd like so she could get ready for teaching. Not used to interacting so much, I had no time to recover. Maryann also expected a lot of sex, sometimes even in the middle of the night. It was all just too much.

I loved my residency and classes required for an MPH at the Harvard School of Public Health; I recaptured the dopamine high of learning and met brilliant and stimulating people. As one of the first residents in occupational medicine, I had the freedom to structure my program. My professors, all male, were support-ive and seemed to want me to thrive. I also made several new friends including, Chris, a vibrant and attractive internist from the South, a few years older than me, with a wry sense of humor.

With the support of my professors at Harvard, I began to heal from the trauma of my internship and was soon jumping out of bed in the morning, looking forward to the classes and interacting with my colleagues—especially one British postdoc-toral fellow.

We met that fall of 1976 in epidemiology class. When I looked over at her in the seat next to me, I noticed her profile—

the outline of her firm jaw, her short auburn hair, her long dark eyelashes, and the distinctive laugh lines next to her mouth.

I resolved to speak to her after class, but she beat me to it. Turning in her seat, she flashed me a dazzling smile. "I notice you take copious notes. Can you share with me what he said about prospective observational studies? I'm afraid I was daydreaming." She had a crisp, authoritative English accent that further piqued my interest.

Who was she daydreaming about? "Sure," I said, rummaging through my papers. I told her what I'd recorded.

"I'm Gillian, by the way." She smiled that smile again—perfect teeth, the lines on the side of her mouth deepening.

"I'm Patricia," I said—then, jumping on the opportunity and because of her accent, "Would you like to get a cup of tea?"

"Yes," she said. "But I prefer coffee."

My stomach quivered—which should have been a warning— as we headed for the cafeteria.

Gillian was thirty-four, a cell biologist, trained at Oxford, and doing postdoctoral work in a lab at Harvard. Able to take courses at the School of Public Health for free, she'd chosen epidemiology and biostatistics. She was intelligent, laughed easily, and we soon determined we shared the same liberal politics and feminist leanings. She gave no sign she was a lesbian.

Coffee with Gillian after class occurred often over the next few weeks, and I looked forward to it. I soaked up epidemiology, wanting to be one step ahead of her in case she asked me to explain any concepts.

I soon realized that was unrealistic—she was too bright and quick to need my help—but she seemed to enjoy chatting with me about her work, weekend adventures, and politics. Still, there was a reserve, an impersonal quality to our discussions. I wanted to penetrate it.

Shortly after our return from Phoenix, while Maryann was out shopping, I told David about Gillian and admitted, "I find her very attractive and intellectual, but I don't lust after her." I announced this as much to convince myself as David.

"Really?" he said, his voice registering disbelief. "That's not like you, Patroosk."

Thoughts of Gillian crept into my mind throughout the day; enhancing the pleasure I took in learning epidemiology. I knew it was dangerous to have such a strong, irrepressible attraction when I was living with Maryann. But my heart wasn't listening.

As epidemiology class ended for the term, I worried I wouldn't see Gillian as often, so I pitched the idea we teach a course together to Harvard undergraduates. I suggested we call it "Women and Cancer," with a focus on the sociopolitical forces that influence women's health care. She agreed with heartening enthusiasm. I made the case to my department chair this should be part of my residency training. He said he'd allow it, provided we held it in the evening, on my own time. Fortune favored us when we secured a room for the class in Adams House on the main Harvard campus in Cambridge.

Before class, as I walked through the Lower Common Room of Adams House, I marveled at the carved ceiling and gigantic marble fireplace. Franklin Roosevelt, Henry Kissinger, and John F. Kennedy had walked its halls. I felt I'd arrived at the center of academic sophistication, a long way from Phoenix College and Arizona State.

I devised most of the curriculum, and we presented our seminars to twenty students, the majority young women, who lounged in overstuffed chairs in front of a fire. I opened the discussion, but when it was Gillian's turn, I sat back in my cushy leather chair and watched her—appreciating her classy, accented English, her regal bearing, and her stylish dress. I noted the dimple in her chin, the attentive tilt of her head as she listened to the questions posed by the students, and her considered responses.

In late February 1977, lying awake at night with a bout of bronchitis, I thought of Gillian. She was not married or dating, but she was often skiing, hiking, or visiting friends on the weekend. She'd talked of her thrill of careening down the ski slope almost out of control; the "almost out of control" part gave me a buzz. I'd gone from admiring and respecting her to thinking about her obsessively—in class, on the bus, and even when I was with Maryann.

In early March, a friend of Gillian's from England came to visit. Sheila was a seal biologist with the same British accent as Gillian. She was charming and beautiful and had known Gillian at Oxford. The three of us met for drinks. Gillian left for the restroom and Sheila confided in me, "I feel I am in Gillian's way much of the time. She's often studying her notebooks even when we're together."

This surprised me. How could Gillian prefer perusing her research notebooks to interacting with this lovely woman? Sheila admired Gillian and had been her faithful friend for many years. I marveled that Gillian's personal reserve extended even to her long-term friends.

A week later, Gillian and I had a stimulating session in the class we were teaching. Usually, the class lasted two hours, but the discussion was lively and continued for an extra hour. At the end, Gillian and I stopped at 33 Dunster Street, an intimate, cozy bar just off Harvard Square, for a drink.

As we sipped our gin and tonics, Gillian's usual polite aloofness dropped away and she leaned in, tilting her head toward me while we talked. I told her how I'd gotten into occupational medicine and how my grueling internship had made me question my choice of medical specialty. She told me about her loss of periods after taking birth control pills and her hopes for a career after she finished her fellowship. It disappointed me to learn she slept with men. But my senses heightened, and my pulse quickened at her nearness across the table, the strong, serious lines of her face, the sudden brilliance of her smile, and her full, throaty laugh.

"My academic visa is almost up. It's so frustrating having to scrounge for a job to stay in the US and to argue that I'm uniquely qualified above all others." She sighed. "Self-promotion is just not my style."

"I'll do my best to help you," I offered, wanting nothing more than for her to stay in the US, to keep having coffee and drinks with me, so I could get to know her more intimately.

It was after midnight when we walked to our cars. I was tipsy, and high from the stimulating class, our intimate conversation, and the nearness of Gillian's face across the table.

I took my time driving back to Boston, hoping to calm down enough to sleep.

Maryann was asleep when I got home but woke up when I crept into bed.

"Were you with Gillian?"

"We had drinks after class."

"For *three* hours?" She turned over, her back to me.

I lay awake for several hours, thinking about the evening. Maryann awoke again later and rolled over to ask, "Did you kiss her?"

"No, of course not," I said. But I'd wanted to.

When I drifted off, I dreamed I was in an old country estate with Gillian, and she was having a problem with her heart. I had to examine her by putting my hand under her left breast to feel for her heartbeat, then laid my ear on her breast to listen. She objected, but at the same time requested it.

I sat next to Gillian in biostatistics class the next day. I loved the elegance of exploring biological phenomena with numbers, but I couldn't concentrate. I crossed and recrossed my legs, fidgeted in my chair, and sat on my hands. With a sidelong glance, I noted the curve of her thigh in her tight jeans and her strong profile. A tingling excitement eclipsed any thought of biostatistics.

At the break I told her a watered-down version of my dream, leaving out the part about my head on her breast. She regarded me thoughtfully but didn't comment.

During biostatistics lab, I spent the entire time coaching her on what to say to my department chair about a potential job because I wanted her to stay in the US. Neither of us could focus on the lab.

When Gillian got busy at work and couldn't have coffee with me or walked out of class talking with someone else, I felt let down. When she told me she went out drinking with the male teaching fellows as she had with me, I bit my lip and turned away to hide my disappointment. I cycled between exhilaration and pleasure when I was with her and depression when I wasn't. With my emotions surging, I knew I needed to turn down the volume of my longing, or I was going to make myself miserable.

My feelings soared upward again when, for my birthday in March, Gillian gave me the record album *Love and Affection* by Joan Armatrading, a lesbian British singer to, as she said, "improve my philistine taste in music". In one of the popular songs, Armatrading sings she is not in love but is open to persuasion. She'd feel freer with a lover than with a friend. Since I looked for any hint Gillian might have feelings for me, I wondered. Was she giving me an indirect message?

Confused, I was eager to discuss my hopes with David. Since he was rarely home, we conducted our discussion through notes left on each other's desks in sealed envelopes.

"Gillian might be giving me mixed messages," I wrote to him. "I'm not sure how to respond."

David wrote back:

If Gillian asked you to join her for a weekend trip to Vermont without Maryann, what would you do? If you went, you essentially

say no relationship is safe from disruption, since there can
always be a more highly desired person. This is selfish. Trust and
security are important, even though you may not appreciate it
right now because of multiple opportunities. I don't support any
efforts not directed toward trying to make it work with Maryann.
You should show some discipline.

He was right. Discipline I had plenty of in my work, but not in my personal life. At least not where women were concerned. There were times when I wanted a woman who was caring and nurturing, but I also wanted a woman pursuing her own high-intensity career, and who I found sexy and desirable. It didn't seem possible to have it all with only one woman.

Maryann continued to demand sex, but I was less and less interested. Often, I begged off, saying I was tired or stressed. She noticed and became cranky and critical. Living together grew increasingly difficult.

One April evening, she exploded with complaints.

"You eat off my plate when you know I don't like it. Sometimes you should deign to clean the bathtub after you shower and pick up your pile of clothes on the chair." She got up close to my face. "You've become *boring.* All you do is read, study, and talk on the phone. I'm tired of your silences and lack of communication."

These withdrawals from the joint bank account of positive feelings we'd shared in the beginning had been more frequent in recent months. Now the account was nearly overdrawn. She was justified in her complaints; I said I would clean the bathtub and pick up my clothes. But we didn't discuss the real problem: my growing attraction to another woman.

The next week, Gillian and I again had after-class drinks at 33 Dunster Street. It began with a long discussion about politics and our families. For the first time, I discussed with her my relationship with Maryann and the recent tension. I didn't have the nerve to tell her the reason.

I misplaced my car key, and Gillian had to drive me home. When I walked through the door, it was 2 a.m.

Maryann flipped on the lamp and sat up in bed when I tiptoed into the bedroom. "Where the hell have you been?"

"Gillian and I stopped for a drink after class and just talked," I said. It was the truth. All the action was taking place in my head and heart, but not with Gillian.

Maryann glared at me, then turned over, not leaving me any covers.

I knew I needed to get a grip and tried to act aloof with Gillian in biostatistics class the next morning. She didn't give me the opportunity; she ignored the free seat next to me and sat next to some guy and talked to him throughout the break.

Gillian remained distant over the following two weeks. Each time she ignored me, I'd slink off to my office to work on my research projects, trying to distract myself from the growing knot in my chest and the fear she didn't like me anymore. I was tempted to talk about my angst with my friend Chris, but had not yet told her I was gay.

Then Gillian turned friendly again. I didn't understand the cause of the change but took advantage of it to invite her to our apartment for dinner. That evening, I sensed Maryann observing our interaction and wondered if my attraction to Gillian was obvious.

But why upset Maryann? I will never be romantic with Gillian. I cared for Maryann. I should come clean with her, I thought.

"I have a crush on Gillian," I confessed the next evening over dinner. "This has happened to me before and it'll pass. She's straight, anyway."

This admission didn't help my relationship with Maryann at all. As I was writing in my journal the following afternoon, she arrived home from work and blew through the house like a bad storm, grumbling about all the windows being shut as she slammed them open.

"Are you writing the things you dislike about me?" she asked.

Before I could answer my writing had nothing to do with her, she snapped, "I don't care, Patricia," and stormed out.

A few days later, she burst through the closed bedroom door while I was studying. "The house is a mess. Am I the only one who cares?"

To keep the peace, David and I scurried around, picking up the papers and books strewn on the couch and chairs.

My efforts did not appease Maryann. "You steal my white socks, and you don't do your share of the laundry."

To improve the strained atmosphere, David and I took Maryann out to dinner. I was on the second day of a total fast. I'd read that fasting reduced inflammation and improved brain function. So far, it wasn't having that effect on me. It was torture watching them eat, my stomach roiling. I found it difficult to focus and conversation was stilted.

"When I was cutting up the zucchini last night, I was thinking it was you," Maryann told me halfway through dinner.

I didn't reply, but my muscles tensed.

"You're a real jerk, Patricia," she said as she continued to tuck into the dinner I'd bought her.

I'd had enough. I threw my half of the tab on the table and strode out of the restaurant.

I was on foot, so soon Maryann and David drove by in her car. She slowed and rolled down the window to heckle me. "Hey little girl, do ya wanna ride?"

I clenched my jaw, ignored her, and continued walking.

When I arrived home, I found she'd locked me out of the apartment. Pounding on the door got no results. The blood rushed to my face and my ears rang as I ran down the stairs. In the street, I shouted up to David's window. He came down and said something to me, but anger impaired my hearing. I stormed across the road to the park where a baseball game was underway, and stood behind the backstop, breathing hard and pretending to watch the game.

David came up behind me. "Patroosk, you're being ridiculous," he said, laughing.

My feelings are ridiculous? He was discounting my experience, just as my mother had done when I was a child. I whirled around and kicked him in the balls.

David doubled over, then straightened up, grabbed me, and

threw me down on the concrete. He straddled my chest and pinned my arms so I couldn't move. I spat in his face and he spat in mine.

This was our first ever physical altercation. Tears filled my eyes as the fight left my body.

The baseball game stopped. An official stood over us, asking if everything was okay.

No, it wasn't. Embarrassed, we both got up.

"We're having a domestic disagreement," I said. "It's all right now."

My ribs felt bruised; I had pulled a muscle in my torso, and scraped my knee and hand. I looked sheepishly at David. "I'm so sorry I kicked you. Are you okay? I wonder what those guys would think if they knew we're both doctors."

David's brief smile turned to a look of concern. "What's wrong with you, Patroosk? You'd better never fast again."

"Yes, fasting makes me crazy," I admitted.

But fasting was only part of the problem. I had unresolved anger left over from my internship, felt trapped in my relationship with Maryann, and guilty about hurting her. Plus, I was in love with a straight unavailable woman. To top it off, I missed being with Cass.

I washed off with a garden hose outside our apartment building and walked off to think.

In another nearby park, I sat jiggling my leg up and down and listening to the sound of children playing. Maryann didn't want me spending any social time with Gillian. That wasn't happening anyway because Gillian had returned to being distant and aloof. She allowed no chance of us being alone together—perhaps because she'd realized I had a crush on her.

Was I thinking like a man? Did I need to touch her sexually to feel close to her? I'd found the urge to do so grew more intense the more distant she became. When I felt unimportant to her, my desire for her changed—became more sexually explicit, even crude.

In early May, Gillian swooped into our last class in Adams House late, snapping off her rain cape. With her knee-high boots, her pants tucked in, and her rigidly upright bearing, she looked like a queen coming in from the hunt. Her eyes looked very dark; her hair wet and dripping. She plopped into one of the overstuffed chairs, her arms wide open on the arm rests, the curve of her thigh visible, her legs crossed, one boot in the air.

Weak with desire, I stood holding on to the back of a chair. But I had to focus; we had a class to teach.

Afterward, I asked her if she wanted to go to 33 Dunster and celebrate.

Gillian hesitated. "No, I need to get back to the lab."

I had been living for the moments when I could be alone with her. After saying a clipped goodnight, I turned away to hide my disappointment.

It pleased Maryann to see me at home at a decent hour that night. I'd attempted to clean up the house before she arrived home from work the day before, even putting flowers on the table. I helped her with dinner prep and lingered to ask about her day. David had forgiven me for my attack, and we'd all settled back into a peaceful coexistence.

With the term ending, I no longer would see Gillian regularly. To my surprise, Maryann suggested we invite Gillian to dinner at our apartment to celebrate. Though puzzled as to Maryann's motivation, I called Gillian, who accepted with enthusiasm.

She arrived looking casual in jeans and a tank top. Conversation flowed easily, and both Gillian and Maryann appeared relaxed. I could not relax, fidgeting in my chair, and picking at my food. My neck and shoulders tensed, thinking about the speech I intended to make to Gillian if we were alone.

At the end of the evening, I walked Gillian down the two flights of stairs. When she reached the landing, I took a deep breath and launched in. "I know you said before you didn't like it when one member of a couple expressed a romantic interest in you." My heart pounded. I stood a stair above her, gripping the railing. She looked up at me, concern in her eyes—or was it fear?

After taking another deep breath, I exhaled and continued. "I debated whether I should say this to you. But I believe you know I'm very much attracted to you. I'm having a tough time with it. I just can't ignore it."

Gillian stared at me, her face inscrutable, and I wondered if I'd misread her. Perhaps she didn't know, and now I was scaring her.

"Even though I'm saying this to you, I expect nothing from you," I backpedaled. "I know this makes you uncomfortable, but we won't be seeing each other over the summer."

Gillian was quiet for several moments and turned her head to the side to avoid my direct gaze. *Had I just ruined our friendship I very much valued?* I was still on the stair above her, my heart pounding, poised to flee.

Gillian looked up at me. "I'm flattered and admire the fact

you can say that. When I really like someone, the last thing I'd do is tell them." She smiled her brilliant smile. "We'll work this out."

I let out my breath, not realizing I'd been holding it. We said good night, and I bounded up the stairs, light with relief. Gillian was still my friend.

I'd gotten my feelings off my chest, and I thought that would be the end. My longing would die down, especially since we would be apart most of the summer with Gillian in England and me in Illinois, West Virginia, and New York City for my research projects and practicum.

But I was wrong.

CHAPTER TWENTY-ONE

I'd been wanting to see Cass for months, so I called her about a week after my admission to Gillian. The following day, Maryann and I drove up to New Hampshire. Although I still had romantic feelings for Cass, I told Maryann we were now just friends; I had become resigned to our apparent inability to be anything more.

When we arrived at Cass's house in Keene, Cass was friendly and warm and seemed glad to see us. But Sara, now ten, was clingy and attention-seeking.

Maryann soon won over Sara with her good humor and antics and offered to help her get into one of the elite prep schools in Boston. Cass appeared relaxed and tanned, her strong, shapely arms and legs bare in the balmy weather. Being around her unlocked memories of holding her as she shuddered with pleasure under me. I did my best to tamp down such thoughts.

Cass appraised me with her blue-gray eyes. "You've gained some weight since your internship," she remarked. "It suits you."

"Yes, Maryann feeds me well," I acknowledged, giving Maryann a smile.

We made dinner together. Maryann entertained us with stories from her classroom, and conversation flowed without strain during our meal of salad and hearty soup. The biggest bonus for me was that Cass and I could interact as friends without the resentment present at the end of our relationship as lovers.

On the drive back, Maryann and I exchanged an easy banter. I thought I would miss her when I left Boston for my summer practicum and research project. Yet, as I stared out the window at the passing small towns, flowers bursting with color in their roundabouts, an aching heaviness filled my heart. It was hard to be grown-up and accept I could not have everything. While I lived with Maryann, romance and sex with Cass was off-limits—and with Gillian, it wasn't even on the table.

I was uncertain what my future would be after completing my Master of Public Health. Dr. Peters said he would keep me around for an additional year while I worked it out and finished my research. I kept my stipend by getting yet another master's degree—in physiology this time.

My plan was to spend the summer working for the Amalgamated Clothing and Textile Workers Union, gathering data for a research project on whether exposure to processed cotton and phenolic resin dust caused a decline in lung function.

During the month the Union sent me to Herrin, Illinois, I worked closely with a regional manager, Paul Restivo. He was about my age, very smart and dedicated. I stayed in a nearby motel, and we spent long hours at the factory, taking environmental measurements, examining workers, and doing pre- and post-shift pulmonary function studies. When not working, we shared meals and talked about our lives. Paul gave me a book about the history of unions in Illinois, *Bloody Williamson*, that opened my eyes to their historical struggle. It was refreshing to have a light, uncomplicated friendship away from Maryann and Gillian.

Paul was a decent and attractive man. One of several I would meet over the years. If I were straight or even bisexual, I might have considered a relationship. But it was too late. I'd already tasted the wine.

Late July and most of August I spent in New York City. My sublet apartment was a fourth-floor walk-up in Greenwich Village. Every morning, I walked to the national headquarters of the Amalgamated Clothing and Textile Workers Union, in an old office building off Washington Square, and awaited my assignment from Eric Fruman, the head of health and safety.

One of them was to go to West Virginia to interview and examine workers exposed to carbon disulfide at a viscose rayon plant. The Union suspected chronic exposure might lead to heart and lung disease.

I was content, absorbed in my work, and thought of Gillian rarely. We'd had no contact. I didn't have a phone. She was in England, and I was too busy to write.

After this six-week respite, Maryann joined me in New York for two weeks. We explored the city together, took in several plays, jogged in the park, and returned to making love. I didn't like New York City—the heat, the humidity, the dirt, the throngs of people, the sirens day and night, and the cockroaches. I couldn't wait to return to Boston in late August. I kneeled and kissed the ground when we got off the plane.

~

Gillian returned to Boston from England to complete her fellowship a few days later. She called me soon after her arrival and asked if I wanted to go to dinner with her. Though I thought I was on my way to getting over her, I accepted her invitation with eager anticipation. Maryann was visiting her family in Connecticut, and David was on vacation somewhere.

Gillian came upstairs to my place to fetch me for dinner. I got the familiar quiver in my stomach when I opened the door and saw her standing there, smiling that smile of hers. She wore a white, tunic-style dress and a pale blue T-shirt, looking casual and relaxed in the warm weather. I followed her down the stairs to her car and told myself to chill.

During dinner at an Italian restaurant, secluded in a corner booth, I recounted tales of my summer in Illinois and New York, glowing with the pleasure of her presence. I hardly touched my food.

"I'm envious you got to work with the unions," she said.

"How was your trip to England?" I asked, fidgeting to quell the tingling electricity in my body. I wasn't so over her after all.

"Oh, my mother was her usual difficult self. I was happy to come home." Gillian shook her head, as if ridding herself of the memory.

I smiled at her. "It's nice you're thinking of Boston as your home."

As Gillian drove me home after dinner, I said with more casualness than I felt, "Wanna come upstairs for a drink?"

When she hesitated, I swallowed hard, steeling myself for rejection.

"I should pack for my move, but I guess I can do that tomorrow. Sure, let's have a drink." She flashed her brilliant smile, and my heart leapt.

We sat on the couch together, a couple of feet apart. She spoke of her childhood and her time at Oxford. I told her about my father's illness and its effect on me growing up. As we sipped our dessert port wine, I suggested ways we could make our Cambridge class even more relevant if we taught it again in the spring.

When Gillian rose to leave, I stopped her at the door and put my arms around her. I intended only to give her a friendly straight-woman hug goodbye, but she pulled me close for a full-body embrace and said, "You're a really nice person—it's so good to see you."

Gillian held on and molded her body into mine. *What is she doing?* My heart raced and my mouth went dry. I wondered if she could feel my heart pounding. I brushed my cheek against her hair and tightened my arms around her. *What does she want?* My knees were rubbery, and I held on to her in part for support as she continued to press her body into mine.

After several confusing moments, I pulled away. "I'm suffering from tachycardia," I gasped.

The intensity of the moment broken, Gillian laughed. "You doctors are all the same."

I took her hand and led her through the bedroom into the bright lights and yellow walls of the kitchen. I needed a glass of water. My legs were unsteady, my mouth full of cotton. I leaned against the counter and sipped my water, my hands shaking. Then I pulled Gillian close and kissed her.

She tasted like Italian food. We carried on kissing, my tentativeness giving way to deeper hunger. *I can't believe this is happening.* As I ran my hands over her strong back, I was only vaguely aware of the glare of the kitchen lights, the countertop pressing against my hip, and the ticking of the clock on the wall.

I pulled away from her. "How're you feeling?'

"Ambivalent."

"Why?"

"Because you have a relationship with Maryann, and I have a relationship with no one. Because you're a lesbian, and I'm not."

I sighed. Either I let a woman move in I didn't love, or I pursued a woman who was not a lesbian, or I pushed away a woman I loved because I couldn't commit—all with the same result: keeping love, risk, and vulnerability at bay.

I pulled her to me. "At this moment, does it matter?"

"When I don't allow myself to think, I enjoy it." She relaxed into me.

I kissed her again, more deeply this time. My tongue detected something metallic, but I didn't stop. Sensing she wanted me to do more, my body vibrated with desire, but I was still uncertain. "I'm a little scared," I said into her hair.

Gillian pulled away so she could see my face. "Why?"

"You caught me by surprise. You're straight. I'm not sure what you want."

"I don't know. It's just . . ."

I unbuttoned my top and put her hand on my left breast. Then I slid my hands under her shirt and caressed her small, firm breasts. Her nipples became hard.

I hesitated, fumbling as if I'd never done this before. It was nothing like how I performed with Cass. I'd had an obsessive desire for this woman for nearly a year. Now, amazingly, she was in my arms. I placed my hands on each side of her face and studied her; her lips parted, her dark eyes half closed, her head tipped back, neck exposed. She looked vulnerable and beautiful.

Gillian laid her head on my breast, and I held her, my heart still pounding wildly.

Then she raised her face and kissed me, pressing hard. Both of us were breathing heavily. I bent backward against the kitchen cupboards as she pressed against my mouth, her legs around my thigh, her skirt stretched tight. *Wow!*

I came up for air. "Gillian . . ."

She pulled back, her eyes unfocused.

"Would you like to lie down?" I asked.

Gillian looked at me for a long moment. My body tensed.

"Yes," she said, "I must get some sleep before packing tomorrow."

I gave her a sleeping shirt and looked away while she took off her clothes. Then she lay on top of the covers in a most alluring position.

"Turn down the sheets and get in," I said, but took my time getting undressed—my thoughts churning, my body tense—before slipping into bed next to her and spooning her from behind.

Lying full length next to her, I froze. This was the moment to take charge—but I did not. The gray dawn crept around the cracks in the blinds, and I let her drift off to sleep.

While Gillian slept for a couple of hours, I continued to hold her and lay awake, thinking. *What does she want? Is this what she means by us "working it out?"* Though her body signaled willingness, I hadn't followed through, as if I were the one conflicted. Her words—that she was not a lesbian—warned me maybe this was not what it seemed, that if I took the bait, I would get hurt.

In the morning, I made her coffee and eggs. Gillian was cool and businesslike, and I didn't touch her. I wanted to ask: *What were you thinking? Are we still friends?* But I didn't.

After Gillian left, I slept for a couple of hours, then wandered around my apartment in a state of agitated confusion. That afternoon, she called and asked if I would come to her place to help her pack, since I'd kept her up half the night. A weak voice called from some distant recess of my brain to be careful. I ignored it. I agreed to come over and brought sandwiches for us.

We packed her kitchen stuff, books, and records. Afterward, we sat cross-legged on the living room floor among the boxes, talking, eating the sandwiches, and drinking wine.

"I've never considered myself a dull person, even though I behaved very properly in my twenties," Gillian told me. She took a sip of her drink.

I stared into her eyes. "I've *never, ever* thought you a dull person." I held her gaze, then leaned over our crossed legs and kissed her. She kissed me back with mounting intensity.

But Gillian had more to say. "This is a pleasant interlude, but I'm doing this lightheartedly. I'm straight, you know. This doesn't represent my true self. I take this less seriously than I would with a man."

Her words knocked me back. I wasn't taking them in, focused as I was on the way she just kissed me. To me, this was very serious. I leaned against the couch, trying to calm my racing heart.

"I just don't get involved with people," Gillian continued as she reached for my hand. "I know you take this seriously, and I don't want to hurt you. In fact, I really like and respect you, and I hesitate to ruin a wonderful friendship."

Hit the pause button! My mind tried to warn me. But I so wanted this woman. I wasn't listening to her words, and I couldn't stop myself. This was not the first time, nor would it be the last, desire would rule over my better judgment.

I pulled her up off the floor and hugged her standing up. Gillian pressed up against me, molding her body to mine, obliterating any good sense I might have left.

"I don't think this is a good idea for the reasons I've mentioned," Gillian stammered, but she didn't pull away.

"I want you. That's all the reason I need," I said, receiving the cues from her body—not her words, not thinking beyond desire and the present moment.

My mouth sought hers and I felt her yield as I became more insistent. Then Gillian pulled away, took my hand, and led me into her bedroom. As we both undressed, I admired her narrow hips and firm, muscular body, and my limbic brain took over. We lay on her bed, me on top. I slipped my fingers between her legs and gasped when I found her wet and responsive. Gillian kissed me and wrapped her legs around me, and I was lost in a blur of touch and feeling.

Eventually, I pulled away, my body tense, and rolled over onto my back. Gillian's words from earlier that evening penetrated like a knife. She'd had the best of me—my friendship, my intellect, my humor, and even my love, but—*She's taking this light-heartedly? Saving her genuine feelings for a man?*

I jumped out of Gillian's bed and dressed in a hurry. "I've got to go," I said, rushing out the door, not giving her a chance to respond. This was going to lead to heartache. I also knew I couldn't stop.

The next morning, I paced around my apartment, unable to stomach breakfast, my thoughts churning.

I'd known I was a lesbian for as long as I could remember. I understood sexuality existed on a spectrum and Gillian might be further along the straight-gay continuum than she imagined herself to be. At least, that had seemed to be the case in those intimate moments we'd shared. Perhaps she could ignore ingrained social pressure and slide in my direction. Without having to label herself straight or gay.

What was I going to do with her? And what was Gillian doing with me?

Then I thought of Maryann. How I had betrayed her. Yes, I'd warned her in the beginning I might be attracted to other women —but I had let her move in and assume we were a couple. Sharp pangs of guilt penetrated my chest. Where was David when I needed to talk with him? Maybe I should see a therapist.

Maryann was on her way home from Connecticut. She'd arrive home around noon. I didn't want to be cooped up in the apartment alone with her and my guilt. As soon as she walked in the door, before she put her bag down, I said, "It's a beautiful day; let's go up to New Hampshire and see Cass and Sara."

Maryann was in a good mood, having enjoyed our time in New York; she agreed. After a quick phone call to Cass, we were on our way.

Quiet in the car, mulling over the events of the previous two evenings, I seethed with sexual energy. Gillian had unleashed the longing I'd had all last year, and I couldn't sit still.

Once we arrived, Cass invited us to stay over for the weekend. Though I caught her looking at me from time to time, Cass interacted with casual indifference. Even if she'd once loved me, she'd decided I wasn't a suitable partner for her. I wondered if traces of love and lust remained. I'd never stopped loving her.

Throughout dinner, Maryann acted proprietary, putting her arm around me, and kissing me in front of Cass. I hadn't told her about my ongoing feelings for Cass but imagined she could tell.

After dinner, we played Scrabble at the kitchen table. I was slow to compose a word, and there was a lull in the conversation.

Maryann looked up at Cass and said, "You know, Cass, Patricia still has the hots for you."

I kept my head down, staring at the board, heat rising to my face. When I glanced up at Cass, laugh lines crinkled around her eyes. She looked at the board and appeared to be trying to suppress a smile. It was true. I would not deny it. Maryann blurting it out and putting it on the table in front of us took some of the energy out of it—at least temporarily.

"I can't take Maryann anywhere; I never know what she's going to say," I said, forcing a laugh. We carried on with the game.

The next morning, I got up early to have time alone with Cass. We talked in quiet voices at her kitchen table, holding mugs of steaming coffee. Still processing what had gone on with Gillian, I told Cass an abbreviated version of it.

At first, Cass found it exciting and encouraged me to talk; but then she abruptly got up and refilled her mug. When she sat down again, she fixed me with her lovely blue-gray eyes.

"Make a choice. You can't have your cake and eat it too."

This was the same warning Cass had given me when I was with her, and also seeing Anna.

I held her gaze. "I'm not sure I have a choice. I don't know what Gillian wants, and I don't feel in control of the situation."

"What do *you* want?"

I sat sipping my coffee, my mind churning with thoughts I could not share. I wanted Maryann's friendship, if not her love; I wanted Cass to still love me and sleep with me; I wanted to penetrate the boundaries of intimacy with Gillian and see where it led. And I wanted no one to be hurt or for any of it to interfere with my work and career. I wanted it all.

If I'd known about Buddhism then, I'd have realized desire is the root of all suffering. And there was much suffering to come.

CHAPTER TWENTY-TWO

The next morning, while Maryann slept in, I considered the ways she improved my life. She bought paper to recover the end tables, cooked most of our meals, set out flowers on the dinner table, put on the good sheets, and kept the house neat. Now though, it felt confining. The companionship we had in the beginning had become frayed. Maryann often told me she loved me and I was the best in bed she'd ever had. But for me, it wasn't enough; I wasn't in love with her.

With these thoughts in mind, I walked into Cass's bathroom later that morning while Maryann was taking a bath. She looked cute—round and cuddly. I toweled her off as a wave of affection for her swept over me followed by a deep pang of guilt knowing I was being unfaithful to her. I knew how it felt to have someone betray me. I didn't want to inflict that pain on Maryann. My fantasies and feelings for Gillian continued with a life of their own, despite my futile attempt to keep them in check. It wasn't fair to Maryann. I would have to be honest with her and end our relationship.

I stayed away from Gillian for an entire week. But when I could bear it no longer, I sought her out in her lab on the top floor of the Dana-Farber Building on the Harvard Medical School campus.

I'd never been there before. It was in the evening and Gillian was alone, looking all-business in a pressed white coat, her radiation-monitoring badge pinned to the front. Her eyes widened when I came in; then she ignored me, scrawling some calculations on a notepad.

I fidgeted for a while as Gillian worked, then said, "Will you show me your office?"

"Okay," Gillian said with a sigh, "but I'm busy. Only for a few minutes."

As soon as we stepped inside her office, I got right to the core issue. "Lighthearted sex with you is unacceptable. Involvement with a woman is an intense, whole-person experience."

Gillian met my gaze, and her face softened. "What I said the other night was too simplified. We should continue this conversation at another time."

I snapped off the light in her office, which was separated from the lab by nothing more than glass windows and took a step toward her. I wasn't sure what I intended to do.

Gillian made a dramatic display of turning it back on. "Jesus, you disrupt my work, and you also insist on disrupting my life!"

She turned and walked away, leaving me standing there under the bright lights. *Uh-oh, wrong move.* But at least I was having some impact. Maybe disrupting her life was good.

The following day, I paced in my apartment, unable to work, wanting to call Gillian but unable to because Maryann was there. She was understandably twitchy when it came to Gillian.

It was past time to analyze the data from my research project, but unusually I couldn't focus. When Maryann left for the store, I succumbed and called Gillian. She sounded indifferent and uninterested. Maryann arrived home while I was still on the phone and shot me an angry look before stomping out of the room and slamming the door.

After hanging up, I leaned forward—my elbows on the desk, my head in my hands—and sighed. *I need to tell Maryann it's over.*

I called Gillian again the next day, and she was more friendly. She agreed to go to a movie with me that evening.

When I told Maryann I wanted to go out with Gillian alone to see a film, she pressed her lips together and folded her arms across her chest. "Suit yourself, Patricia, but don't expect me to tolerate this indefinitely."

I didn't expect her to. But I didn't yet have the capacity, or the courage, to tell Maryann our relationship was over.

Sitting next to Gillian in the theater watching *Annie Hall*, my thigh just inches from hers, I remembered how it felt to touch her.

When the movie I'd paid little attention to ended, I asked her out for a drink. Gillian hesitated. *Is she avoiding the discussion she said we should have later?*

"Okay, just one drink."

We had difficulty finding a place that was open but eventually landed at the Café Vendome. We had two gin and tonics and talked about mundane things. I said I wanted to fly to Europe in the summer now that the fares were cheap. Gillian warmed to the idea and proposed that we go together—or at the very least, she would give me the address of her sister in London.

We stayed at the bar talking until it closed, but I wasn't ready to let her go—not without discussing what had happened between us. Gillian wasn't ready to go either, because she suggested we walk. Strolling along Commonwealth Avenue, we eventually sat on a park bench on the green strip between the east and westbound lanes.

I swiveled toward her on the bench and got right to the point. "Why did you come on to me?"

"Because I enjoy you and you'd been away, and when you returned, I was glad to see you. Then you hugged me, and I just responded to the way you felt." She shrugged.

"You let the genie out of the bottle," I said, "and I can't stuff it back in."

Gillian looked away at the cars passing, the headlights intermittently illuminating her face. "I've thought about what happened a great deal. I'm confused about what I want." She paused, then studied me. "I don't want to be gay."

"Part of my attraction to women is aesthetic," I said, wondering if Gillian could relate. "I just find some women beautiful."

"I can appreciate the beauty of some women. Some men are beautiful, too."

I considered this. "That may be true, but for me, it would be like trying to appreciate the stars while blinded by the sun."

Gillian raised an eyebrow and smiled. "I've always sought emotional and physical satisfaction from men, but my affairs have been intense, shifting-sand interludes. The ones I've been attracted to have not been interested in me."

"I can't imagine that!" But I could see how Gillian would intimidate men.

David hadn't identified as gay for very long and had spent years in denial, I told Gillian, hoping it had some relevance to her. Cass had been married with two daughters. "Who you love is complicated and can change over time," I said, then bit my lip. I knew intellectual argument was useless in affairs of the heart.

Gillian considered this for a moment. "I know this is going to sound cold and rejecting, but I don't feel attracted to you."

Ouch! But how could I sync Gillian's words with the way she'd responded? I was quiet, waiting, staring at my hands clasped in my lap.

"I enjoy being with you immensely, and I'm still confused about what I want. I don't want to mess up your relationship with Maryann. Especially when what I can offer is so uncertain."

What Gillian could offer was everything I'd ever wanted, but I didn't say this.

Enough words. I rose, pulled her up off the park bench, and held her close, wanting to feel her body express its own truth. Gillian did not disappoint; she pressed herself into me in the way she had that August night.

Then, remembering we were in the middle of Commonwealth Avenue, we moved apart, still with arms around each other's waists. We walked like this, swaying as if drunk, until Gillian let go and held my hand as we crossed the street to her car. Once inside, we kissed until Gillian pushed me away. "You really *are* crazy," she said.

Right.

It was 3 a.m. when Gillian drove me back to my apartment in Brookline. Even before we pulled up in front, we saw Maryann pacing the sidewalk.

"I'm getting out of here," Gillian said. "Let me know what happens. Call me."

I jumped out of the car, and she drove off, leaving me with a furious Maryann.

Before I could say anything, Maryann grabbed me and pushed me into the bushes.

"Did you fuck Gillian?" she yelled, her face contorted and ugly.

I recoiled at her crude language and aggression. "No, it wasn't like that."

"I've been here for two hours, pacing the street, wondering where you were, worried something happened to you."

"I'm sorry, I should've called," I said as I pulled myself out of the shrubbery and brushed off my clothes.

I took Maryann's arm, and we walked up and down the sidewalk. "We got physical when I came back from New York," I admitted. "I can't help it. I'm in love with Gillian, even though she insists she's straight."

This was not how I'd wanted to break up with Maryann. She looked at me with pain in her green eyes, her lips quivering, and guilt overwhelmed me. An instant later, anger replaced the hurt and her face contorted.

"I can't believe you'd do this!" Maryann hissed. "I've been living in a fantasy world with you. I thought you were special. But you're just another cheating dyke!"

I just stood there, inwardly shrinking, her accusation piercing like shards of glass.

"If you see her again, we will definitely break up, and if you don't, we'll probably break up, anyway."

I teared up, remembering the pain when Cecilia betrayed me and the pain I was causing now. "I'm sorry, Maryann."

"All the effort I put into our relationship has been one-sided. I went to Connecticut thinking I was going to split up with you. But then I remembered what made me want to stay. You know what you want and where you're going."

Professionally, yes.

I didn't want to hurt Maryann further. Nor did I envision hurtling off into a tenuous and emotionally damaging affair with Gillian. I did my best to comfort Maryann and said I wouldn't see Gillian anymore—at least while we were still living together.

Just like an alcoholic who promises not to drink but knows she won't be able to resist the craving.

I didn't call Gillian for three weeks. Then I ran into her on the quad in front of Harvard Medical School—and instead of avoiding her, I followed her. Gillian looked elegant in her form-fitting jeans, billowing white blouse, and scarf.

When I caught up, she said she was in a hurry, no time to talk. She didn't ask me what had gone on with Maryann. I slipped a note I'd written earlier into her hand on the Dear Fuckface stationery Maryann had given me, asking her to call me.

Gillian didn't call me. I called her. She was cool and distant. Still, I asked if she would join me for a coffee break at four o'clock and she agreed.

As I was leaving to meet her, my department head nabbed me in the hall with questions about my research. This was important, too. I told him of my progress on the rubber workers study, as well as my new research on mortality in jewelry workers. I tried to be concise as possible, looking at my watch.

I was late; Gillian frowned at me when I arrived.

"I'm busy and can't talk now unless it's urgent," she said, no trace of warmth in her voice.

I sighed. "Why is it so hard to gain an audience with Your Indifferent Majesty?" I existed in a limbo state with only intermittent positive reinforcement—sometimes I got friendliness, other times I got deep freeze. It didn't occur to me to protect myself.

"I've got to get back to the lab," Gillian said, ignoring my crestfallen face.

I moped around for the next week with no contact with Gillian. Maryann and I endured a tense coexistence, mitigated only by David's presence. I'd started seeing a therapist, and she challenged me to examine why I was drawn to unavailable women, and how it might relate to my relationship with my mother.

One evening, when Maryann was out, I called Gabrielle at Stanford University. She'd been my best friend in college—driven, climbing the academic ladder. We'd not talked for months, but always picked right up where we left off. Gabrielle had had experience with affairs, lots of them, with men, which we'd discussed at length over the years.

After initial greetings, I said, "I'm so confused. I need your advice. I'm obsessed with a straight woman who slept with me and now is ignoring me. I'm still living with a woman I don't love in the way she needs."

"Oh God, not good. Let me get a glass of wine," she said.

I told Gabrielle the story, including all the things Gillian had said to me after our recent encounters. Gabrielle listened, then sighed and said, "You're going to get hurt. This will not turn out well. You should back off from Gillian. Break up with Maryann, if you must."

"I've been trying to," I said, disappointed.

Gabrielle doesn't know how Gillian felt when I held her, how she responded, how she encouraged me with her body—if not her words. Gabrielle's warning influenced me, though, because I focused on my research project over the next couple of weeks and did not see Gillian.

At the end of two weeks, unable to contain myself any longer, I made sure there was no one around one evening and burst into Gillian's office. "I think I'm in love with you. You're a huge, big deal in my life. I think about you all the time, and it's distracting me from everything else important."

In the movies I'd grown up with, bold, dramatic proclamations of love always had a good outcome—such as the *Sound of Music*, when Julie Andrews falls into the arms of Christopher Plummer after he admits he loves her. I'd identified with the man in these torrid scenes—not so much his maleness, but his power. But that was not happening here.

Gillian put down her pen, sighed, cupped her chin in her hand, and looked at me. "I'm sorry; I'm responsible for this mess, and I regret it. In all honesty, I can only say you're one of my best friends and I enjoy spending time with you."

Gillian's words landed like a blow, and a hard lump formed in my chest. I didn't know what to say.

"It's true you've broken down certain barriers with me that other people haven't," she said, her face softening.

It sounded a little better, but a fist still clutched my heart. I searched her eyes.

"I have nothing to offer beyond friendship."

That's not how it felt when you kissed me. The fist gripping my heart and the lump in my throat prevented me from saying it out loud.

"Any decisions you make regarding Maryann shouldn't be based on my actions or what I have to offer," she said, her voice becoming more crisply authoritative.

"Maryann's making her own decisions independent of me, I'm afraid." Unable to stop beating my head against the wall of Gillian's resistance, I persisted, "Do you ever think about being with me?"

"Yes," Gillian admitted. "But I'm emotionally distant from people—independent, isolated, and somewhat lonely. I think about practical problems. Not much about people, sex, or friendship."

A wave of tenderness made me reach out and touch her face. "But you have such a wonderful sense of humor; I've felt your warmth, your passion. I just can't accept distance is what you really want."

"I have to get back to work." Gillian turned away.

There was nothing more I could say or do; I left her office. Tears blurred my eyes. I took the elevator down to the first floor and walked out into the crisp October night, the wind swirling the leaves around my feet.

For the rest of that term, I focused on my research, socializing only with other friends and colleagues at work. I stopped procrastinating and told Maryann I could not be what she wanted and needed. We should end our relationship as lovers. She had already decided that. She planned to move out at the end of the term. I accepted her announcement with resignation and relief but felt bad about myself for the way it had unraveled.

Gillian's words had been discouraging. She appeared resolved to view those two nights in August as an aberration. I couldn't put the way she'd been with me out of my mind. Once again, I caught up with her as she walked through the quad.

She was wearing tight jeans, her knee-high boots, and a silk blouse open at the neck. She looked stunning. The wind blew her hair across her eyes as other people hurried by.

"Okay, *what?*" Gillian said with obvious impatience.

"I'm still in love with you." I knew I sounded like a besotted adolescent.

Gillian sighed, looking annoyed. With her voice low, she said, "Jesus, whenever I so much as make a friendly overture toward you, you make it into a big deal. Can't you just be a normal friend?"

"First of all," I said, "I'm *not* normal. I've *never* been normal. I'm a woman who loves women—you in particular." I bit my lip, hoping I wouldn't tear up. "Second, your overtures were more than friendly."

Gillian still looked annoyed. "You insist on imposing your feelings and desires on me and pressuring me to respond. You're so fucking arrogant! Haven't you ever had a woman turn you down?"

I thought for a moment. Cecilia had betrayed me. But had anyone ever turned me down?

"No," I said. But it was happening now. I just wished Gillian didn't look so devastatingly beautiful doing it. Her words stung, and I backed off—yet again.

～

For the next three weeks, I wrote letters to Gillian I threw in the trash. I covered my hurt with anger over the fact she'd crossed the line of friendship with me that late August night—when I wasn't expecting it, when I thought I'd recovered from my crush on her—almost. It had brought to the surface my lack of commitment to my relationship with Maryann, and I was the one who'd had to suffer the consequences of hurting her the way I had.

I sent Gillian a note: "I've not yet achieved a state of sublime indifference."

Gillian wrote back: "In the old country, the remedy is cold showers and hot tea."

In mid-January 1978, after several weeks of not seeing one another, Gillian invited me to ride with her to a work party thrown by colleagues from the Harvard School of Public Health.

Even though I knew I shouldn't, I agreed.

That evening I dressed in black gaberdine slacks and a red silk blouse and tied a black and white scarf around my neck. When I opened the door to my apartment, Gillian looked at me with approval. "You're looking very elegant."

Still wary of her, conversation was stiff in the car.

More women than men attended the party. Gillian asked me to dance since other women were dancing together, but I declined; I couldn't bear to touch her.

I spent most of the evening talking with a medical student interested in participating in my research and got a little drunk on punch, as I wasn't driving. My inhibitions and resolve were fading with the alcohol and the late hour, and when Gillian and I got in her car to leave, I moved across the bench seat and kissed her.

Gillian didn't resist.

"You know you really are crazy," she said.

"I know. The risk-reward ratio isn't favorable. Maryann and I broke up, and she's moving out."

"I'm sorry." She sounded sincere.

I took her hand and put it against my cheek. "I'm glad I got to know you, broke down some of your barriers—did what we did."

Gillian held my gaze. I thought she was going to kiss me again. Instead, she said, "And I'm really glad I got to know you."

"I don't think about you in a romantic or sexual way as much as I did before, but I want more than friendship," I told her.

Gillian took her hand back, and looked away. I waited in tense silence. She turned toward me again. "I'm not sure, but I think I do too."

Wow! That jolt of excitement again. *Be careful*, my brain said.

"I don't care whether you consider yourself straight or gay," I said, struggling to articulate my thoughts. "Can't we just carry on—just me and just you—without you having to undergo a crisis of identity?"

I yearned to be Gillian's lover, to make a life with her, to work together on meaningful projects, both of us successful in our careers. This was unrealistic, as long as Gillian continued to insist she was straight and kept me (and others) at a distance. Until she beckoned, and I came running, like a dog.

I leaned toward her.

"You know you're crazy," Gillian said. "You're going to get in trouble with yourself. This situation has caused a lot of pain. We should spend some time apart. I'm not sure what I want."

"Shut up," I said with tenderness. I took her in my arms and kissed her. She kissed me back as the windows fogged up.

A couple of weeks later, I realized that in my lifetime, Gillian and I would not go beyond kissing in cars while she protested it meant little to her—she was not a lesbian. In our relationship—for which I had no name—Gillian had all the power. I was clear about what I wanted from her; she was conflicted about what she wanted from me. I had to accept that what I desired most, her love and commitment, were unattainable. Although Gillian and I were to have more intimate moments, I would respect the boundaries of friendship she'd set, and never speak of what had gone before.

My therapist was right. I had a thing for women who were unavailable. Even Cass—who I still loved and who had once loved me—had life circumstances that made her not wholly available. But Cass still captivated me. I wondered. *Is it too late to try again?*

CHAPTER TWENTY-THREE

I'd completed most of the field work on two of my research studies and was nearing the end of my second year at Harvard, taking a few classes but spending most of my days in my office or the computer lab analyzing data. My life had less structure and more free time.

When Maryann moved out in early 1978, I called Cass. Now that I was single again, she agreed to see me. I planned to drive up to New Hampshire on a Friday in February, but there was a record snowfall in Boston, and I was delayed by twenty-four hours.

The next day I dressed for her in my tweed jacket with the suede patches on the elbows and shoulders and black slacks. When I arrived, Cass suggested we go to the theater to see *Saturday Night Fever*.

Though offended by the mistreatment of women in the film, we both liked the music and dancing. I could hardly wait for the movie to end and kept my hand on Cass's thigh on the way home, tense with wanting.

With the snow falling outside the window of Cass's bedroom, we made love.

A few days after my return to Boston, Cass called. "I don't enjoy cleaning up after you," she said, having second thoughts since the weekend. "I see no future in our relationship if you can't be monogamous."

❦

Several weeks later, Cass agreed to see me again when her car broke down on a business trip to Boston and she had to take the bus home. I tried to make up for being a disappointment to her in past years in small ways by buying expensive asthma medications for her, paying to get her car fixed, and driving it up from Boston.

On the way to Keene, Cass's car broke down again. I trudged through the spring melt to a service station in New Ipswich and returned with a couple of young guys in a truck to tow it back.

Once the car was on the hoist, the mechanic—an ancient man with gnarly hands—spat on the floor and growled, "Looks like you have a broken wheel bearing."

"Can you fix it today? I need to be in Keene this afternoon." My shoulders slumped at the thought of missing out on an evening with Cass.

I called to say I would be delayed. There was no answer.

Several hours later, it was nearly dark, but I was on the road again.

I arrived at Cass's house, let myself in with the hidden key, and found it empty—of people and of food. Weary and disappointed, I drove to the store, bought some groceries, and collapsed in a chair in the living room to wait and read.

When Sara and Cass returned, Cass gave me only a terse greeting.

"Your car broke down on the way, a broken wheel bearing," I explained. "It took hours for it to be repaired. Sorry I'm late."

"Well, you'll have to make your own dinner," Cass said. "We've already eaten."

Her lack of appreciation stung, but I let it ride and got up to fix a salad in her kitchen.

Almost immediately, Cass lay on the couch and fell asleep.

After eating alone, I made up her bed with fresh sheets from the laundry, put a folded set on the arm of the couch for me, sat down across from her with my book, and expected to sleep alone. I studied Cass instead of reading, her worry lines faded in sleep. She looked so lovely and vulnerable. Was I in love with her? Could I make her life easier?

Sara roused Cass and urged her to go to bed. I took a chance, followed her, and climbed in beside her, my body tense with desire. She turned over, her back to me.

I rolled her over to face me.

"I'm sorry, but do you expect sex when I'm so exhausted?" she said.

"No, but a little talking would be nice. Do you even care I'm here?" I'd had a difficult and frustrating day myself. I'd so wanted to spend the evening with her, to reclaim the magic we'd once shared, for her to forgive my inconstancy.

Cass rolled away from me. "I'm just too tired to care right now. I'll probably care in the morning."

I spooned her and cried quietly against her back, releasing the tension that had built up from the day's obstacles and the frustration of wanting her.

"Why are you crying?" Cass asked, her voice muffled by the pillow.

"My frustrating day. And relief you'll care I'm here in the morning."

Cass turned over and fell asleep with her head on my shoulder. I drifted off to sleep as well.

⌇

Later, I woke up with Cass on top of me. She'd come alive with passion, all mouth and hands, only allowing me to receive, shifting the balance of power. This thrilled her. When I made love to her, she told me it felt better than ever.

The tension dissipated; we could talk. We discussed events of the previous weeks; her worries about her job and daughters, the aftermath of my breakup with Maryann, my frustrating affair with Gillian until the birds started chirping, and we fell asleep again.

I continued to visit Cass in March and early April, and we enjoyed an easy companionship, not just making love, but also interacting with her friends and Sara. On one visit, I spent the entire week with Cass and Sara doing ordinary things—shopping, making potato soup, working in the yard, listening to music, dancing in the kitchen.

I loved Cass, always had, but I couldn't commit to being only hers.

I am not sure what scared me about it. Perhaps I didn't want her to expect me to rescue her, though Cass never implied she wanted me to. Maybe I just couldn't handle the combination of emotional and physical love and being as vulnerable as I had been with her. Perhaps I still had not gotten over the trauma of Cecilia's betrayal. Maybe I thought Cass was too old for me— laughable, since she was only thirty-seven, ten years older. But she had children and different priorities. I didn't want to compete with her daughters for her time and affection.

In truth, I was just not finished exploring the world of women. Within a few weeks, I was back at the Saints.

By late spring, Cass had broken it off with me again. I sat on my bed at home, desolate and alone, wondering why I couldn't manage my personal life better. I didn't want to lose Cass, but I could not be what she needed then. The front door opened, and I heard David dump his things in the hallway. I waited for him to walk through my bedroom to the kitchen, but he just went straight to his bedroom and closed the door.

He was already in his sleeping shirt when I knocked and came in. He could see I was on the verge of tears, so he patted the bed next to him and I sat down.

"I've messed up my life," I sobbed.

"Oh, Patroosk," he said putting his arm around me. "I know it seems that way. I can understand your being enamored with Gillian. She's elegant and sophisticated, but out of reach. And Cass . . . such a lovely woman. I really like her." He paused for a moment, thinking. "Maryann was difficult for you—such a powerful personality, an in-your-face sort of person. Still, if you were living together, you owed her your loyalty."

He was right. I winced, flooded with remorse for the way I had betrayed Maryann, knowing I shouldn't have let her move in. But I didn't want to be consumed with guilt just then; I wanted comfort.

"I have to say, Patroosk, I admire that you put yourself out there. You're brave and take risks and have interesting experiences with women, even though you're feeling lost right now."

"Thanks, Wease," I said, trying to focus on the positive. "What would I do without you?"

He offered the solace I was not getting from the therapist to whom I was paying hundreds of dollars, and who challenged me to be accountable for how I was hurting myself and others.

Perhaps I should remain alone to better understand my motivations, what I needed, and what I could offer another, rather than chasing after the next romance high, searching for the right woman, the right balance. But that was not to be. Not yet.

PART IV

THE RECKONING

"Let me fall if I must fall.
The one I will become will catch me."
—THE BAAL SHEM TOV

CHAPTER TWENTY-FOUR

With Maryann out of my life, Gillian ambivalent, and Cass and I unable to get our timing and priorities in sync for a relationship, May 1978 found me seeking distraction at a Gay Women Professionals' meeting in Boston.

Standing in the brightly lit kitchen of someone's house with my glass of wine nearly empty, I thought of leaving and set my glass in the sink, then turned and bashed into the shoulder of a woman I hadn't noticed before. We were the same height, six feet, but despite the faded denim jacket hiding her body, I could tell she was powerfully built, with broad shoulders for a woman.

She smiled at me. "Sorry, I didn't expect you to turn around so suddenly." Her voice was deep, husky.

Still taking her in, I said, "No problem, I was just leaving." But then I thought—*perhaps not.*

With her prominent jaw and wide, big-toothed smile, the woman was not beautiful in a feminine way, but she was striking. She had startlingly blue eyes that conveyed intelligence and cunning, and she wore her dark blond hair to her shoulders. *I know you*, I thought, but couldn't recall meeting her before.

I poured us each another glass of wine and we talked for at least an hour, standing near the sink, other women coming and going around us. Her name was Dani. She was thirty-two—four years older than me—and was going to photography school in Boston though she lived in Cambridge. Before leaving, to my surprise and pleasure, Dani gave me her phone number.

My desire to remain alone, to figure myself out, faded. I wanted to pursue Dani with enthusiasm but told myself to take it slow. After a few unplanned encounters, either at the Saints, or at women's meetings, Dani offered me a ride home one night. I hesitated before getting out of the car. The way she looked at me shook my resolve, tempting me to do what I had always done, hoping for a better outcome.

Dani unhooked her seatbelt. My pulse quickened, and I unhooked mine. She leaned forward and kissed me tentatively, then moved toward me on the seat. A rush of excitement filled my body. I reached up, my fingers in her hair, and pulled her to me for a longer, deeper kiss.

As necking became more intense, Dani backed away. "Move slowly," she warned. "I'm vulnerable right now."

Was she just out of a relationship? "Okay." I took a deep breath and let it out, counting to six to calm myself. "You set the pace."

After saying goodnight, I jumped out of the car and bounded up the stairs to my apartment, confident I would see her again. It wasn't only physical. There was something about Dani that stirred my soul.

A few days later, Dani invited me to her place in Cambridge. It was not her house but belonged to an elderly couple with old Boston money who still lived downstairs. He was a Professor

Emeritus of physics at MIT and his wife was always saying she was sorry before almost every sentence. Dani rented one of their many upstairs rooms but had the run of the stately Cambridge home on a quiet tree-lined street, the house full of eighteenth-century antique furniture.

I got a ride to her house from a colleague, and when I arrived in the evening after dinner, Dani greeted me at the door in tight white jeans and a form-fitting black shirt accentuating her long, lithe body.

We walked to the theater to see the movie *Madame Rosa*, about a woman who lived in a sixth-floor walk-up in the Pigalle. She was a retired prostitute, Jewish, and an Auschwitz survivor who served as a foster mom to children of other prostitutes. Dani cried during the film, and we walked out without speaking, strolling up Massachusetts Avenue to Harvard Square. How sensitive she appeared, her emotions so close to the surface.

Dani and I sat on a bench in Harvard Square. I ignored the people passing by and gave her my rapt attention as she told me about herself. Her first girlfriend was Uta, a German psychologist who Dani met while she was working as a horse-riding instructor at a Girl Scout camp. After she got a breakup letter from Uta, she was so devastated she slit her wrists.

"How old were you?" I asked.

"Just nineteen," she said, looking pensive.

Dani followed Uta to Europe and tried salvaging their relationship, to no avail. In Germany, she had a brief affair with a man named Bob but feared getting pregnant.

"I can so identify with you there," I said.

Dani's most serious long-term relationship was with Jane, whom she lived with for several years, until Jane left Connecticut to move to Boston for art school. When Dani chose not to join her, Jane returned to dating men.

Dani had several other affairs with straight women. Her most recent one was with Susan, a woman she'd waitressed with at a Mount Washington hotel in New Hampshire before deciding to come to Boston to attend photography school. Dani thought she'd ended the affair when she left New Hampshire, but it was proving more difficult than she expected.

Finally, Dani talked about her passion for art and photography.

"All of this has made me strong," she explained. "I acted and got hurt and confused, but now I know the pain isn't unbearable—that it'll happen again, and I'll be able to take it."

"I can understand that." A wiser woman than I might have noticed warning signs in her narrative, but I was already so drawn to her—her intensity and her ability to accept risk, including starting over to follow her passion for the art of photography. It differed from the disciplined trajectory of my life, at least professionally. Dani removed her aviator glasses, wiped her eyes, and looked at me straight on with her intense blue eyes. I still didn't touch her or kiss her, but heat rose to my upper chest and face as waves of attraction drew us together.

Dani reached for my hand, and we walked back to her house in Cambridge. She invited me upstairs, and as soon as she closed the door, I lost my resolve to let her make the first move. I stepped toward her, took her face in my hands, and kissed her. Her lips were soft, responsive, and slightly salty.

Pulling Dani onto the bed, I told her, "I'm dying to stretch out with all six feet of you," as I rolled on top of her.

Dani put her arms around me, saying it felt good to be totally covered. But she appeared hesitant, and I raised up and looked into her eyes.

"You're the first gay woman I've ever been with," she admitted.

Surprised, I rolled off her, propped my head on my elbow, and stared at her. "But you've seduced straight women; and isn't that harder?"

Dani ignored my question and smiled at me. "You have really nice eyes," she said in a husky, exciting way as she reached for me.

Frustrated by clothing, we undressed in a hurry. Dani wanted to be on top, so I let her, and we made love. I luxuriated under her long body, my fingers digging into her broad shoulders and smooth muscular back.

Afterward, we looked at each other naked, both smiling and shy. I got dressed, kissed her goodbye, and caught the train to Boston. As I bumped along in my seat on the Red Line, I pondered why I found this androgynous woman so alluring. I had not expected to be drawn to a woman like Dani: a seducer of straight women, a woman with the strength and stature of a man, a woman who wanted to be on top. I thought about Virginia Woolf's *Orlando*, which I had read that month. I imagined Dani like Orlando, an aristocratic man who loved nature and dogs, lived for centuries, and ultimately became a woman.

Whatever else she was, Dani was a woman magnet, straight or gay, and could be trouble.

The train jolted to a stop, and I got off.

One thing Dani had said to me while we were sitting on the bench in Harvard Square stuck with me. When she was young, she'd identified as male and hated being born female. I found that curious. I envied men their privilege, their lives made more comfortable by supportive women who did most of the work (while they took the credit). But except for their physical strength, I didn't think of men as strong, nor did I envy men's bodies. I never thought of myself as male. I was happy Dani was a woman.

Uneasy with the intensity of my attraction to Dani, I let a few days pass before I called her. When I did, she said she felt dizzy and depressed, but she had to pull it together to play softball and then visit her family in Connecticut over the weekend. I invited her to come to the Harvard Medical School campus to meet me before her game.

I noticed Dani before she saw me. She wore her softball out-fit, showing off her tan muscled legs and arms—*gorgeous*, I thought. I snuck up behind her and hugged her. Dani swung around and held onto me. People turned their heads to look at us as they passed. I decided we were too public, so I suggested we go stand by the wall in the shade.

Just guessing, because Dani had said earlier she was trying to end her relationship with Susan, I said, "Are you upset about Susan? You don't want to hurt her because you know what it's like?"

Sure enough, Dani admitted she felt guilty getting involved with Susan in the first place, just because she was horny, and regretted the pain she'd caused when she ended it. She leaned against me; I put my arms around her, and she cried a few tears into my shirt. I wondered if the relationship had meant more to her than she let on.

I wanted to be there for Dani, but I also felt the mounting

tension in my body as I held her. We were still visible to passersby on the medical school quad. Even with her height and Amazonian physique, Dani didn't pass for a man. I was still not out to my professors and colleagues. I enjoyed their high regard and didn't want it to jeopardize it.

After several minutes, Dani pulled away. She wiped her eyes on the back of her hand. "Thanks, I just needed to flow with it."

"My pleasure," I said. "I'll walk you to your car."

I was reluctant for her to leave, and I guess Dani was, too. Arriving at her car, parked next to the quad, she turned briskly around, looked me directly in the eyes, lowered her voice with husky intensity, and said, "Get in for a minute."

We both did, and she kissed me, pressing me hard against the seat. My body was at the edge of a cliff and falling, but I recovered and pushed her away. "I can't do this here."

"Okay." Dani sighed and leaned back.

"Call me as soon as you return from Connecticut," I ventured as I opened the door to get out.

"Can't wait," she said, smiling.

Over the next weeks, our affair became so incendiary I had little time to think, so caught up as I was in a whirlpool of emotion. Images of our time together floated through my mind like a movie:

Dani pinning me against the wall behind her open bedroom door and French kissing me while her housemate was climbing the stairs to her room.

Dani hitting the softball out into left field for a home run when I came to watch her play, and thinking she was a real athlete.

Dani turning the clock around while we were making love.

Her wide-mouthed smile.

Her lips like Mick Jagger's lip syncing the words to "Miss You" in the car.

Dani walking everywhere with a bag of film and a camera around her neck.

I'd encountered no one like her, nor had I fallen so hard.

David met Dani one weekend when he wasn't on call. The three of us sipped an after-dinner port wine in the living room. He was unusually quiet, and soon excused himself and retreated to his room. I imagined he found her outward confidence and flamboyance overwhelming; her androgyny confusing. Later, he said. "Be careful, Patroosk."

David should have known I wouldn't listen.

Buoyed by the euphoria of falling in lust or love, spring was magical. We visited a friend's farm in New Hampshire and while Dani shot photos of artfully arranged plants and random pieces of wood, I found a long rope, and lassoed her cowboy style. Much stronger than me, she soon freed herself, threw the rope over me, and pulled me down on the grass. Inspired, Dani snapped photos of me tangled up in rope. Later, she superimposed a large white goose on the image and presented me with the result, entitled "Silly Goose."

On other occasions, we both scrabbled on the floor with her three dogs—riled up, growling, tugging, and barking along with the canines—until Dani flipped on her back with her head in my lap, smiling up at me.

The disco song "Love is in the Air" came on the radio as we were driving down Memorial Drive one afternoon in the thick of rush hour traffic. Dani veered to the side of the road and slammed the car into park. She turned the radio up full blast, pulled me out of the passenger door, and danced with me in the grass. We laughed and held on to each other as cars honked—a few offering thumbs-ups and waves.

We both loved to watch the latest films, and Dani got so engrossed she would grip my hand or hide her face on my chest. Sometimes, I would look over and see tears streaming down her cheeks. Dani experienced things so intensely, it was contagious. I cried along with her.

Was it love, lust, or curiosity I felt for this unusual woman? Likely all three. Even though I hungered for her touch, sex with her wasn't magical in the beginning. She bore down on me with her long body and lean, hard weight like a guy, doing what I assumed she was used to doing with straight women. I gently steered her to a better balance.

One evening in June, a few weeks after we started dating, I had a sore throat, but Dani wanted to come over, anyway. We went to see a mediocre Polish movie called *A Woman's Decision*. The best part was her hand on my leg during the film.

I thought Dani would leave afterward, but she asked for a few minutes together alone. I didn't have the willpower to turn her away and take care of myself, and she followed me upstairs to my apartment. It was stiflingly hot. Before I could open the windows, Dani kissed me and pulled me down on the bed, aggressive, her long fingers pushing inside me almost to the point of pain.

After making hot, sticky love, I would have liked to linger in her arms, but Dani jumped up right away. She had to meet Susan, who would arrive from Vermont that evening.

Susan? I thought she had broken up with her. Dani didn't explain. She kissed me at the door and said, "Bye, baby," in a macho way that left me stunned.

I sagged against the doorjamb, watching her go. I had twinges of doubt, but I failed to heed them, too imbued with oxytocin and other hormones of love and attachment.

A week later, when I arrived at Dani's softball game, further doubts surfaced. The day was hot and muggy, the field dusty, and the air rang with women's shouts. Dani's muscular arms and shoulders glistened with sweat. She was late so she couldn't play, but as we stood together watching behind the backstop, I noticed she paid rapt attention to the movements of a fellow player, Donna. Jealousy burned in my chest. *Is Dani ogling that woman? Without even trying to hide it?*

After the game, Dani and I drove back to her house, where more women showed up from the Gay Professional Women's group, and I drank two glasses of wine—enough to loosen my tongue.

"Do you have a crush on Donna?" I heard how brusque my voice sounded, but Dani didn't even flinch.

"No, of course not."

I didn't believe her. Perhaps it was because of my own wandering eye.

When Dani drove me back to my place in Boston that evening, I was quiet, still trying to reconcile what I'd observed with her words of reassurance.

Dani was leaving for Sweden on a trip with her grandfather in two days. She'd asked for time alone with me. Upstairs in my bedroom, she kissed me and undid my blouse, but I couldn't relax into it, my mind still churning.

"You have a crush on Donna," I blurted out like a teenager. "And I can't stand it."

Dani jerked away from me and sat on the bed; her brow furrowed. "What right have you to limit me?"

What right? None. Especially given my recent history and wariness about investing too much in a relationship with only one woman. But what were *our* rules?

Dani exhaled. "I've been jealously guarding these last few hours to be with you. I need to feel your passion and go to Sweden on a high note."

I sat down next to her and wrapped my arm around her. Dani relaxed into me, laying her head on my shoulder.

"Sorry," I said. "I find myself not wanting to share you."

After a few moments, I got up, poured us a glass of wine each, and put Beethoven's 6th Symphony on the record player. Dani got her wish in bed. I knew I'd miss her terribly while she was away.

Once in Sweden, Dani wrote to me:

Dear Patroosk,

Until I find something that fits, perhaps you'll allow me to borrow David's appellation. We are in route to Stockholm via the inland waterways. I got in a few good shots. Speaking of "desire," I flashed back upon our few days together before I left and wished

*you were here to crawl into one of the tiny bunks. We wouldn't
mind the rain.*

I smiled when I read it. Dani thought of me, even with the
distraction of other tall, elegant Swedish women.
She wrote again:

*I sent you a picture of Margit, as I saw the poster over your bed.
Right now, I am in the mood for chilled white wine, a white
bearskin rug, your white skin next to mine, and the golden sun
setting on the ocean . . . with Pachelbel or Chopin playing.*

Every other woman in my life faded into the background, and I
fell deeper into Dani's thrall, her absence only increasing my
desire. Had I finally found the right woman? To provide all that
was missing from my focused and ambitious life? Could I commit to loving only her?

CHAPTER TWENTY-FIVE

I n June 1978, when Dani was still in Sweden, David and I were having brunch at TGI Fridays, sitting at our favorite table with the high-backed wicker chairs. David said, "I can't stand the thought of our sleazy landlord rummaging through our drawers again."

I took a bite of my eggs Benedict, frowning as I remembered catching the creep red-handed going through my underwear drawer when I came home one afternoon. "Yeah, the bastard."

"We should buy a house." David snapped open the real estate section of the *Boston Globe*, perusing the houses for sale.

I did the math. With our combined incomes, we could qualify for a mortgage. I had discretionary income for the first time in my life, but I'd spent most of it. David was more frugal. He had at least a few thousand dollars in the bank.

"Why not?" I agreed. "If you lend me money for half of the down payment."

David nodded and kept looking.

We pulled our chairs together and circled prospective "House for Sale" ads. We found one for sale by owner near the Harvard School of Public Health in Jamaica Plain, and right after breakfast, drove over to see it.

It belonged to a Greek family. The grizzled patriarch showed us around, walking us through the upstairs, the three bedrooms, the light-filled sun porch, and the immaculate basement. When he was out of sight and earshot, we gave each other an enthusiastic thumbs-up. We told the owner we'd buy it—even before seeing the spacious downstairs apartment rented to an elderly woman, Mrs. B. We'd never bought a house. It was the first one we'd looked at, and we didn't even negotiate the price.

The owner called in his wife, took out a bottle of ouzo from the dining room cabinet, and we sealed the deal—not with a written contract, but with a round of drinks.

As we drove away in a daze at our daring, David reminded me he was leaving on vacation to Costa Rica in a few days, which would require me to take care of the house-buying details, including signing the contract. I didn't mind; busying myself with the purchase would keep me from missing Dani so much.

David and I were about to make our fourth home together, and I took for granted he would always be there. He'd tolerated Maryann living with us. I hoped he would tolerate Dani living with us should it ever come to that. Both outsiders, both gay, David and I had formed a lasting friendship based on trust. We were life partners in the sense that we had soldiered through the grueling years of medical training, sharing experiences, and supporting each other. Hopefully, our friendship would withstand and compliment my partnership with a woman like Dani, whose career aspirations and temperament so differed from my own.

When Dani returned from Sweden in late June, she called and invited me over. I donned black jeans, a new silk blouse and earrings, borrowed the Mustang from David, and drove way too fast to Cambridge. When I arrived, she threw open the door and kissed me, heedless of her elderly landlady in the living room behind her. She took my hand and led me to the back porch, where she'd set out a candlelit dinner.

She'd laid the table with the correct positioning of silverware, napkins, and glasses. The meal consisted of baked mushrooms stuffed with crab meat and cream cheese for an appetizer, paired with a California Sauvignon Blanc. Sea bass followed with mashed potatoes and grilled asparagus. By the time we opened the pinot noir, I could barely refrain from kissing her, even with her landlady still in the living room behind us.

While Dani was in Sweden, she chose a new moniker for me: Laki. This was a shortened version of the Swedish word for doctor. I had never liked the name Pat and preferred Patricia, which Dani found too formal. "Do you like it?" she asked.

"Sure, it's fine," I said, although I hoped I was much more to her than a doctor.

I told her about the house.

"That's great," she said. "We'll have more privacy."

I hoped this meant Dani intended to spend time with me at home and didn't resent David's continued presence in my life.

Our talk during dinner remained on an intellectual plane and ranged from a discussion of Lillian Hellman's *Pentimento* to the importance of ritual and table manners—until I'd had enough.

"This conversation is getting too abstract for me," I said, wanting to feel Dani's body on mine. "Why don't we go upstairs for dessert?"

We left the dishes for later—much later.

That July, the experience of being in love swept me away. It thrilled me Dani could love me in return. I could be open with her, I desired her, and she was my intellectual equal. Those weeks I described in my journal as being full of depth, yearning, and happiness. Dani complemented me and we fit. Fragmented images came to me during quiet moments when I sat at my desk in my office, trying with limited success to concentrate on my work:

Dani in a rakish scarf and jacket, not caring we were touching in public.

Dani driving her car with one hand on the wheel and the other on my upper thigh, making me dizzy.

Her eye for good photo composition.

Dani's thoughtful, strong, patient look when I told her of my own turbulent struggles with my identity as a lesbian and later as a doctor.

She observed the colors in the evening sky, the shape of the clouds, the light on the water, or the fish in the beak of a bird, all the time keeping her hand on my knee or her arm over my shoulder. I saw the world through her keen photographer's eye—encircled by her love.

In our lighter moments, she loved teasing me. When I got too obsessive about something, Dani'd announce, "News flash, news flash, Laki is obsessing," exaggerating and mimicking my words and facial expression. I had to laugh, my worry forgotten.

It was all *so much*—she was so much; we were so much—but we hadn't talked about the shape our lives would take, whether we might live together, whether we should be monogamous.

One night, after we'd made love, I cried—with happiness in the way Dani expanded my life by loving me, and pain that I'd loved and lost before. But I believed we could overcome everything, including our differences. There were no difficulties we couldn't vanquish together.

One evening in August, while lying in bed in the afterglow of lovemaking, I told Dani I loved her.

At first, she was quiet, and fear gripped my chest that I'd told her too soon. The next thing I knew, tears filled her eyes.

"Why are you crying?" I looked into her eyes, more intensely blue with tears.

"I feel your love." She snuggled into my shoulder. "And I'm happy."

Dani soon fell asleep, but I lay awake, thinking. Dani consumed much of my time and attention. I was behind in analyzing data for my research projects and doing little reading to prepare for the possibility of returning to finish my internal medicine residency—at a different hospital than my internship, of course. Despite the tumult of my love life, my work came first, my ability to compartmentalize honed over a lifetime. But sometimes this was impossible with Dani.

I thought about a conversation I had with Mom after she'd met Dani during a visit to Boston that summer.

"You should be careful," Mom had warned. "Dani might expect you to support her. She won't make much money as a photographer."

I'd stiffened. *Why is Mom trying to sabotage my relationships?* "I hardly think so," I'd retorted. "Dani's quite independent."

I had very little money anyway, and no savings. I'd bought Dani a couple of small pieces of gold jewelry and a leather camera case, but she'd never asked for those things. She was often short of cash, but rather than borrow money, she skipped meals to buy the photography equipment she needed.

247

Mom always assumed women were after my money, especially after I finished my medical training. She felt trapped in her marriage to my father—bound to him because she thought she could not raise two daughters as a single parent on the income of a secretary; and then, after we left, because he needed her care. It galled me that Mom believed women would just be with me for my financial potential, even if her fear came from a desire to keep me safe.

I knew Dani was not the sort of person whose love I could buy, and I had very little buying power, anyway. As a lesbian feminist, she wouldn't want to take on the role of a traditional wife, supported by her spouse. This emulation of the patriarchy was to be avoided by any self-respecting feminist, and none of our friends would've approved. Still, Dani allowed me to make dinner for her, pay for dinners out, and keep the liquor shelf stocked.

Dani had her own mother problems that summer. Settling herself on the couch in my living room a few days after I told her I loved her, she said, "I know I'm a disappointment to my mother sometimes—not married, not the girly girl she had hoped for, and still going to school. I want to be an artist, Laki, not just a commercial photographer."

I put my arm around her. "Mothers can be so vexing." I offered. "You're beautiful in your own way, and you're already a talented artist."

Dani relaxed against me as we both sipped chilled Chardonnay, waiting for her lasagna to come out of the oven. Cheese and tomato smells permeated the living room.

Nestled in the crook of my arm, she said, "I used to have the talent of detachment, but I've lost that. I just get on my feet when *wham!* something else comes sailing along, and I am knocked on my ass again." Dani propped her feet up on the coffee table, looking thoughtful.

"One day a sensitive, generous, powerful woman walks into my life and says, 'Come here.' I say, 'Okay, but on my terms.' The sun breaks through, and I see this lovely woman as she is: a gift, and the wrapping is gorgeous." Dani reached over and tousled my hair.

It seemed odd; her talking about me in the third person. I didn't think of myself as gorgeous, but I delighted in her affirmation. Still, I felt some apprehension. *What are her terms?*

"I'm still bouncing off walls while she looks on in puzzled bemusement," Dani continued. "How long will she hang around? And will she want to intervene and change me?"

I'd like you not to look with such interest at certain softball players, I thought.

"I know she's exhausted by all this action and not sleeping. I note this out of the corner of my eye and cautiously approach, tail in a position of question, ears alert."

I laughed at her dog analogy. Dani exhausted me in a good way from nights spent in her arms. "Your intensity is one thing I love about you," I reassured her. "I'm not going anywhere."

The oven timer dinged, and Dani jumped up to take the lasagna out. I lingered on the couch, basking in the contentment of her care.

In mid-August, after we'd been dating for nearly three months, Dani invited me to Connecticut to meet her family. I found her mother handsome and sensuous, her father quiet and sweet. I especially liked his furry dog, Deidre. On a side table, I noticed a picture of Dani when she was younger and had long, waist-length hair. She looked so different from the way she presented to the world now. Her mother asked Dani if she'd worn her skirt in Sweden; I didn't even know she owned a skirt.

I met her beloved little brother, Richard—whom she'd talked about so much and who was not at all little, but even more powerfully built than Dani. He and his wife took Dani and me for a ride in their boat, and I observed the affectionate interaction between Dani and Richard, who had a calm, practical, competent demeanor.

Dani and I went for a walk on the beach near her parents' house. Seagulls filled the air with their raucous cries overhead as she gave me background on her family. I asked if her brother and his wife had wanted any children.

"Yes," she said, "very much so. But they couldn't. It disappointed me when Richard's wife kept having miscarriages. It would have been the closest I'd ever come to having a child."

I was quiet and kicked a few small beach stones in front of me as we walked. Taking a deep breath of the salty air, I said. "Maybe I should sleep with your brother, since he looks and acts so much like you. It would be like getting pregnant by you."

Where the hell did that come from? Did I have regrets about not having a child? Or did I think a child would further bind Dani to me?

"Really?" Dani stopped walking.

I stopped.

Dani just stared at me. She must have known I was hooked; I had to be to even consider having a baby with her brother. I don't think she thought my proposal was preposterous, but she appeared at a loss for words.

I must've been temporarily insane. The last thing I needed to do in my career trajectory was get pregnant. I feared pregnancy—and besides, how could I think her happily married brother would consent to such an arrangement?

"Well, maybe that's not realistic," I conceded, stunned by my impulsive offer.

Dani put her arm around me and held me close as we continued walking. I remained quiet, thinking. I was living my life outside the heteronormative box as a lesbian, as a doctor, perhaps even as a polyamorous woman living in a platonic relationship with my gay male friend and colleague. But my desire for a stable home with a woman grew ever stronger—whether she pursued a career or played a more supportive role to mine, or both.

In Boston in the seventies, while the free-wheeling sexual revolution was conducive to having affairs, it wasn't conducive to monogamous couplings among lesbians, except for a lucky few. I hadn't been ready before with Cass and Maryann. But was I ready now?

CHAPTER TWENTY-SIX

Despite the lusty intensity of that first summer of 1978 with Dani, an undercurrent of fear and insecurity ran through me and surfaced as a smoldering, sulky jealousy. Dani picked up on it and I sometimes suspected she was cautious about what she said to me when describing her activities when we weren't together. As a child, I'd learned to expect pain and loss when I had to compete for the affection of someone I loved. To squelch my anxious feelings and accept with confidence that I had won Dani away from all others was new for me. It would take time to trust it was true.

One very warm evening in August, Marianna, Dani's former roommate and girlfriend, who was visiting from New Hampshire, came downstairs to see us off as we were leaving the house. Dani kissed her goodbye on the mouth—a little too long—and the green-eyed monster gripped my chest.

Once we were in the car, I challenged her, "Why'd you kiss her on the mouth?" I tried to keep my voice even.

Dani turned off the motor and faced me. "She's a dear friend. And I haven't seen her in months. Why does it matter?"

"It burns me up inside when I feel I can't trust you." My throat tightened, the hot car closing in around me.

"Laki, dearest," Dani said, taking my hand in both of hers. "What's a kiss compared to the love we share? Do you have so little faith in me that my friendship with another woman is threatening to you?" She regarded me with wide-eyed earnestness.

"I can't stand you kissing other women that way." I kept my voice strong to mask the shakiness and vulnerability inside. "It looked more than friendly." I turned aside and stared out the window. *She loves me. Why was I doing this?* My fear rose from something old and deep.

"You're tired, and that's part of your reaction." Dani squeezed my hand, then pulled back.

Is she trying to explain away my feelings? Deny my reality? I remained quiet, staring without seeing at the two girls playing badminton in the yard. Fighting the tears that threatened my composure, I resisted the urge to jump out of the car and take the 'T' home. Sweat trickled between my breasts.

Dani gripped the steering wheel and looked straight ahead. "I won't let either of us destroy the love we share. Don't act as if you own me. I'll go away from you—yes, even you, for whom I've waited so long."

The muscles at the back of my neck were tight and my head ached. I said nothing. Dani started the car, the air conditioning came on, and she drove. I'd blown it with my fear. Dani would become even more guarded. How could I bear sharing her with other women or losing her altogether?

One of us would have to change. I hoped it would be her.

That night, I wrote in my journal that Dani was like the ocean waves I couldn't catch and hold. To show my feelings of jealousy and distrust would only make her more cautious with me. I didn't want her to be cautious. To know all facets of her, to crack open the parts she might hide from others, was my desire. Then, I might also let her see those parts of me.

Society's attitude toward homosexuality had gradually changed. It had been five years since it had stopped being considered a mental illness by the medical profession. The gay rights movement was gaining ground and visibility. Boston's annual gay pride parade was now in its eighth year.

Years of hiding who I was and my love for women had become intolerable. Some of my colleagues at the Harvard School of Public Health may have seen me with Dani, who was uninhibited about showing affection in public. Also, I felt secure in my position as a resident and research instructor. My professors liked me and supported my research, which they too had a stake in. Although my sexual orientation might still be interesting to some, I no longer thought their knowing I was a lesbian would threaten my future at Harvard or my subsequent career options.

One August evening, I brought Dani to an academic party at someone's house. She was flamboyant, could dress with flair, and people liked her. *It would be fine.*

I was busy conversing about work with a colleague in the living room when I became aware I hadn't seen Dani for half an hour. I excused myself and went into the kitchen after I heard her laughter. She and two or three of my male colleagues had their shirt sleeves rolled up and were comparing their flexed biceps.

Dani's were bigger.

∽

Despite Dani's height and lean, muscular body, it was her womanly traits that turned me on. She had curves in all the right places, and she was discovering a new and exciting erotic responsiveness.

I began to assert my preferences in bed. I'd play Dani's luscious, womanly body like a fine musical instrument until she lost control. Only then did I let go with her and feel my own pleasure, the intensity heightened by the waiting. This dynamic, my taking the lead, was new to Dani, but she came to accept and enjoy it.

Still, there was a mounting tension between us—not about sex, but about trust. Passionate about her art and photography, Dani would sometimes stay away for several days at a time. I filled in the blanks with my worried imagination. I tried to fight this mounting possessiveness by telling myself she loved me and was monogamous, even though she'd never promised it.

Just before Labor Day, we took a trip to Provincetown, a gay mecca. We sat in a bar with the back open to the beach, someone playing Paul McCartney's "Ebony and Ivory" on the piano, and a soft, warm breeze caressing my skin. Same-sex couples were lying on the shore, sitting on the stools outside, and wandering in for drinks, wearing only scanty beachwear. I relaxed into the comfortable warmth of being in the majority.

I looked with interest at the passing fauna. And so did Dani. As the bar began filling up in the late afternoon, I lost track of her.

I drummed my fingers on the table. *Where is she? Who is she with? Is she cruising?*

When Dani returned to my side half an hour later, I said curtly, "Let's go for a walk."

As dusk settled in, we walked along the beach, Donna Summer disco music drifting out from the bars we passed. "Sometimes I just don't understand where you go in your head," I blurted out.

Dani shrugged. "What does it matter? I'm here with you."

The muscles at the back of my neck tightened, and I took shallower breaths. Tension had been building inside me for weeks. I couldn't stop myself, though part of me cried out, *don't!*

"Sometimes I think you don't really love me."

Dani stopped walking and stared at me; her face contorted with hurt. "How can you say that? How can you not feel my love for you?"

Right away, I regretted what I'd said. Later, Dani told me what she'd heard was her love wasn't enough, was never enough, tapping into an old wound and an emotional third rail. My saying what I did felt to her like I'd plunged a knife into her chest. She had done everything to show me she loved me with her entire being.

Dani withdrew a piece of her heart from me then, although I wasn't aware of it at the time.

CHAPTER TWENTY-SEVEN

That summer, David noticed with envy how much I was enjoying my residency in occupational medicine at Harvard. He, meanwhile, was dragging home from Boston University Hospital at all hours, exhausted, irritable, and lonely.

Concerned about David's unhappiness, and his indecision whether he wanted to take on a fellowship, or even practice medicine at all, I invited him for a jog around Jamaica Pond. Halfway, we stopped for breath. "Why don't you apply to become a resident in occupational medicine at Harvard?"

"Why not?" he said after only a few moments.

"Great, you can sell the Mustang back to me," I said, as we resumed jogging.

David was accepted into the MPH program, and by the fall, we were engaged in our respective pursuits at the Harvard School of Public Health, pleased to have our professional lives tracking together once again. Harvard also granted me another paid year as a research fellow and instructor. In our free time, we toiled painting and furnishing the new house.

Late that year, I considered finishing my internal medicine residency. I had already done the first year as an intern. I just needed to complete two more years of residency to become eligible to take the Internal Medicine Board Exam for certification.

Board certification was unnecessary for medical licensure

and the ability to practice. Still, it was an important credential required by healthcare organizations and insurance plans as a condition for participation. Patients also valued it. Because I was board-eligible in occupational and environmental medicine, several months of that residency might be transferable. Not having to struggle through the full two years of internal medicine would make it more doable. Also, I wanted another chance to prove to myself I was a real doctor.

I worried, though, about how an internal medicine residency might affect my relationship with Dani and my ability to keep up with her needs. At present, my research at Harvard absorbed and focused me during the day and I arrived home still full of energy. Because I wanted Dani to spend more time at my house, I cooked for her or shared meal preparation with David—seafood or chicken with vegetables and mashed potatoes, as Dani didn't eat red meat. After dinner, we'd drink Tia Maria or Cointreau and listen to music, read, and talk. Internal medicine residency would drain my energy and make me more needy. Did I want to tip this balance?

Our first Christmas together, Dani invited me to go with her to Old Saybrook, Connecticut, to visit her family. She'd told her parents we were close friends, but I wasn't sure they were aware of just how close. I was now out as a lesbian to my family and friends and was no longer hiding my sexual orientation at Harvard. I wondered how her parents could not know, given Dani had no boyfriends. What if we were to live together? What would she tell them about us?

On the porch bench, drinking tea to warm up after our walk

with her father's dog in the snow, we picked up an earlier conversation.

"Laki," Dani said, taking my hand, "when I've needed you, you've been there for me. Your ability to perceive things with clarity and good sense serves as an anchor for me."

I rubbed her back and leaned against her strong shoulder, thinking I was better at perceiving other people's issues than my own.

"You say I provide *joi de vivre* for you," she continued, "but you provide stability for me, and we fit together."

As we were undressing for bed, Dani came up behind me, put her arms around me, and pressed her body and breasts against my back. I shivered, anticipating what was to come. "Feel my love for you, Laki."

How could I not believe her—believe in us and our future together?

The first six months of 1979 passed without conflict. Dani and I slipped away to Maine in the spring as the weather got nicer, and I bought her a ring she told me she was proud to wear on the ring finger of her left hand. During the day, while Dani was out shooting photos, I was finishing up my research on mortality of jewelry workers and lung function in workers exposed to phenol-formaldehyde—all part of discovering environmental causes of disease for prevention. I was content with my life, though I still worried what would happen when our routine changed.

For the final two years of internal medicine residency, I chose a Tufts University–sponsored program at a community hospital. It was likely to be more humane than my internship at Boston University Hospital—plus, it was nearby, and I could walk to work. Though I agonized over my decision to return to the demanding world of residency training, I decided to go for it. I wouldn't be cooking at home, just grabbing food when I could in the cafeteria at the hospital. But I had faith in Dani and in us. I'd start in July.

David had enjoyed the past year getting an MPH at the Harvard School of Public Health and catching up on sleep. We'd stripped the lead paint off the walls, repainted, and completed several other house improvement projects. But all was not well at home.

The tension building over the last few months for David erupted one late May evening. Unaware he'd been waiting for a certain television show to come on, I turned the channel to something else just as his program began. His reaction—changing it back, throwing down the remote, retreating to his room, and slamming the door— surprised me.

"What's up with you? Why're you so angry?" I asked when David emerged in a calmer state a few minutes later. I'd turned off the TV and sat at the kitchen table eating a TV dinner.

David sat across from me, rubbing his arms. I took a bite of my TV dinner, waiting for his response.

"I think the underlying problem is you don't care about the house. You're over-committed to too many projects and priorities and are anxious about starting your residency. Lately, I feel you take advantage of me." He got up and paced around the kitchen.

"How?" I asked, taking another bite.

"I make sure we've paid all the bills, arrange for house insurance, shovel the walkways when it snows, take out the garbage, and buy most of the groceries and supplies." He walked to the sink to turn off the dripping tap.

I jiggled my foot up and down under the table. What David said was true. A sense of foreboding took away my appetite.

"I hung all the pictures, installed the dryer and picked up the washer from Dani's house. I also measured the windows for curtains, arranged for the final lead paint inspection, and fixed the faucet. I'd be more enthusiastic if you were more available to help, Patroosk."

David stood at the sink staring at the faucet, which continued to drip.

I took a few more bites of dry, processed meat loaf. It was disgusting. I pushed it away, moving my head around to relieve the tension in my neck. "I know. I'm sorry. The last few months, I've left much of the house chores for you, and I've been spending too much time at Dani's. I'll try to be more responsible."

"I do most of the cooking unless you cook for Dani. I don't think you even—"

The list was growing too long. I'd already apologized, but David looked on the verge of tears.

"I worked hard on removing the lead paint from the walls, and I do shop and cook sometimes," I protested.

"Yes, you do some work, but it is usually a joint venture with Dani and me," he said, sitting down at the table again. "I can't endure it any longer. You can lead your separate life with Dani. If you want to sell the house right away, I'll agree." His shoulders slumped, and he leaned back in his chair, looking down.

His offer landed like a blow. I reached across and put my hand on his arm.

David raised his eyes to meet mine. "I've loved you more than anyone else in my life. That makes this conflict even more painful."

Tears welled up. *I'd been such an ass.* "Is there not anything I can do?"

He shook his head. "It's too late. I've already made my decision. I'm leaving."

In late June 1979, David left for Washington DC to become one of two physicians in the Office of Occupational Medicine at the Occupational Safety and Health Administration (OSHA) just as I plunged into a whirl of sleepless nights, long hours, and ever-increasing responsibility for other people's lives.

David's departure was a cataclysmic change in my home life, and I didn't realize at first how unhappy it would make me. When I came home from the hospital the first week of residency to find his coat gone, his briefcase not by the door, the cupboards bare, and his room empty, I slumped in a chair, despondent. I missed our talks and his quirky sense of humor. Since medical school, David's friendship had been the rock-solid base I'd relied on no matter what was happening in my love life. I'd taken him for granted, not realizing friendship isn't just about shared experience but also requires mutual care, trust, and compassion. I had failed the care and nurturing part of late, expecting it just go one way—toward me.

I sighed and poured myself a glass of wine. The next couple of years were going to be hard.

CHAPTER TWENTY-EIGHT

I began the second of three years of residency in internal medicine that July 1979, anything but confident. It had been three years since I had worked in a hospital setting, and now I was overseeing several interns. On daily rounds, I was the one interacting with the attending doctors, other residents, and interns, coordinating recommendations from the consulting specialists.

In the pocket of my three-quarter-length white coat I carried a peripheral brain, a small, spiral-bound book of interpretation of lab results and abbreviated information on various medical problems. The book grew tattered from hourly use. Every spare moment, I stole away to the resident's lounge to read about my patients' conditions. My internship had been a struggle for survival, with little positive learning. I was determined to become a better doctor during my residency.

It took all my energy, all my concentration to cope with this world of disease and death. The harder I worked to gain confidence as a doctor, the more I lost confidence in my ability to hold on to Dani.

One Saturday evening in September, after being on call all night, I arrived home to find Dani had left her dogs in my house, and they'd pooped and peed in the kitchen and on the living room rug.

I threw my stuff on the chair by the door. "Shit!"

Tempted to yell at the dogs, I realized it wasn't their fault. Exhausted and seething, my head aching, I cleaned up and took the dogs out. As I was climbing the stairs, Dani pulled up in her car.

"Where the hell have you been? Don't you even care about your dogs?" I demanded.

"Sorry, I got caught up in work and couldn't make it over last night," she said.

I said nothing, taking some deep calming breaths.

Dani felt pressure to produce work to sell, to get a supplementary job, and to figure out what she wanted to do with her life. When I could, I tried to be supportive, listen, and offer suggestions—but now we had competing needs. Dani desired a sense of herself as an independent person, free to pursue whatever took her fancy and to react to whatever moved her, like a leaf in the wind. What had seemed such a good fit before wasn't working now.

A couple of weeks after the dog incident, we were sitting on the couch in my living room drinking coffee—me slouched against her, her arm around me—watching the fall leaves drift past the window and listening to Harry Belafonte on the record player.

Dani got up to refill our coffees. When she sat down again, her expression changed; she looked troubled.

"Thank you for your support last week when I was finishing up my work for finals." She paused.

I remained silent and took a sip of coffee.

She turned toward me. "You're gone so much; it's as if you

have taken another lover. Then, when you're here, you're dissatisfied and unhappy. Something needs fixing—in me, in you, in our relationship."

Uh-oh. My shoulders tensed. What she said was true. But I didn't want to start the day acknowledging this painful reality. "Is it fixable?" I dared to ask.

"Maybe, maybe not." Her voice caught on the last word, but she continued. "Sometimes I feel on very shaky ground because we clash so much. We can't seem to listen to each other."

My stomach clenched at the thought it might not be reparable. "What do you want from me, Dani?" I managed, keeping my voice level.

"I think we need outside help."

The record ended, the needle lifted, and it was silent, except for the rushing sound in my head. If only Dani was more available to me, there'd be fewer clashes. Where could I find time to see a counselor? I had stopped seeing my therapist six months earlier. I wasn't sure I had the mental and emotional strength to confront the residual wounds of childhood—the impact of my father's illness and absence, my mother's denial of the validity of my feelings, my fear of betrayal—all of which influenced my present reactivity. I may have made a mistake returning to residency training. I believed it was my fault our relationship was floundering.

By late fall, the increasing emotional distance between Dani and me had sucked the energy and joy out of my life as we now confronted the reality of each other. I took Dani up on her suggestion to seek counseling. I preferred to see a couple's therapist with acceptable credentials. Dani wanted to see a lesbian-feminist therapist. We couldn't find anyone that met both of our criteria. We compromised by seeing two therapists: Linda, who was a credentialed couple's therapist associated with a major teaching hospital, and Nancy, a lesbian feminist who practiced therapy.

After our second session, Linda suggested we might reestablish closeness if we went away together during my upcoming vacation with no outside distractions.

Following her advice, Dani and I took a trip to the Yucatan in November 1979. Mexico was not my ideal choice because of my fear of flying, but Dani wanted to go there for warmth, sun, and photography, and I agreed.

We explored Mayan ruins, where Dani focused on taking photos. To explore the hinterlands and small villages, we rented a small motorbike and roared off down dirt roads, passing huts of grass and sticks, dirt floors, hammocks, barefoot children, and scrawny dogs. Villagers stared, wide-eyed, as two very tall, very pale women flew by with their knees up high on the tiny motorbike.

I hoped Dani and I might resume our passionate lovemaking, but that was not to be. We made love, but it felt perfunctory and efficient, like we were an old married couple. Since I equated lust with love, I worried again she didn't love me. I had little experience with how desire and passion may wax and wane over time, even in the healthiest of long-term relationships. I needed the intensity and drug-like high of our first months together to feel secure, that we were still solid, committed, and that Dani would stick with me through my residency.

We sat in a restaurant a week into the trip, surrounded by families speaking Spanish. I stared past Dani at the reds, greens, and golds of the painting on the wall, and a heavy sadness threatened to overwhelm me. She was concentrating on unwrapping her tamale and didn't notice my change of mood.

"I want to feel in love again," I blurted out.

Dani looked up, searching my face, worried.

Regretting my statement, I backpedaled. "I mean, it would be wonderful to experience again the passion we had in the beginning."

"Yes, it would," she said, tucking into her food.

I was afraid to pursue it further; Dani might say passion was no longer present leaving me without the addictive highs I relied upon to counter the ever more frequent lows and keeping me from having to address the deeper, emotional wounds preventing true intimacy.

The next day, we traveled to Isla Mujeres, where we snorkeled. Distracted from my earlier sadness, I drifted for hours among the corals, following the darting schools of blue and yellow tang and an occasional angel fish, crab, or lurking moray eel. I became so enthralled with the colorful marine life, I forgot to reapply sunscreen and got a severe sunburn.

Sex was off the table after that.

When we returned to Boston from Mexico, we established a comfortable rhythm. Dani was at my house when I returned most evenings I wasn't on call. On my outpatient rotation, I had enough energy to shop and cook for us again and we spent quiet evenings at home reading, talking, and listening to music. Our

lovemaking was tender, if not as passionate as it was in the beginning.

However, my contentment was short-lived.

Around the holidays, Dani acquired an Egyptian Pharaoh hound
she named Buto to replace the two puppies she'd given away and
her elderly border collie, who'd disappeared. Buto curled her lips
into a lovely smile when she was happy and served as an excellent
prop for Dani's photos, as she sat in a regal pose. As Dani was too
distracted to care for Buto consistently, she often stayed with me
and slept in my bed more than Dani did.

In late February 1980, I was in the middle of a fast-paced
emergency department rotation. On my feet all day and most of
the night, stabilizing and admitting sick patients, I needed a quiet,
relaxing time and TLC when I got home. Often, however, I returned to an empty, cold house with no food in the refrigerator
and not even a dog to curl up with.

Then Dani disappeared for a week. I called her house, and
the landlady told me she hadn't been home for three nights after
a woman named Helinka had been there for dinner.

My gut clenched. *Is she having an affair with Helinka?*

Dani arrived at my place at the end of the week with Buto, who
bounded up the stairs and over to her food bowl, expecting treats.

Before Dani could put her bag down, I confronted her.
"Where've you been?"

She gave me a defiant look. "Seeing friends."

"Right, friends with benefits?" My eyelid twitched.

She flared. "You are too demanding and confining; you won't
even let me have friends."

This wasn't true. I wanted Dani to have friends, but I also wanted priority with her time. And I didn't want her to sleep with any of her friends. Including her photography school chums, her softball team, and her contacts from various feminist groups, she had a much wider social circle than I did. I'd become isolated— one of the many downsides of medical training.

I'd had a couple of glasses of wine while I waited for her to show up—this was becoming an ever more frequent way of unwinding in the evenings for me—and I had little restraint.

"I don't mind you having friends," I said, "but I'd like you to be with me when I'm available."

Work was so stressful, I could've benefited from down time alone, looking after myself and reading up on my patient's medical problems. Instead, I lamented the lack of care I received from Dani.

In the late seventies, we didn't know any lesbian couples who had been together for more than a few years. There was no encouragement from our straight friends or family to stay together in a long-term, committed relationship. There was little support for monogamous coupling from our lesbian peers either. Anything resembling the patriarchy was to be avoided by any self-respecting lesbian feminist. Still, I'd hoped Dani and I might build a life together after I got through this residency. My expectations were tracking much like my earlier relationship with Cecilia.

Both of us lacked the skill of compromise and negotiation required to maintain any successful relationship. It was all or nothing. One either gave in to the other's demands and resented it, or stubbornly resisted, as Dani had been doing lately.

That evening, I mustered the courage to say, "I want us to be monogamous."

269

Dread gripped me. When Dani took her time responding, tears welled up, and I couldn't hold them back.

"I guess I'm just not the marrying kind." Her voice was hard.

My head pounded, and my stomach roiled. Perhaps I'd contributed to her attitude by not trusting her. My return to residency had made me more needy—of safety, love, and care. My tears flowed, and I did not try to stop them.

Dani picked up her bag, called the dog, and left. I slumped on the couch. *How had things gone downhill so fast?*

Before I knew it, it was March. I was about to turn thirty and was the senior medical resident on call, covering the whole hospital.

An ambulance arrived in our emergency room in the middle of the night, bearing a toddler whose body had been burned over 80 percent. His skin was a sickening gray, his hair and eyelashes gone, his eyes swollen shut. I held his hot, gray head in my hands while another resident intubated him before his airway became too swollen to breathe.

Rage fueled my ability to function and direct his care. His mother had left the toddler alone in the house with a faulty heater that had caught fire. Firefighters found him cowering under his bed. *How could she?*

The surgical resident did a cut-down on his tiny, charred ankle to put in an intravenous line to replace the fluids that would soon seep from his burned skin; he no longer had any boundaries, no protection between his inside and outside. If he survived—and he probably would not—he would undergo years of indescribable suffering.

When he was stable and I could leave the treatment room, I

fled to the supply closet, tears stinging my eyes. I banged the wall with my fist. *How could a mother let this happen?*

His mother was in the waiting room, crying hysterically. A nurse found me and asked if I would order a sedative for her. The thought flashed through my mind. *Let her suffer. Let her marinate in the anguish of what she's caused by her neglect.* But it was my job not to judge, but to relieve suffering. She would have a lifetime to confront the horror of it. I ordered the sedative.

I left another resident in charge at the hospital and rode the ambulance with the burned toddler to the Children's Hospital Burn Unit. He was unconscious—sedated—and had a tube down his throat. The thought of the suffering he would endure over the weeks, months, and years if he survived sickened me. It would be better if he did not survive, but that was not my call to make. As we jostled through the rain-soaked streets of Boston, I spoke to him softly, placing my fingers on a small patch of skin that wasn't burned, tears blurring my vision.

I came home after that thirty-six-hour shift at the hospital with images of the little burned boy running through my mind. I dropped my coat and bag on the floor, too depleted to hang them up.

My shoulders drooped when I saw Dani on the couch, drinking a glass of wine and reading a book. There was no sign of dinner.

Drained and out of sorts, too tired even to open the fridge, I plopped next to her on the couch and propped my feet on the coffee table.

"Couldn't you have made us dinner?"

Dani put down her book and sighed. "Laki, I feel oppressed by your demands and unspoken expectations. I love you and need your love; but I also need my freedom."

What a line. It sounded like she had rehearsed this—something from her therapist—and I didn't want to hear it. I slouched farther down on the couch and put my arm over my eyes, wishing I could shut everything out—not see that burned boy, not feel anything.

"Life with you is a scale of weights and balances. If I don't watch and argue, you'll trample me with your needs, your desire to be taken care of. I want to do that sometimes, because I love you, but I want to be your lover, not your servant."

Anger rose in my chest. It had taken all my strength to care for that child, and my heart ached with sadness. I wanted dinner, peace, and her loving arms. Was that too much to ask?

"You're hardly my servant."

Dani sipped her wine. Angry silence hung between us as I counted my breaths to five and tried to calm myself.

Sensing this, Dani continued. "I want us to have a peaceful life together. I know your work is hard right now and full of pressure. I wish you would find the strength to deal with it. You are asking too much from me to be all good things to you, to make the rest of your life bearable."

That was clear. I created tension in the little time we had together. Life with her was so impassioned and enthralling when we got along. I didn't want to drive her away.

"Okay, I'm sorry."

I pulled her close, and she put her head on my shoulder.

CHAPTER TWENTY-NINE

In early March, while going over the latest admissions with the intern, Josh, I met Mr. Manley, a man in his late seventies. He'd just been transferred from one of the nearby nursing homes with dehydration and difficulty breathing. He was emaciated, his ribs visible, and I could see the muscles between his ribs and in his neck contracting with every labored breath. His lips were cracked, and his tongue shriveled; he was so dehydrated Josh couldn't start an intravenous line. We searched for a vein and had to poke him several times before we could thread one in. I also had to insert a needle in the artery of his thin wrist to draw blood gases. All of this he tolerated in listless silence.

When Josh and I could sit at the central desk to review Mr. Manley's admission orders, I noticed a Do Not Resuscitate stamp on the front of his chart. Despite his terrible blood gases showing severe respiratory distress, we would not transfer him to the ICU.

I turned to Josh, a serious, asthenic man who looked too young to be an intern. "You've listed no family contacts. Call the nursing home, get his details, and make sure we can contact the family when it's time."

Mr. Manley was still alive the next night I was on call. I found him in his room, lying on his side, struggling to breathe, his mouth open. A silver thread of drool slid down the side of his chin. I placed my hand on his shoulder and called his name, but he didn't open his eyes or respond.

I walked to the main desk and opened his chart, but no contacts were listed.

I paged the intern. "Where're Mr. Manley's contacts? The family needs to be called."

A nurse looked up. "He has no family."

I stared into the middle distance. How must it feel to come to the end of your life, connected to no one? To go alone and disconnected into the void of death?

That night, every time I walked by Mr. Manley's room, I found him lying on his side, never changing position, his rib muscles still contracting. His breathing had become erratic, with long pauses followed by snoring sounds called Cheyne-Stokes breathing. The end was near. Who had he been and whose lives had he touched? Who were his people? Where were they now?

I thought about my own death. My parents would no longer be alive, my sister far away, my love life uncertain. Childless, would I, too, be alone when I died? I shuddered.

Needing to be there with him. I walked into his room and put my hand on his shoulder as he took his last breaths. Glancing down, I noted the time on my watch—2:10 a.m., the time I would record on his death certificate.

The sadness of that moment stayed with me all the rest of the night, and for years to come. I didn't believe in religion's promise of an afterlife. But neither could I be sure what happened to this man—what might happen to any of us—after death. Was there some form of continuation?

As a human invested in my identity, I hoped there was.

⤸

The day after my thirtieth birthday in mid-March (which I spent on call in the emergency room), Dani and I dined at one of our favorite restaurants in Cambridge, The Peacock. It was an intimate, homey restaurant with dimmed lights and candlelight that served fresh, local seafood with an excellent wine selection.

Mellow after a glass of California Chardonnay, I said. "Are you coming over this weekend? Do you want to drive up to Maine? We could eat lobster at that restaurant in the little cove." I thought getting away from the city might inspire more closeness between us.

"I can't, Laki. I promised Helinka I'd go sailing with her." She said this matter-of-factly, as if she had a hair appointment.

I stiffened—was I losing her? Tears burned my eyes. As I took a couple of swallows of my Chardonnay, I realized she'd told me this two days earlier. I gripped my glass of wine hard and looked over her shoulder at the heterosexual couple behind her, laughing and having a much better time.

Dani outlined the base of her wineglass with her fingers. She looked up with a pleading look in her blue eyes. "We both love each other. But all day, I've been nursing a dull ache in my chest."

I stayed quiet while Dani sipped her wine. *Was she breaking up with me?*

"I question what I've done with my life, and what I will do," she said. "I wonder who I am and how I affect others. All these questions involve you, Laki."

Really? Couldn't we just have a pleasant weekend together in Maine? "How?" I asked as the server came to top up our wineglasses.

275

Dani waited for the server to leave. "Monogamy. You view it in terms of relationship, whereas I view it in terms of identity. I've told you I need validation from others, people who know me well. If I care for someone, we might make love. It doesn't mean either of us is going to 'fall in love' or change our life."

This sounded like psychobabble to me—a way to justify being polyamorous and uncommitted.

The food arrived—sea bass on a bed of lentils for her and a salt-cured pork chop and mashed potatoes and green beans for me—but I didn't feel like eating. We were silent until the server left. I mulled over whether Dani thought making love with me didn't mean she was in love or going to change her life, or whether she was referring to other women.

"I see monogamy as confinement. I won't let you or any other person limit me in that way. I may go for extended periods of time sleeping with only one woman, but that doesn't change me into a monogamous person. I don't want to be obligated through love, friendship, honor, or money." Dani took a bite of her food and looked at me as if she expected me to challenge her.

My limbs grew heavy as I sank into my chair. My food sat untouched.

I'd seen monogamy as confinement when I was with Maryann, hadn't I? When I wanted to sleep with Gillian and Cass? Now I was the one evoking feelings of confinement in Dani when my heart ached for us to be exclusive.

"I used to think monogamy was confinement until I fell in love with you," I said. "I don't think I can be open with you knowing you're having a similar experience with someone else."

I took a big gulp of my wine and wiped my eyes with my napkin as I glanced over her shoulder at the straight couple. They were just leaving; his hand was at her waist, and she was smiling up at him.

I would give anything to feel that way again with Dani. Was it not possible for two lesbians to sustain commitment?

CHAPTER THIRTY

N ear the end of March, David invited me to join him in DC for a couple of months, having confirmed that a temporary assignment for me was possible. He was grateful to me for suggesting he do the residency at Harvard and had forgiven my neglect of our house. His work was stimulating, and he was much happier. David's position, which had been interim, became permanent.

I proposed to the chief of medicine that six weeks working for OSHA's Office of Occupational Medicine in Washington, DC should be part of my internal medicine residency. I was well-liked at work, and he'd called me "a damn good resident." The chief accepted my proposal.

Before I left, Dani and I met with Linda, our therapist. "Dani is not finished with you yet," she told me. "She's still very emotionally attached." Linda thought time apart might give us better perspectives.

At the end of March, when I drove to DC in the Mustang, David greeted me at the townhouse he rented with a big hug and dinner ready to serve. Over crab cakes, salad, and wine, David described his work projects. Jimmy Carter was the president. OSHA had just been formed and many dedicated scientists were on board to promote workplace health and safety. David's excitement was infectious.

"Can't wait for you to meet Victor," he said. He was the first physician to join the Office of Occupational Medicine, a graduate of Harvard.

Indeed, Victor was impressive, a massive bear of a man with an unruly shock of black hair and a trim black beard. Knowledgeable and irreverent, he punctuated his statements with swear words and a raised, bushy eyebrow.

We divided work projects equally among the three of us. The Director sent me to Kellogg, Idaho, to investigate an allegation Bunker Hill Co, a lead smelter required women who wished to work in the smelter to undergo sterilization before an offer of employment. Studies showed the lead contamination in the surrounding soil was so high the kids at a nearby school had lower IQs than similar students further away.

I had to drive an unmarked car because anti-government sentiment was strong in rural Idaho. Shooting at my car might become sport for the locals. Uneasiness compelled me to walk with haste from the parking lot into the plant. I spent a couple of weeks there, interviewing and examining employees in the union hall while industrial hygienists took measurements inside the smelter. All of it confirmed the company's complete disregard for health and safety.

Our team's report resulted in a huge citation and fine for the company and a commendation for us for a job well done from the assistant secretary of labor. Bunker Hill would eventually be shut down and become one of the largest toxic Superfund sites in the country.

ॐ

Back in DC, with no night call and more discretionary income, David and I often dined together in upscale downtown restaurants. We always found things to discuss: our work, our personal lives, politics, and our plans.

One evening, when we were dining at the Monocle, David asked me, "Why do you stay with Dani? It seems like she just makes you unhappy."

"She does lately, but I can't give up." The same perseverance that had served me so well in my professional life kept me hanging on to Dani, even though our relationship goals appeared incompatible.

"I'm sorry, Patroosk. Maybe you should leave her and come here—join Victor and me in the Office of Occupational Medicine. I'm sure they would hire you."

"I don't know . . ." The thought of leaving Boston, Dani, Gillian, and my other friends made me lose my appetite.

Still, it was comforting to be with David again. Our easy camaraderie returned as we shared the cooking, shopping, and cleanup. He assured my skirt was not on backward and the stove turned off before we rushed out the door. We shared the same office, and could discuss our projects, giving each other advice on the science and politics. I bounded into work eager to discover the latest health concern, the next place I could apply my fresh skills in preventive medicine.

I got to know Victor, our brilliant colleague, with his New York accent and colorful, irreverent comments. Convinced of our importance, we identified harmful exposures to prevent disease in the nation's workers.

The hurt I'd suffered almost daily of late in my relationship with Dani faded; it was a taste of what it might feel like to leave her.

While I was in DC, Cass came to visit. She'd gone to work for a new company and had been in New York visiting her eldest daughter. When Cass arrived at David's townhouse and greeted me with warmth in her voice, the desire to feel her in my arms again returned with such power; I had to turn away. Why should I be monogamous with Dani when she was not, when she caused me such pain? I hoped Cass might stay the night with me. I wanted to lose myself inside her. It had been so long since I'd experienced the lustful abandon we both enjoyed when we were together.

Once we were alone in my room, I took a step toward her. "I want you to stay."

Cass looked tired. The stress of her new job, which required a lot of travel, and the responsibilities of a single parent etched worry lines on her still lovely face.

Cass took a step back. "I can't anymore."

Her rejection landed like a body blow, and tears filled my eyes.

Cass's face softened. "I still find you an attractive woman, but I don't feel the same."

Why had I thought Cass would always be available? With the same level of lust, if not love, she'd had for me for years? She had her own life, her own needs, and for all I knew, she might have started seeing someone else. For years, I would regret that we could not get our timing right for a relationship.

～

While I was away, Dani called me several times. As soon as I returned to DC from Idaho, she came to visit.

Dani arrived in the evening and joined David and me for dinner. David had cooked coq au vin, and I'd added garlic mashed potatoes and a salad. He sat, saying little as Dani talked about her doings in Boston. David gave me a knowing look across the table. I gave him a reassuring smile. *The visit will be okay*, I said with my eyes.

Afterward, in my room, Dani exclaimed, "Laki, how I've missed you!"

She flopped on my bed, still dressed, and propped herself up on one elbow, looking at me. I sat on the edge next to her. She raised her arm and ran her hand through my hair.

"So, your life is going well. I'm happy for you. I allowed myself to miss you only a reasonable amount."

"I missed you too."

Dani got up, and I watched her undress, enjoying her lithe body, the sharp definition of the muscles in her limbs, her flat abdomen, and the flare of her hips. "Nice." I smiled, turned on just by the sight of her.

Dani threw her clothes on the chair. "I've been working out. Your jock is all toned up."

I got undressed, and we lay down together. Dani snuggled against me, and my body responded to her touch. "While you were gone, I couldn't be with anyone else, so I came to your house, and it helped."

"What else are you doing to take care of yourself?" I ran my hand along the smooth skin of Dani's long, muscular back.

"I worked out and took saunas. I'm learning how to soothe myself when I am at my lowest points and I'm keeping myself busy."

I continued to run my hands over her body while Dani talked. My brain was on vacation, my body in control.

"I've decided I'll do photography—artistic, not commercial, but only photography, even if I starve." She snuggled into me again. "I love you, Laki. I hope you know that. I've many interests and want to live life to the fullest. I want you to understand and accept me—truly accept me."

I held her tight and glanced at the clock: 10:30 p.m. I had to get up early. Would we have time to make love?

Dani wasn't finished yet.

"I'm flaky, creative, impractical, and enthusiastic about many things. It can work for us. If you can see me as the person I really am, I'm more than willing to try, Laki."

But that person is non-monogamous, incapable of commitment.

"I'm willing to try too," I told her, wishing she'd stop talking and kiss me. Whatever our conflict, whatever my doubts, sex almost always made things better.

Dani nibbled my neck, and that was all it took—no more talking.

The next day, Dani, David, and I visited the Torpedo Factory Art Center—a large, converted munitions plant that was home to the nation's largest collection of working artists' open studios under one roof—in Alexandria, Virginia.

The prospect of joining these artists excited and energized Dani and she filled out an application for one of the artist's studios. Her work would be judged before acceptance. It was a gamble, but one she thought well worth taking if I moved to DC. And if she came with me—just too many ifs.

When Dani departed for Boston, I stopped worrying about our relationship and focused on the stimulating work at hand.

While I was in DC, David bought a townhouse in Logan Circle.

As the time for my return to Boston drew near, I accompanied him to take possession of his new home. It was in a gated community, in a rough part of town on its way to becoming gentrified. "It has a second bedroom with its own bathroom," David said, his blue eyes twinkling. "You could come to DC when you've finished your residency and work for OSHA. You would be welcome to live with me here."

I looked out the window of the second bedroom. A group of young Black men gathered around a garbage can fire, the flames casting shadows on the wall. *Perhaps.* The idea of living and working with David again tempted me. I could benefit from the stability he offered and had learned my lesson about not taking his friendship for granted.

CHAPTER THIRTY-ONE

When I returned to Boston and my residency in May 1980, the blissful reunion with Dani didn't last long. Soon, she was canceling dates with me, and often wasn't home when I called. Suspicious Dani was sleeping with Jennifer, a woman on her softball team, the distance between us widened, even if we were in the same metropolis. Dani had more freedom, more support, more girlfriends.

Over the previous couple of years, Gillian and I had maintained a platonic friendship. She liked Dani. We would have dinner together or see a movie. In late May, I was on my own in one of those thirty-six-hour stretches when I wasn't on call or at the hospital. Dani was away somewhere with one of her girlfriends. Gillian and I went out to an Italian restaurant for dinner, then to my house afterward.

To flaunt my "philistine taste in music," I put country songs on the record player: Loretta Lynn, Brenda Lee, and Patsy Cline. We drank wine, and I played her the songs that had gone to my heart. As the evening progressed, Gillian talked more freely and laughed more easily. I sat a safe distance from her on the couch but could not forget how much I had once wanted her.

Then it was 2 a.m., and Gillian rose to leave. As she pulled her coat off the chair, I turned her around and put my arms around her, wavering between a straight-woman hug and something more. Gillian dropped her coat and held me, pressing her body against me in that familiar way I could not resist.

I couldn't let her go. Patsy Cline played in the background. I sought her mouth progressing down her neck as her breath caught. Confidence replaced the fear and self-consciousness I'd had before. I had no obligation to Dani, nor did she expect it. There was nothing holding me back. I took Gillian into the bedroom, and we undressed. Then I lay on top of her, her bare skin warm and smooth, my excitement mounting as I breathed in the familiar, fresh scent of her perfume and touched her wet center.

When it was over, I lay with my head on her chest, and she stroked my hair.

Gillian was awake before me in the morning, sitting on the edge of my bed, looking down at me, her expression pensive. I rubbed my eyes and sat up.

"I didn't intend to stay last night, but you inveigled me," she said.

I laughed. It sounded obscene. "Is that even an actual word?" I jumped out of bed, slipped on my bathrobe, and looked it up in my grandfather's massive and worn 1898 dictionary. It meant "enticed."

"I think you inveigled me, too," I said, smiling at her.

At the end of June, there were only six months left in my internal medicine residency. A year earlier, my professors at Harvard had been grooming one of my male colleagues, a year behind me, for a career in academic medicine. I wondered why they'd chosen him, as I thought he was uninspired and colorless. It was hard to know whether sexism and homophobia influenced their choice, or whether it was a personal failing on my part. Still, I persevered in finishing up my research and submitting my papers for publication, even as I worked long hours at the hospital.

DC looked increasingly attractive. I'd lost faith in my relationship with Dani and my future at Harvard. I sent in my application to join David at OSHA.

My sister Terri came to stay with me in Boston for a couple of months that summer of 1980. It was a welcome visit. She often left a crock pot of something delicious warming for me to eat when I dragged myself home from the hospital long after dinnertime. Terri took care of Buto and did the grocery shopping. She liked Dani, even helping her frame her photographs while I was at work.

One evening over dinner, Terri asked, "Is everything okay with you and Dani?"

"Not really," I admitted. "Our lives are so different, and I'm afraid we're drifting apart."

"I think she still cares for you." Terri was concerned and motivated by a desire to support me, but I didn't want to discuss my strong suspicion Dani was sleeping with Jennifer.

That week Dani was busy preparing for a show of her photography. After dinner, Terri drove to Cambridge to help her set up her opening exhibit.

The night of Dani's opening, Helinka gave her a bouquet of balloons and Nancy, her lesbian therapist, brought her a dozen yellow roses.

Roses from her therapist?

Dani's entire softball team showed up, including Jennifer. I wandered the venue with Terri managing only a few words with Dani.

Terri and I had prepared my house for an after-opening party. The living room filled with Dani's friends and admirers. Dani danced with Jennifer in the living room while Gillian and I sat on the sun porch and talked about everything except the state of my relationship with Dani. Later, I learned Gillian had taken Dani aside at the party and warned, "Patricia is a really nice person. Don't hurt her."

Though I'd never talked with Gillian about my difficulties with Dani, she must've noticed something that inspired a desire to protect me. I also hadn't told Dani about sleeping with Gillian. Perhaps I thought Dani wouldn't care, and that would hurt even more.

In late July, Terri returned to Phoenix to plan her wedding to a man she'd been dating for a couple of years. I tried, unsuccessfully, to imagine having the same opportunity with a woman.

A few weeks later, OSHA sent news they had accepted my application. I arranged to start the job after completing my residency in December. The American Board of Internal Medicine had counted six months of the Harvard residency toward eligibility for the internal medicine boards.

I hadn't told Dani yet.

That night, Dani and I argued over the phone about her ever-increasing unavailability. She was not living up to her promise of spending two days a week at my house. Once again, she broke our date.

"You are a totally selfish bitch!" I slammed down the phone. Not a persuasive way to make a request, but I'd run out of patience.

Two nights later, Dani showed up. She'd spent the last few days helping to set up the Judy Chicago Dinner Party exhibit. She dragged in and slumped on the couch with a deep sigh. I was just out of the shower, my scrubs in a heap on the floor. I threw on jeans and a sweatshirt while Dani poured herself a full glass of wine, plopping down again on the couch.

I noted her dour expression and sat across from her, Buto at my side, bracing for the onslaught. "Obviously, you have something to say."

"Yes, Laki. When I was exhausted and needed care, all you could think about were your own needs. I worked all day photographing the sculptures and helping to set up the Judy Chicago Dinner Party—the lights and the display of every plate and place setting. It was an amazing, uplifting experience. That's where I got my energy, *not from you.*"

Why is it my job to give her energy? I was at the hospital working all night while Dani and her friends were on the streets doing guerrilla art. The Judy Chicago Dinner Party celebrated women finding their place at the table, just as I was finding my place in medicine. Wasn't I doing my bit for social justice for women by investigating and exposing their health hazards in the workplace?

I fled to the kitchen and poured myself a glass of wine. I took a big swig and leaned against the counter.

Dani walked up behind me.

"I'm afraid of this overwhelming power you have over me. I know I give you that power. I don't know why."

What power? I rummaged in the refrigerator for something for dinner. Nothing there. I took a jar of peanut butter from the cupboard, banged it on the counter, and slammed the door shut. Dani had complete freedom: the ability to sleep undisturbed at night, to come and go as she pleased. She could engage in the exciting world of Boston feminist politics with her art or run off to Martha's Vineyard with Jennifer. Slapping the peanut butter onto a piece of bread, I tore a hole in the center.

Dani invaded my personal space. "You're a bulldozer," she said. "You overpower me. But I need you. Maybe because you're so strong. Even at your weakest, you're incredibly strong."

I didn't feel strong or powerful. I felt hungry, tired, and cranky. And I'd reached my limit of tolerance.

CHAPTER THIRTY-TWO

In July 1980, I was two weeks into a rotation in the high-intensity, high-demand environment of the ICU/CCU as a senior medical resident. When on call, I covered the house and was in charge of managing every cardiac or pulmonary arrest in the hospital.

I was older, confident now I could handle any unstable, sick patient that came through the door. Night duty was still demanding. I rarely got any sleep on those shifts, which contributed to my lack of tolerance for Dani's inconsistent attention, absences, and neglect.

On a hot, humid day in early August, I'd had enough. Driving over to Dani's house in Cambridge on my Sunday off, I ruminated over yet another broken date the night before; Dani had promised to come over, but canceled at the last minute, claiming she had work to do.

I let myself in with the hidden key and climbed the stairs to Dani's room with resolve. I needed to do this for myself, to gain control of my life.

It surprised her to see me, and fortunately Dani was alone, poring over photographs laid out on her desk and wearing faded jeans and a turquoise terrycloth T-shirt. She looked up at me and smiled, and I almost lost my resolve. I took a deep breath. "Dani, we need to talk."

We sat on her bed, my heart pounding as I gathered my strength.

"I can't stand this anymore, having you flit in and out of my life."

Dani looked thoughtful. She turned her knees toward me and leaned in, her blue-eyed gaze intense.

"I want only you, to make a life with you. I can't tolerate your romantic involvement with others." I searched her eyes. "I don't want to hurt constantly or be humiliated and lose my self-respect." I had to hurry now. I could choke.

Dani put her hand to her mouth, her eyes still locked on mine.

"I can't do this anymore." My chest tightened, my heart ached, and I looked away from her intense blue eyes at her bathrobe, hung on the hook behind the door, so I wouldn't cry.

I heard her make a stifled choking sound and looked back.

Her face crumpled and her eyes filled with tears. She sobbed like a child.

I'd expected her to argue or defend. Not this. I grabbed a handful of Kleenex and handed them to her. I took her in my arms and stroked her hair. She cried into my shirt, blew her nose, and settled back with her head on my chest.

The tension drained from my body. "I heard what you've been telling me about being overwhelmed by my needs and your requirements for independence and acceptance," I murmured into her hair. "I know I demand too much from you."

Her tears gave me reason to hope.

Dani was no longer crying. In one swift motion, she pushed me down on the bed, kissed me, and undid my jeans. She told me she loved me; our love was still strong; our passion held more power than any other emotion, than any other person. I couldn't leave.

My head throbbed, but I let Dani undress and make love to me, my resolve joining my clothes in a heap on the floor.

A couple of weeks later, Dani took off with Jennifer to the Michigan Womyn's Music Festival. My world turned gray; I ate very little and slept poorly, even when I had the chance. Still, she'd said before leaving we would go to Connecticut together when she returned to visit her family and see her older brother's new baby.

When Dani returned twelve days later, I was on call. The hospital operator paged me to say a woman was in the lobby waiting for me.

Dani smiled and took my hand when I came downstairs. We walked outside the entrance to a treed area where she kissed me; although I was so stiff, she might as well have been kissing a tree. We strolled down the hill and sat on a bench while Dani told me about her trip. She and Jennifer had stopped at an idyllic lake in Canada. They'd hooked their sleeping bags together that night to keep warm.

My chest constricted. *Why is she telling me this?*

Dani shifted on the bench and put her head in my lap. I was glad the trees obscured us, so I wasn't being observed by the hospital staff. Then she delivered the gut punch. She and Jennifer had driven fifteen hours straight to Connecticut to see her older brother and their new baby.

I shifted her head off my lap and sat up, my stomach in a knot.

"Did your mother ask about me or us?" I didn't want to know how Dani explained her relationship with Jennifer.

"She did. She asked if I was going to DC with you."

"What did you tell her?" Blood rushed in my ears.

"That I was."

I said nothing.

I remembered I was missing *Morning Report,* the summary of what had happened with each patient on my team the night before. I rose from the bench and hurried away from her.

Dani followed me to the hospital entrance, giving me a run-down of which nights she was free in the following week or two, and which nights she was spending with other people. I didn't want to hear it. I left her without saying goodbye and returned to curious looks from the interns as I listened to the rest of *Morning Report.*

Over the next couple of weeks, I was sure Dani continued to sleep with Jennifer, so I made an appointment to see Linda who said it will be hard with Dani. She advised me not to attach importance to the women Dani was seeing, to trust her, and to not let her know she was hurting me. Have an affair if I wanted. Hang on and see it through.

What bogus advice! An affair? The last thing I needed. The night with Gillian had been a one-off. I wondered if Linda would've given the same advice to a heterosexual couple.

I didn't think so.

∽

After work one hot August evening, I retired to the couch alone and thought of Vicki, a southerner who worked at the Centers for Disease Control in Atlanta. I'd met her at a conference in DC that spring, where I'd taken and passed the examination to become board-certified in occupational medicine. She was older, funny, and wise.

I called Vicki long-distance and told her about my distress over Dani.

Vicki sighed. "If you're standing under a tree and getting shit on, you got to move out from under the tree, honey," she told me. She thought I had intended to break it off with Dani when I returned to Boston from DC.

"I can find a nice southern woman for you," she suggested.

Nice offer, but I didn't want a nice southern woman. I wanted Dani.

I felt better after talking with Vicki, but then Dani called to say she had to change our date night because she forgot she was getting together with women from the Michigan Womyn's Music Festival. I smacked the wall with my palm and banged down the phone.

I thought of going out, but decided I'd rather stay home alone. It was the right choice. Sitting in the sunroom of my house and watching a nature program on TV was more satisfying than the continuous push-pull of my relationship with Dani.

I didn't need to have an affair—my old way of coping. I just needed to learn to take care of myself. After fixing a nutritious dinner and relaxing for a while in my own company, my mood lightened, and I daydreamed of someday traveling to Africa to track mountain gorillas. Somehow, I would heal the bottomless pit of need Dani had opened in me.

❦

Even before I admitted it to myself, I dropped by the chief of medicine's office and told him I was breaking up with my partner and having difficulty concentrating. I wasn't being as attentive and efficient as usual, and I didn't want him to think less of me. He and several other physicians on staff had supported me as a resident. I enjoyed performing well and their positive recognition.

I hadn't yet told Dani I was going to DC without her. I needed time to get used to the idea. Perhaps it was karma I had fallen in love with a woman incapable of giving me the security I needed, given how I had behaved with Cass and Maryann. In a moment of self-sabotage, I considered leaving my residency.

The chief was a man in his late sixties. He looked at me from behind his desk with a concerned expression. "Is there anything I can do within our structure to help you?" he asked.

This unexpected kindness floored me. Over the years, I'd realized although misogyny in medicine still prevailed, there had been exceptions—men who had supported me and desired my success. I swallowed the growing lump in my throat. "I feel like giving up and leaving town," I said, looking at my hands clasped in my lap.

"It's commendable you express your feelings," he said. "You're the sort of person who is committed to your career and I can't imagine you giving it up, even though I know residency is stressful."

"The stress of residency was the nail in the coffin of a relationship doomed, anyway." Though tempted to leave, I knew I couldn't, not after all the sacrifices I'd made to get this far. Tears stung my eyes.

"Do you need a few days off?"

I said no, I'd prefer to work, but then I looked into his kind eyes and admitted, "When I finish my residency, I'll have something. At the end of this relationship, I'll have nothing." I wiped my eyes on the back of my hand.

"Not nothing," he said. "Just intangibles."

In late September, the leaves were turning red and gold, and the nights were chillier. I drove over to Dani's house in Cambridge and climbed the stairs with determination. This time, she would not sway me. I brought Buto with me for support.

Dani was on the phone but hung up when she saw my face. Flushed, achy, and slightly nauseated, I was coming down with the flu and wanted to get this over with.

"Let's go for a walk." She would not seduce me into changing my mind this time.

"I don't have time," Dani said. "Let's sit on the porch."

We descended the stairs together, Buto clattering behind us, her nails clicking on the hardwood floor.

Dani wore jeans, an open-collared shirt, and her jean jacket despite the warm day. Her pockets were stuffed with photographic equipment. We sat across from each other on the wicker chairs. She looked me in the eye, picking up my determined vibe.

"Dani." I took a deep breath and slowly exhaled. "I'm leaving you. I'm going to Washington alone."

This time I was ready for her tears. I stood my ground and made no move to touch her.

Buto licked her hand.

"Is there nothing I can do?" she choked. "I won't sleep with friends anymore."

Isn't that the main issue? "Really? What about Jennifer?"

Dani hesitated, stopped crying. "I can't make that decision now."

At the risk of losing me, she would still sleep with Jennifer? The tightness in my chest spread to my throat. I rose to leave, then turned to face her.

"Then I'll decide. You have two weeks to wrap up your affair with Jennifer."

"That's not fair," she pleaded.

I whirled around and headed for the door, calling Buto to come.

I drove home, my heart aching with little hope she'd change. It was gut-wrenching giving her up. The good times were exhilarating in a way I had rarely experienced with anyone else. Despite all the pain and disappointment, I still loved her.

CHAPTER THIRTY-THREE

November 7, 1980 was my last night on call. During a lull in the wee hours of the morning, I read *The Wall Street Journal*. Ronald Reagan had just been elected president in a landslide and announced he would make decimating OSHA one of his first priorities. This didn't bode well for the future of the Office of Occupational Medicine, not to mention the rest of the country.

Just when my freedom from the demands of residency shimmered on the horizon, the elections empowered the moral majority in their quest to limit the freedom of women, gays and lesbians, as well as abortion choice. Lying in my windowless on-call room, I couldn't shake a sense of dread. Major change was afoot that would undercut all the transformation and hope I'd witnessed in the last two decades.

The next night, I sat drinking sherry with Mrs. B., my elderly downstairs tenant, because, as usual, Dani was late to arrive. Mrs. B.'s tiny, humpbacked figure bustled over to refill my glass. I reflected with her on my accomplishments in my twenties: I'd graduated medical school with honors, survived internship, and earned two master's degrees from Harvard. I'd completed two residencies with boards in occupational medicine and board-eligibility in internal medicine. I'd published two research articles, with another on the way. I had confidence in myself as a doctor, a clinician with good diagnostic skills, and compassion for my patients. I had learned to trust my instincts, my knowledge, and my judgment.

"But my personal life is a mess," I said, swirling the amber liquor in my glass.

Mrs. B. nodded knowingly. She was not so deaf she didn't hear the comings and goings, the fights with Dani, the slamming of the front door.

Before I left the hospital the following day, I admitted a twenty-seven-year-old man to the ICU with end-stage liver disease from alcoholism. In the emergency department, he had puked blood all over my scrubs from his hemorrhaging esophageal varices. His blood would not clot because his liver was not making the ingredients for clotting, so he just continued to bleed. We were pumping blood into his veins as fast as he was bleeding it out. The surgical resident inflated a balloon in his lower esophagus, stabilizing him, and I was free to leave.

I changed out of what had been my favorite scrubs—men's scrubs, of course, since I was so tall—and threw them away before leaving the hospital.

I was limp as a wet dishrag when I arrived home, looking forward to a glass of wine and a nature program on TV.

Dani was there, eating a TV dinner at the kitchen table. I frowned, annoyed to see her, and wished I'd gotten my key from her. She had her mouth full and greeted me with a curt nod.

Why is she here? I tensed with anxiety that she was gearing up for another pointless discussion. In the six weeks since I'd given her the ultimatum about wrapping up her affair with Jennifer, she'd given me no sign she had.

"Can we dispense with our usual hand-wringing diatribe this evening?" I asked before she even opened her mouth.

Dani put down her fork and looked up at me. "I don't understand myself for getting involved with a woman who is so totally egocentric." She took in a forkful of processed mashed potatoes.

"I'm the one who's egocentric?" Dani was the most solipsistic woman I'd ever met. Was this her way of justifying her affair? "You're so caught up in your own world, you have no idea what I'm going through. You said you'd be here at eight o'clock last night. You didn't show until ten when I needed to be in bed asleep."

I paced the floor, preparing to go on a rant.

Dani cut me off. "You see only that I've wronged you by sleeping with Jennifer and that's all you care about. You *can* be caring, loving, and generous—it's true. But I've seen it happen only when it holds an advantage for you." She took a swig from the glass in front of her, half-full of something amber-colored.

"It's hard to be caring and loving when you're running off to the Vineyard with Jennifer, sailing with Helinka, out to the bar with your softball team. You hardly make any time for us when I'm not working. Have you fed the dog?"

"No, not yet."

Buto looked up at me, her gaze expectant. I walked to the cupboard and got out her kibble, filling her bowl. She was out of water, too. Sensitive to our tone, she didn't leap on her food.

Dani ignored our dog and carried on.

"Maybe you thought you could push me around. But I drew the line—my refusal to ditch friends so you could control me. Yes, I've slept with another woman because you weren't fulfilling needs of mine. Sexual needs were at the bottom of the list, Laki. More important to me is acceptance with unselfish, unconditional love. I didn't have to bargain for it like I have with you."

I snorted. "So, you've found a woman who is giving you unselfish, unconditional love like an infant at mama's breast? Even when you disappoint her, as you no doubt will?"

Dani gave me a dark look, got up, opened the cupboard where I kept the Cointreau to top up her drink. I wondered just how much she'd had before I'd come home. Was alcohol fueling this?

As she reached for the bottle, I walked over, caught her wrist, and squeezed it—perhaps a little too hard. "Don't—no more."

Dani looked surprised, then defiant as I stared her down. My heart pounded. She could overpower me in any physical confrontation. I held on to her wrist and felt her close her fist. *Is she going to hit me?*

Then she lowered her arm, and I let go.

She stayed put, still close. "Never have I experienced such overwhelming aggressiveness as I have with you."

Who is she talking about? "This aggressive ogre is hungry."

I moved away and rummaged for something to eat in the refrigerator. I found only wine, mayonnaise, and ketchup. The freezer yielded a spinach soufflé, but it would take an hour to bake. I settled for snacking on stale peanuts while I warmed up the oven for the soufflé.

Dani still hovered, but I was fed up.

"I'm so tired of this. Of you making me into a raging ogre who ignores your sensitive feelings and thwarts your creative energy. Go fuck whoever you want, yourself included."

I flounced into the sunroom, turned on the reading lamp, took out a magazine, and flipped through the pages, too tired and upset to read.

Dani spoke softly to the dog in the kitchen, urging her to eat. Soon I heard Buto crunching her kibble and listened for the sound of Dani leaving.

She didn't leave. She followed me into the sunroom and sat in a chair near me, her face partially hidden in shadow.

"Last week, I relived the most awful years of my life," she said, her voice shaky. "Years of depression, attempted suicide, and the odd looks from people who knew. You didn't have a ghost of understanding. You only expressed hurt and anger I spent the weekend with Jennifer." Dani looked on the verge of tears.

I remembered there was a time when she'd turned to me for solace and comfort, and I'd been happy to give it. Over the past year, though, I'd been less available both physically and emotionally. So had she. Whose fault was that?

"Sorry, I've run dry of unselfish, unconditional love." I returned to flipping the pages of my magazine, not looking at her.

Dani banged her fist on the table between us, rattling the lamp. "You insist on monogamy from me. But what about you cheating on Maryann? Most important to me is *approval* of who I am. I get approval from you if I bend myself to your will. But it's all conditional, Laki."

I looked up at her. "You'll find it will be conditional with Jennifer too. Are you so naive that you think a woman will be there to love and comfort you, no matter whether you meet her needs as well?"

I winced inwardly, realizing that's exactly what I had wanted of Cass. I buried my face in my magazine.

Dani jumped up and snatched the magazine away. "I could say many bitter things, Laki, but I would only dislike myself for it. I love you even now. We can be such great friends and we play together better than anyone I know. That's hard to give up. But it's gone too far. We've hurt each other too much."

Her tone had softened, but I ignored it. She'd slept with Jennifer. She was still sleeping with Jennifer. That was all I could hear. I was finished with her. Blood pounded in my head. Also tempted to say further things I might regret, I realized there was no point. It was over.

"Just go," I said.

Dani headed for the door, grabbing her coat and bag on the way, forgetting about Buto.

"Leave the key!" I shouted to her retreating back.

The door slammed, rocking the walls. I slumped in the chair. Only then did I cry.

After a good cry, I poured a glass of chardonnay and thought of my doomed relationship with Dani. Could she ever really see me? My sensitivity and vulnerability, my real—not imagined—strengths, and my genuine love for her? But satisfying my need for love and security with Dani this past year was like trying to buy a cantaloupe at the hardware store.

Why do we persist in relationships that are one-sided, unsatisfying, or abusive? In the last year, my self-esteem had suffered; perhaps I even felt undeserving of committed love, or thought it was impossible to achieve as a lesbian. I'd become addicted to the roller coaster of highs and lows—the lows when she didn't show up when I most needed her and knew she was with someone else. The dopamine high when she returned after a period of neglect, when she told me how much she loved me, and when we had great sex.

I'd become a prisoner of my hope. I'd believed how Dani was

during the first blissful months of our relationship was how she really was and would continue to be. I'd believed the reason she'd changed—to become resentful, angry, and philandering—was my fault. Perhaps it gave me a sense of control, false though it was.

I would leave Dani, breaking the cycle of addiction in the only way I could, and my heart ached. My soufflé sat untouched on the table. I called Buto and flopped on my bed with my arm over her, not bothering to undress before drifting into a troubled sleep.

CHAPTER THIRTY-FOUR

T hree weeks later, I threw my ID card on the counter, strode out of the hospital, hopped into my Ford Mustang, and drove to the security gate. The guard in the booth gave me flak about not having my ID card to park for free, but I didn't care.

Through the window, I yelled, "You won't ever see me again. I'm outta here!"

He frowned and opened the gate. I roared away.

The date was November 30, 1980, and it was the last day of the third year of my internal medicine residency.

In the weeks since our last fight and breakup, Dani and I had reached a truce and acknowledged our impasse. I had no expectations, and she could relax and express the affection for me she still had. But there was only the thinnest veneer over my pain.

David had arrived from DC. He and Dani were at the house when I screeched up to the curb. I burst through the door and yelled, "I'm done, forever!"

I tore off my scrubs but kept them for a ritual burning later.

After I'd showered, Dani knocked on the bedroom door. "Dress up. We're going out."

In a happier mood than I'd been in for a long time, I put on my flowing black velvet pants, red silk blouse, contact lenses, earrings, lipstick, and heels. When I emerged from the bedroom, Dani wore a white tuxedo, with a lavender cummerbund, and looked dashing as she put tall yellow candles in silver candelabras and lit them. One by one, some of my best friends—Gillian, Chris, and Paula—came up the stairs, also very dressed up.

We all sat in the living room and chatted by candlelight. I was about to suggest drinks.

"There's someone at the door, Patroosk," David said. "Better go down and look."

David had always been easy to read, and tonight was no different. I suspected something was up. Dani walked with me to the door. A long, off-white, gleaming Rolls Royce with a silver emblem on the hood stood at the curb, complete with a driver.

"Wow, this is a surprise!"

Dani beamed at me. I smiled back at her. This was Dani at her best.

We got our coats, and Dani took a picture of me standing in front of the car. Then we climbed in—Paula, Gillian, and me in the backseat, Dani and Chris in the jump seats facing us. David sat up front with the handsome gay driver. The driver pulled out chilled champagne and glasses and we sat back in the luxurious, walnut-lined leather seats and toasted one another.

"We have an itinerary tonight," David announced as we sipped our champagne.

Our first stop was the hospital I thought I'd said goodbye to forever just a couple of hours earlier. When we approached the booth, the same guard was on duty. I leaned out the window of the Rolls and handed him a glass of champagne. He laughed and waved us through.

We drifted past the ER—my least favorite place—and toasted the two nurses free enough to dash outside, then past the guard again, collecting our glass.

As the limo floated by the Harvard School of Public Health, I could see the lights on the fourteenth floor where my office used to be. I wondered who was there now, working late. Gratitude filled me for the opportunity to forge an alternative career path and for the supportive colleagues I'd met there. I expected some would remain friends for life.

The driver stopped and pulled out a third bottle of champagne. We were all tipsy by now—just as well—because the next stop was Boston City Hospital and Boston University Medical Center, where David and I had suffered through our internships.

We floated down East Newton Street to the entrance to University Hospital. David and I raised our middle fingers to salute the chief of medicine and other tyrants of our internship. We'd survived that ordeal, scarred but not broken, and I had regained confidence and trust in my abilities as a doctor.

We did not linger with disturbing memories; instead, we proceeded a couple of blocks to East Springfield Street, where we found our former rented townhouse and a new building next door where the other one had burned to the ground while I slept.

Cruising Washington Street to the Boston Common, we enjoyed the Christmas lights on full display. A lump formed in my throat for the city I would soon leave behind. It had been so exciting when I first arrived here from Salt Lake City, caught up in the youthful intellectualism, feminist culture, history, and East Coast hustle. Here I was with some of my closest friends—people I loved. I couldn't bear to think I might be leaving forever.

Our limo cruise ended on the Boston waterfront. The driver left us at the Chart House, where a colleague and her husband were waiting at a reserved table upstairs. David and Dani sat on either side of me. The three of us had Alaskan King crab, while the others had oysters.

Soon, a young man in a tuxedo arrived bearing a bouquet of balloons. He read a card wishing me success in my new job and new life. Dani grinned, and I smiled back at her, squeezing her hand. This was so Dani—an extravagant, grand gesture with a flourish.

We drove back to the house in Gillian's car with the balloons. It was so cramped I had to sit on the floor. At one point, Paula leaned over and whispered in my ear she had loved me for years and if I wanted her to marry me, she would. I thought she'd had too much wine, but I smiled up at her, pleased with her affection.

When we arrived home, Paula and Chris had to leave amid a flurry of hugs and kisses goodbye. Gillian came upstairs with David, Dani, and me. While David retired to his room and began sorting his clothes for packing, Gillian sat on the couch between Dani and me—my arm around Gillian, her head on Dani's shoulder, the three of us chatting.

Dani jumped up and said she was going to bed. Surprised she was staying the night, I didn't object, as I felt mellow in the warm aftermath of an enchanted evening.

Lingering on the couch, my arm still around Gillian, I was not inclined to move. She shifted closer and lifted her face to kiss me softly at first, then more ardently. I heard a floorboard creak in the hall. I couldn't tell if it was David or Dani but didn't wait to find out. I pulled Gillian off the couch and walked her out onto the front porch.

Gillian hugged me and I was tempted to kiss her again, but my better judgement prevailed.

"Having you here, this whole evening, it was perfect."

309

After we said goodbye, I climbed the stairs, undressed, and got into bed with Dani. I put my arm over her, but she was out cold. I had trouble getting to sleep, adrift on an island of happiness in a sea of sadness.

CHAPTER THIRTY-FIVE

In early December, Dani was putting together another show of her photography and asked for my input. We had a hurried dinner at a seafood bar. After I'd dropped her off in Cambridge and was halfway home, I noticed she'd left her jacket and keys in my car. I drove back to her house, let myself in through the unlocked door, and climbed the stairs to discover Dani and her lesbian-feminist "therapist," Nancy, were sitting across from each other having "therapy" by candlelight in Dani's bedroom.

I stumbled back a step, swaying. We stared at each other, wide-eyed, not speaking for several moments.

"Very professional, Nancy," I let the tone of sarcasm linger.

I turned and strode out before either of them could say a word.

The following week, I gave myself a going-away party. Even Cass came. My living room and kitchen buzzed with colleagues and friends—talking, drinking, and dancing. Friends hugged me and wished me well in my future life—until after midnight.

Dani had the good sense not to show up to the party after I'd seen her and Nancy together. Around 1:30 a.m., after my guests departed, Dani arrived with Nancy who brought me flowers with a card that read, "If I am going to be unprofessional, at least I will do it with élan." I tossed them in the garbage. They wanted to engage me in a discussion about Dani's inability to give me what I needed.

I snorted and looked at them as if they were barking mad. "Get out."

"Laki, let me stay," Dani pleaded. "I need to talk with you. Nancy's leaving."

Without a word, I walked into my bedroom, closed the door, and placed a chair in front of it. I sat on the bed, my breath short, a wave of nausea sweeping over me.

I waited until I heard them leave. Then I got up unsteadily and locked and dead-bolted the front door.

A few days later, while preparing for the movers, I stood in the living room contemplating the dieffenbachia David and I had bought for our apartment on East Springfield Street when we'd first arrived in Boston. It had only one leaf then and now it was six feet tall. It had grown substantially during my time in Boston—but had I? I'd had several love relationships with women, none of them lasting. I'd fallen far short of my ideal: a monogamous, committed relationship of equals. Still, I now had confidence in my abilities as a doctor.

Buto kept me company these last few days and gave me her lovely smile when I patted her with affection. I put Barbra Streisand on the stereo and played "The Love Inside" over and over and cried as I packed. My tears were not only for Dani but also for Cass, Gillian, Maryann, and Cecilia, all the women I'd loved and lost.

Once I finished packing, I slumped down on the couch.

Later that night, I planned to have dinner with Gillian, but we ended up at different restaurants. I went to the Shanghai in Brookline. She went to the Shanghai in Chinatown. I waited and waited until I finally ordered and ate my dinner alone. It wasn't until I got home, and Gillian called that I realized our mistake, and we both laughed.

When I hung up, I wondered if she cared I might leave Boston forever. I'd stopped trying to get the kind of love I thought I needed from her. Gillian was skittish, like a wild animal. I needed to stay still, let her approach, and not try to catch, hold, or define her.

In the morning, the packers came. Mrs. B. called me downstairs for breakfast, but I couldn't eat. Back upstairs, I leaned against the wall, my legs weak, watching the crystal my mother gave me, my books, my record player, my vinyl records, and my clothes all disappear into boxes.

When the packers left at noon, I threw up.

I awoke at 2 a.m. Virgin snow covered the naked tree limbs outside my window and muffled the noise of the city. I took Buto out for a pee and relished the silence. As I watched her rolling in the snow, a lump formed in my throat. I would leave her behind too. Back inside, we curled up together in bed.

After the movers came for the boxes and packed the truck, I loaded Dani's stuff in my Ford Mustang and stopped downstairs for lunch with Mrs. B. My limbs moved as if I were underwater. Disoriented and empty, my life felt unreal, my future uncertain as I drove to Dani's house in Cambridge to bring her Buto and the few remnants of our life together. In practical terms, it had been easy to unravel our relationship—no joint property, no children, separate friends, only a shared dog. We'd only had love to hold us together, and that was not enough. Resigned to our breakup, I'd been able to interact with her over the past six weeks, but I knew the thin veneer over my hurt could crack with little provocation.

Dani greeted me at the door with a glass of French liqueur. We climbed the stairs, and I sat in the one chair in her room, drinking in silence, as she finished her work. I noted her intense concentration, the way her muscles flexed in her tanned forearm and the way her shirt stretched across her broad shoulders. I loved her even more as I prepared to leave her.

Just for an instant, doubt gripped me.

"My friend Debbie told me at my party we're an interesting pair—that we need each other, and it would be a mistake for us to break up." I took another sip of liquor; it burned my throat.

Dani turned to face me, and sighed. "No, Laki, it's not a mistake. We're both tired, and Debbie doesn't understand what we've been through."

The next morning was bright, clear, and cold with snow still on the ground. I put on my brown tweed jacket with the suede patches on the elbows and took my new professional leather briefcase to head downtown to meet the buyer we'd found for our house—a minister's wife—for the closing.

The sale yielded more money than David or I had ever seen in our lives. I had negotiated an agreement with the new owners for Mrs. B. to continue to live in the house for as long as she was able, without an increase in rent.

Afterward, the minister's wife took me out to lunch—we'd become friendly in the last few weeks—and as we waited for our food, I confided, "My occupancy of the house coincided with the beginning and the end of a tumultuous but significant two-and-a-half-year relationship." I could say that without tearing up; acceptance was settling in.

Looking at me with kind eyes, she put her hand on mine. "Patricia, when you close one door, you often open another." She described meeting her current, and ideal, husband just months after breaking it off with another man.

I doubted I could love another woman any time soon. Still, her kindness cheered me, and I felt less gloomy as I took the T back to what was now someone else's house and packed my remaining items into the Mustang.

Dani invited me to dinner at The Peacock and to spend my last night in Cambridge, offering to gas up my car for the long drive to DC. I doubted the wisdom of this and almost declined. In the end, I put on my black slacks, red silk blouse, and earrings—looking better than I felt—and mentally prepared for the evening ahead.

I lingered in the house, walking through every room, grateful for some of the happy memories: the excitement of buying the place with David, and the happier times with Dani, Gillian, Chris, Paula, and other friends. I would miss Mrs. B., who often popped her head out her door and called upstairs for me to come down and have a cup of tea when I felt lost and alone.

By the time I arrived at The Peacock an hour later, my neck and shoulders were tense and aching, my throat tight.

Consuming a glass of wine didn't help. I crossed my arms

over my chest and leaned back in the chair. "So, have you bonked your therapist yet?" I asked, deliberately being crude.

Anger flashed in Dani's eyes. "You don't understand."

"I understand she's a fraud and you're a fool."

"Fuck you, Laki."

We finished the rest of our meal in angry silence.

I thought I should leave her there, but I had nowhere to go. When we arrived at Dani's house in Cambridge, her elderly landlady was away, and the house was dark. I could hold it together no longer—a torrent of pain broke through the protective layer. Alone, I staggered into the kitchen, leaned against the counter for support, and tried to get a grip. My thwarted desire to build a life with Dani, her betrayal with Jennifer, and now Nancy, my repeated inability to find and keep the love I wanted—all crashed down on me. I bent over the sink and cried my guts out in the dark, feeling untethered, unlovable, and adrift, as if I'd severed the line to a spaceship and was floating away into the lonely void of space. The pain was old, deep, and inconsolable. I couldn't stop crying the tears of a child who knows love is the only thing keeping her alive.

So focused on a certain kind of love—the wild, passionate lust I thought should last forever—I was blind to the love all around me: the love of my friends, Chris, Paula, Gillian, and Mrs. B.; the love of Cass, who still cared; and even the love of Dani, when she put conflict aside and arranged for my celebration at the end of my residency. Most important now was the enduring love, stability, and sanctuary David offered when I needed it most.

I climbed the stairs to find Dani in bed, turned away from me. I slipped in beside her and turned my back. Spent from crying, I fell into a deep sleep.

༄

In the morning, I was more rational. We agreed I shouldn't have been so sarcastic; she shouldn't have been so angry.

"I couldn't let myself believe it was the last time you would be in my bed or that you are really leaving me." She teared up, sniffed, and wiped her nose.

"Perhaps it was our method of coping," I told her.

I dressed and hugged Dani goodbye at the door. When I got in the Mustang, the gas gauge showed empty. I sighed and shook my head. Dani had not filled it like she'd offered. Nor had she filled that void in me yearning for a love I could depend on. The car sputtered to life. I'd have to take care of my own needs.

I wouldn't see Dani again for forty years.

I had a final lunch with a friend that day, and by the time I'd cleaned, loaded, and gassed up the car, it was 4 p.m., and it was a nine-hour drive to DC. As I climbed the stairs of my house for the last time, Ms. B. poked her bird-like head out of the apartment below.

"It's too late for you to leave now Patricia. Have dinner with me and leave when you're fresh in the morning."

We had hot toddies, and Mrs. B. cooked a fish dinner. I slept on clean, crisp sheets in her spare bedroom. She woke me from a deep sleep at 6 a.m. I popped upstairs to look at the empty house and the dieffenbachia for the last time. Then I kissed a tearful Mrs. B. goodbye, gave her the keys, and took off for DC.

I listened to Al Stewart's 1976 song "Year of the Cat"—the haunting words and the wail of the horn—and thought of Dani, the passion, and the pain of her.

◦⌐

The day I left Boston forever, well-rested with my Mustang pointed toward Washington DC, optimism crept in to replace despair. Throughout my life, disruption became a source of reinvention. During my twenties, I'd been neither dependable nor honorable, expecting my partner to provide the love, acceptance, and care I should have given myself. That would have to change. Then, I might find a woman to love who'd be capable of commitment.

Boundaries exist, I mused, to protect tender feelings. Within the bounds of trust and loyalty, love can grow. When those boundaries are breached, trust fades and may never return—and along with it, the ability to engage fully in loving another. I knew that now.

Dani had held up a mirror for me. I had work to do to become a better friend to myself before I could love another. To learn to accept vulnerability without fear. To ask for what I needed but not to overwhelm, not to demand. To realize that lust is not love. They might exist together for a limited time, but love is far more valuable and enduring.

During the tumultuous years in my twenties, there were a few special people with whom I truly connected. I hoped they would remain my friends for life.

I would become the woman I'd want to be with.

EPILOGUE

I t was spring 2019 when I immersed myself in my journals and letters from my twenties. When I did, I couldn't believe how deeply I experienced, once again, those old feelings from forty years ago. Several of the characters in my story remained friends—David, of course, as well as Cecilia, Cass, Gillian, Chris, Gabrielle, and Dee.

Though we don't see or talk to each other often, friendships lasting decades have perks: having seen one another through multiple transformations, you bear witness to each other's lives, and you know each other well enough to forgive and accept each other's flaws. When you talk, you can easily pick up from where you left off. The foundation of trust is already there. And because you understand each other, you can share your deepest thoughts.

Ten months after leaving Boston, I traveled on a business trip to London and met the woman who would eventually become my spouse. We could not live together until many years later and had to immigrate to Canada to do so. I became the trustworthy, monogamous person I aspired to be. This time, the woman I chose as my partner is capable of the same.

My medical career took off after Boston, taking me to Washington State after I was fired for being a lesbian in 1984 from a high-level corporate position headquartered in North Carolina. Nevertheless, I thrived as a physician specialist in Seattle, eventually starting my own medical consulting company. I mostly (though not completely—it's difficult to give up one's identity as a doctor) retired after a forty-year medical career. I am grateful for the richness of my working life. A residual desire to help, to understand human strength and frailty—particularly my own—still motivates me.

While writing this memoir, I reached out to those characters who remained lifelong friends. I also tracked down Dani after forty years of no contact. Each of their lives has taken a different course. Cass married a man and has forever kept our relationship secret. Cecilia and Gillian have stayed single for many years. Cecilia became a professor of English and a department chair at a university. David embraced his sexuality and found love in partnership with a bright, witty, and cultured man. Dee married a fabulous woman whom she has been with for thirty years. Dani has been single for decades, running her own landscaping business and building her own house. Our talks over several months brought new perspectives to our relationship of forty years ago.

Sadly, Susan never knew how much she influenced my life.

I must credit my wife for her forbearance during the writing of this memoir. She has no desire to read it, but told me when I began, "I love the result. I don't need to know the recipe."

For decades, I have been completely out as a lesbian. I married the love of my life in Canada in 2006, a privilege I never thought I could enjoy in my lifetime. In Canada, we are part of a tight community, mostly heterosexual. Our sexual orientation is a complete non-issue for these friends. Still, I keep close ties with a community of lesbians in Seattle I've known for over thirty years. We no longer band together as an ostracized minority. Today, we gather as friends who have watched society change before our eyes.

I never take for granted the positive evolution of most of the world's attitude toward LGBTQ+ people since I first knew I was gay and thought I might be the only lesbian in Arizona. I haven't forgotten the gains are fragile. We could lose our rights and freedoms and return to that dark time if we let a culture of hate and intolerance for differences prevail.

ACKNOWLEDGMENTS

I would like to thank those who first encouraged me to write: my friend Melanie Dawson-Whisker, her sister Liza Dawson-Whisker, and my first writing coach, Susan Meyers, PhD, of Seattle University. My classes at Hugo House in Seattle, taught by Theo Nestor, Steve Almond, and Christine Hemp helped stoke my enthusiasm. Hugo House was also where I made the contacts to form the Lake Forest Writing Group: Sara Kim, Linda Lockwood, Helen Wattley-Ames, Anu Garg, and Connie Ballou.

I would like to acknowledge the patience and encouragement of Brooke Warner, my mentor and coach for a six-month memoir writing class and boot camp led by her and Linda Joy Myers. I thank authors Laura Munson, Lynne Schmidt, Steve Almond, Judy Kiehart, and Morgan Elliot, who provided feedback on drafts of my manuscript. Cecilia Lim, Professor Emeritus of English helped me "kill my darlings" and provided valuable insight. Thank you, She Writes Press/Spark Press staff, including Shannon Green, Krissa Lagos, the designers, and other editors for helping me publish. Thanks to Michele Karlsberg for publicity.

I thank my friends David, Chris, Cecilia, Dee, Dani, Gillian, and Cass, with whom I shared relevant portions of drafts, and who helped corroborate my memories of those times with laughter, and sometimes, tears.

I thank my wife Linda for her love and patience with me during the writing of this memoir. It wasn't always easy for her to witness my forays into the past or understand my desire to reveal my story to the world. Her support reinforced my belief she is the right woman for me.

Finally, I would like to thank you, my readers, for inspiring me every day with your feedback and your stories.

ABOUT THE AUTHOR

photo credit: Frances Litman

PATRICIA GRAYHALL is a medical doctor and the author of *Making the Rounds; Defying Norms in Love and Medicine* as well as articles in *Queer Forty* and *The Gay and Lesbian Review*. After nearly forty years of medical practice, this is her debut, very personal, and frank memoir about coming out as a lesbian in the late 1960s and training to become a doctor when society disapproved of both for a woman. She chose to write using a pen name to protect the privacy of some of her characters, as well as her own. Patricia lives with the love of her life on an island in the Pacific Northwest, where she enjoys other people's dogs, the occasional Orca and black bear, hiking, and wine with friends.

In Search of Pure Lust: A Memoir by Lise Weil. $16.95, 978-1-63152-385-4. Through the lens of her personal experiences as a lesbian coming of age in the '70s and '80s, Lise Weil documents an important chapter in lesbian history, her own long and difficult relationship history, and how her eventual dive into Zen practice became a turning point in her quest for love.

You Can't Buy Love Like That: Growing Up Gay in the Sixties by Carol E. Anderson. $16.95, 978-1631523144. A young lesbian girl grows beyond fear to fearlessness as she comes of age in the '60s amid religious, social, and legal barriers.

Parent Deleted: A Mother's Fight for Her Right to Parent by Michelle Darné. $16.95, 978-1-63152-282-6. A gripping tale of one non-biological, lesbian mother's fight for shared custody of her children—an intimate, infuriating, and infectious story of perseverance, sacrifice, and hope in the face of debilitating adversity.

The Longest Mile: A Doctor, a Food Fight, and the Footrace that Rallied a Community Against Cancer by Christine Meyer, MD. $16.95, 978-1-63152-043-3. In a moment of desperation, after seeing too many patients and loved ones battle cancer, a doctor starts running team—never dreaming what a positive impact it will have on her community.

Stories from the Tenth-Floor Clinic: A Nurse Practitioner Remembers by Marianna Crane. $16.95, 978-1- 63152-445-5. When a nurse practitioner takes charge of a senior clinic in a Chicago subsidized housing building, she finds herself doing much more than providing medical care.

Stay, Breathe with Me: The Gift of Compassionate Medicine by Helen Allison, RN, MSW with Irene Allison. $16.95, 978-1-63152-062-4. From the voices of the seriously ill, their families, and a specialist with a lifelong experience in caring for them comes the wisdom of a person-centered approach—one that brings heart and compassion back into health care.